Menno Simons

and the

New Jerusalem

Menno Simons

and the

New Jerusalem

by
Helmut Isaak

PANDORA PRESS

Library and Archives Canada Cataloguing in Publication

Isaak, Helmut, 1939-
  Menno Simons and the New Jerusalem / by Helmut Isaak.

Includes bibliographical references.
ISBN 1-894710-69-X

  1. Menno Simons, 1496-1561. 2. Anabaptists--Doctrines--History--16th century.
3. Mennonites--Doctrines--History--16th century. I. Title.

BX8143.M5I83 2006   230'.97   C2006-904571-2

MENNO SIMONS AND THE NEW JERUSALEM

Copyright © 2006 Pandora Press

Published by Pandora Press
33 Kent Avenue
Kitchener, Ontario N2G 3R2

All rights reserved.

ISBN 1-894710-69-X

All Pandora Press books are printed on Eco-Logo certified paper.

Design by Cliff Snyder

Cover Illustration: Woodcut illustrating Revelation 21, from a rare coloured edition of the Froschauer Bible (Zürich, 1531). Courtesy Conrad Grebel University Archives.

13 12 11 10 09 08 07 06   12 11 10 9 8 7 6 5 4 3 2 1

Table of Contents

Acknowledgments 7

Preface 9

Introduction 11

— CHAPTER ONE —

The Social and Religious Context for the Emergence of Anabaptism in the Netherlands 17

— CHAPTER TWO —

Menno and Münster: A Vision of the New Jerusalem. 31

When did Menno join the Covenanters? 31
Menno and the Münsterites: The *Blasphemy of Jan van Leiden* 34
    The authorship of the Blasphemy. 34
    Menno and the Münsterites: evidence from the Blasphemy 37
    When was the Blasphemy *written?* 40
    Menno and the Münsterites: Menno's baptism 43
    Conclusion 44
Menno and Münster in light of the *Meditation on the Twenty-Fifth Psalm* 46
Münster from the Perspective of the *Fundamentbook*, 1539-1540 and 1554/55 48
Menno's Indiscriminate "No" to Münster and the Münsterites in his
    Later Writings 52

— CHAPTER THREE —
The Heavenly Jerusalem has Descended Upon this Earth 57

"The Word became Flesh": The stepping stone to the New Jerusalem 58
    Incarnation: Melchior Hoffman and Münster 58
    Menno's doctrine of the "Celestial Flesh" 62
Unless a man is born again, he cannot enter the Kingdom of God 67
    Regeneration and Restitution in Münster 67
    Menno's Doctrine of Regeneration and the "Spiritual Resurrection" . . . 68
Genuine Repentance and New Life in the New Jerusalem 72
Conclusion 76

— CHAPTER FOUR —
The Eschatological Anticipation of the New Jerusalem 79

Spiritual and Individualistic Anticipation of the New Jerusalem 79
The New Jerusalem after Münster 83
The New Jerusalem, built on the Right Foundation 86
Completing the Foundation 93
    The cutting off and shunning of the unrepentant sinner 93
    True Christian faith as the instrument of transformation 94
    A holistic vision of the New Jerusalem 96
The Anticipation of the New Jerusalem in Menno's last decade 98
Menno's Understanding of a Christian Magistracy 104

— CHAPTER FIVE —
Conclusion 109

Appendix: Evidence of Menno's authorship of the Blasphemy 113
Notes 117
Select Bibliography 149

Acknowledgments

I want to give recognition to all those who have been involved in the financing, supervision, and proofreading of this manuscript. From my home church in Vancouver to Amsterdam and Waterloo, from Columbia Bible College and Columbia Kitchen Cabinets to Vernon, people from many different walks of life have been involved in this project. I wish to offer special thanks to Professors Irvin B. Horst and the late Sjouke Voolstra for their encouragement and support. During my stay in Waterloo, Professor Werner Packull helped me keep a critical distance from the exciting results of my early research. David Giesbrecht, librarian at Columbia Bible College, not only gave me the keys to the library but also supervised my struggle with the English language. Janet Jones dealt with the impact of the disorganized style of Menno's writing on the manuscript. Professor Walter Klaassen and Professor Arnold Snyder read the manuscript more than once and offered many valuable suggestions.

—*Helmut Isaak*

Preface

Much has been written about Menno Simons over the last century, and there has been major disagreement among Mennonite scholars as they interpreted his life and writings. How should this dour Frisian priest and reformer be understood? What was at the heart of his concern in his voluminous writings? Was it his unorthodox teaching on the Incarnation? Was it his concept of the church? Was it an individualistic spiritualism? Or was it his gradually growing understanding of the Kingdom of God as Helmut Isaak argues in this book?

This conclusion, however, represents not just another key concept as the centre of the thought of Menno Simons. For all its brevity, this work seeks to combine and integrate all other previous serious attempts at a uniting concept into an overall vision which occupied Menno Simons from the time of his conversion until his death. Isaak performs this task, not with detailed refutation of the scholars who preceded him, but rather by an extraordinarily careful attention to the writings of Menno Simons.

He has written what in the book is called a spiritual biography of Menno Simons. The tendency, especially of earlier American Mennonite scholars, was often to use Menno's works as though they all had one date, and to conclude that Menno's views of the church, for example, were much the same throughout his life. That happened partly because they used the collected works of Menno Simons, published in 1681 as the *Opera Omnia*, as the authoritative text.

It is precisely at this point that the present work distinguishes itself. The author bases his conclusions on a careful reading of the first editions of Menno's works and comparing them with the revised versions of those same works published years later. The original texts and the revised versions prepared later by Menno himself, reflect the development and also the changes in his thinking. Menno's writings were not produced in a quiet study, the writer's desk surrounded by many shelves of theological and biblical works. They were written out of experiences of inner turmoil and uncertainty, out of the verbal and physical turbulence of religious controversy, and out of the need to make Catholic and Protestant clergy and governments understand Menno and his followers and to persuade them to abandon their enmity and oppression.

Isaak argues that through all of that, Menno was reaching for an integrated view of a reformed society in which church and state, the spiritual and secular spheres of the Christian life, functioned together as in the Old Testament unity of king, priest, and prophet. The function of government was to keep order, to suppress false teachers, and to do it without violence. Even toward the end of his life he called on governments, not so much to lessen the suffering for his followers, but to be a truly Christian government. This unified, quite traditional, ordering of society, was what Menno called the kingdom of God. He never gave up on that hope, except that towards the end the Kingdom had become for him synonymous with the suffering church, and it was now a matter of waiting on God for the vision to unfold.

The work is very tightly argued, linking the ongoing experiences in the life of Menno to the development of his thinking. Readers may be surprised by the argument that Menno was baptized as early as 1534 and did not leave the Catholic church until nearly two years later, and even more that he referred to the Anabaptists of Münster as his "dear brothers and sisters" until it became politically dangerous. They will be interested to learn that Menno's understanding of the Christian life began with a quite individualistic spiritualism, and moved only gradually to the view that the Christian life was lived in the Christian community, the disciplined church, with its baptism, Lord's Supper, and ban. Perhaps it was the waning of his expectation of a reformation of all of society that contributed to the rigidity and dogmatism of his later years.

Helmut Isaak has moved the work of recovering Menno Simons ahead, in considerable measure. Anyone working on Menno from now on will need to engage this work.

Walter Klaassen
Saskatoon, Saskatchewan

Introduction

The few details known about the life of Menno Simons can be summarized fairly quickly. Born in 1496 in Witmarsum in Friesland, he was ordained a Catholic priest in 1524 when he was 28 years old. He served as parish priest in the town of Pingjum, near Witmarsum, from 1524 to 1531, and from 1531 to 1536 at the parish church in Witmarsum. According to his own testimony, Menno had doubts about the miracle of transubstantiation almost immediately. He was not alone in this. He seems to have been influenced by the so-called Sacramentarians, who were numerous and influential in the Netherlands at the turn of the sixteenth century, and who shaped the religious world Menno inhabited. The execution of the Anabaptist Sicke Snijder at Leeuwarden in 1531 awakened Menno to the issue of infant baptism, and raised questions about the biblical foundation for the traditional practice. Still Menno continued fulfilling his duties as a priest.

In 1534 and 1535, Melchiorite Anabaptists succeeded in taking the city of Münster in Westphalia. There is good evidence that Menno's brother joined this movement and perished in the siege of the monastery of Oldeklooster in 1535, an event that probably was decisive for Menno's later choices. Finally in January, 1536, well after the Münsterite kingdom had collapsed, Menno left the Catholic church and accepted baptism at the hands of the peaceful Anabaptist leader Obbe Philips, who also later ordained him an elder in the movement. Menno recalled this momentous turning in his life with these words: "And so I, a miserable sinner, was enlightened of the Lord, was converted to a new mind, fled from Babylon, entered into Jerusalem, and finally, though unworthy, was called to this high and heavy service."[1]

The image of the New Jerusalem runs like a winding river throughout Menno's thought and writings, and forms the thematic focus of this study. Menno had left Babylon and entered Jerusalem, and he dedicated himself from that point on to the building of the New Jerusalem. After his ordination as an elder he was faced with the task of guiding the confused and scattered Melchiorites and Münsterites, always with an imperial price on his head. He worked in Groningen for the next four years, then two years in Holland and three in the archbishopric of Cologne. The last thirteen years of his life he spent in Holstein, where he was relatively safe. With his excellent knowledge of Scripture, he was able to provide much needed biblical foundations for the New Jerusalem for his dear brothers and sisters who had placed their hopes in the promises of the prophets of Münster. In spite of the high price on his head he managed to minister to his fellow covenanters as an itinerant teacher, pastor and elder. Constantly hiding and moving from one place to another he also wrote an impressive number of pamphlets, meditations, and theological writings, many of which were published in his lifetime. These writings where later collected and published in two major editions: in 1681 as *Opera Omnia* and in 1956 in an English translation as *The Complete Writings of Menno Simons*.

What were Menno's theological commitments, what motivated him, and what guided him throughout his life? A clear answer is difficult to ascertain, for several reasons. In the first place, Menno quite deliberately painted his intellectual biography in a way that disconnected him as much as possible from less savoury elements in the baptizing movement. So, for example, the few autobiographical details he tells us in his own writings, many of which are summarized in the first paragraph above, were written later in his life in reply to the Calvinist reformer, Gellius Faber. In that writing Menno defended himself against the charge that he was a Münsterite. But were his later statements entirely true? If we were to follow Menno's own depiction, it would seem that he had no more to do with the Münsterites than did, say, John Calvin.

A second difficulty has been that much of the scholarly work that has been done to identify the central tenets of Menno's theological discourse, has been carried out most often by Mennonite historians who have had a vested interest in the answers, and whose findings often reflect their own time in history and their own theological orientations. Influenced by Pietism, Johannes Deknatel wrote in 1746 that Menno was "the most formidable founder of our church, comparable to Luther and Calvin in their churches. For Menno was not only exceptionally talented, blessed, zealous and suited to his task; in addition he was not an uneducated man."[2] For Karel Vos, writing in 1914, Menno was the long-term spiritual leader of the Dutch Anabaptists. He credits Menno with developing the foundation for the basic theological tenets of the later Dutch Mennonites (*Doopsgezinden*).[3]

Both Deknatel and Vos saw Menno as a spiritual leader of the Dutch Mennonites; the great 19th century Dutch Mennonite historian W. J. Kuehler did not agree at all. In his view, Menno did not belong to the great spiritual leaders of his time. Kuehler believed that Menno's writings had only historical value, and he was convinced that none of his liberal Mennonite brothers and sisters in the Netherlands would ever consider consulting Menno's writings for theological orientation or spiritual edification.[4] The Mennonite Brethren movement, which started as a Mennonite schism in the 1860s in Russia, to the contrary, claimed to stand in the true spiritual succession of Menno Simons. Their document of separation from the "churchly" Mennonites is almost entirely a literal or paraphrased quotation of Menno's writings.[5]

Writing in the third decade of the 20th century and from his vantage point in North America, Cornelius Krahn was more appreciative, coming to the conclusion that Menno's ecclesiology helped to shape the congregational ecclesiology of the later Mennonite communities in Prussia, Russia and the Americas.[6] For Walter Klaassen, Menno was the first reformer of the Netherlands, just as important for the Mennonites as Luther and Calvin had been for their denominations.[7] Most recently, Sjouke Voolstra's study of Menno Simons considered his understanding of penance, justification and restitution, together with *Gelassenheit* and spiritualism, to be the central themes of his theological discourse.[8]

This present study is built on the careful work of scholars who have gone before, but it asks slightly different questions by approaching the sources in a unique way. In this study we will pay very special attention to all of Menno's writings in order to identify as much as possible, the source, beginning, growth and change of his theological and biblical ideas. We are setting out to shed more light on Menno's intellectual biography, using as our central source of evidence, his writings themselves. The fact is that we possess significant writings from Menno that date from before his departure from the Catholic church as well as writings from early and late in his Anabaptist ministry. We will pay special attention to Menno's early writings of the 1530s and 40s and compare these with the editions of these writings that he revised and published in the 1550s. In these careful comparisons we will find evidence that considerably fills out our understanding of Menno and his changing ideas.

The idea of the New Jerusalem was fundamental for Menno, from the start of his Anabaptist writing. What did the "New Jerusalem" mean to him in these earliest writings, and where did his image originate? Did Menno have something to do with Münster after all, in spite of his later denials? What did regeneration and restitution mean for Menno, after Münster? What did Menno mean when he said that he left Babylon and entered Jerusalem, and that the New Jerusalem had already come down from heaven? Did Menno's understanding of the community of believers as the New Jerusalem change from the 1530s to the 1540s and 50s? How did Menno understand the people of the New Jerusalem to be related to the rest of the world? Did this understanding change over time? Did Menno believe that it was possible for there to be a Christian society and a Christian government? If Menno in the early 1540s was ready to take on the reformation of the Netherlands, why did he sound like a separatist in the 1550s?

A close reading of Menno's writings, while not providing complete answers to all of these questions, will go a long way toward better understanding Menno's core convictions and the way in which he changed his mind, as the circumstances of life around him also changed.

Until Menno left the Roman Catholic Church in 1536 he could have been called a sacramentarian priest, as were many of his colleagues. The first chapter will examine sacramentarian expectations and the struggle for an "evangelical town" in Menno's time. Although Menno claimed that he did not owe anything to anybody for the development of his theology, does the evidence bear out the claim? Might Menno's vision of a Christian society have been inspired by a writing such as the "*Summa der godliker scrifturen,*" written by J. J. van Toorenbergen in 1523? Or was Menno perhaps acquainted with Jan de Bakker, ordained a Catholic priest in Utrecht in 1521, whose testimony during his trial at The Hague in 1525 anticipates almost all of Menno's later theological tenets? The first chapter will explore these and other questions pertaining to Menno's early years as priest in Pingjum and Witmarsum.

Chapter 2 takes up the question of Menno's relationship to the Anabaptist reformation of Münster, and his response to it. In this chapter we will inquire about the importance of Münster for Menno and his followers. What influence, if any, did the Münsterite doctrine of regeneration and restitution have on Menno's own theology? Why did Menno need to write a tract on the *New Birth* in 1539, after he had already defined his understanding of regeneration in 1534, in his *Spiritual Resurrection*? What was the impact of Jan van Leiden's self proclaimed messianic kingship on Menno's understanding of the kingdom of God? Did the early Anabaptist society of Münster as the claimed anticipation of the New Jerusalem help shape Menno's own understanding of a Christian society with a Christian government? Why did Menno feel the need to revise the first edition of his *Fundament-book*? What light does Menno's *Meditation on the Twenty-Fifth Psalm* of 1539 shed on these questions?

The second part of this study, comprising chapters 3 and 4, will concentrate on the theological foundation and changing character of Menno's understanding of regeneration and life in the New Jerusalem. Comparing Menno's early *Meditation* and *Fundament-book* to later revisions, we will focus on visible shifts in his theological understanding of the anticipation of the New Jerusalem. Does his understanding of spiritual regeneration change after he leaves the Catholic Church? How does Menno's understanding of the kingdom of God as the all inclusive Christian society change when he becomes the leader of the persecuted Anabaptists in the forties and in the fifties? Is Menno not after all a perfectionist, when he claims that a regenerated, baptized member of the church does not sin anymore? Is the strict ban an indispensable part of the community of believers without spot our wrinkle? Why is Menno in the 1550s satisfied with a blameless minority church, when in the 1540s the reformation of the entire Christian Church was the goal? Do these possible changes reflect also Menno's own life as evangelical priest, or as leader of the growing Anabaptist reformation in the forties and as the elder of a peaceful, but separated Mennonite fellowship in the fifties? What happens to the death penalty in the fifties? Did Menno's dream of a Christian—Mennonite!—nation with a Christian government ever change? These are some of the questions to which we will try to find answers in our study of Menno' writings. In doing so we will also pay close attention to what Menno says, and what he does not say.

It is well known that Menno's writings are not very readable. He is repetitious and often disorganized. Nevertheless, reading and rereading Menno's writings from different perspectives and following the formation of his theological thinking through its various stages, yields concrete results, and helps round out the intellectual and spiritual portrait of this notable Reformation leader. In pursuing this careful reading of Menno's writings, we have needed to consult the first editions of Menno's early writings. They are not readily available and certainly are not to be found in J. C. Wenger's English edition of *The Complete Writings of Menno Simons*. Nevertheless, only by consulting the entire Menno corpus and paying careful attention to the shifts and changes evident over time can we hope to trace the evolution and maturation of his thought.

CHAPTER ONE

The Social and Religious context for the Emergence of Anabaptism in the Netherlands

Menno Simons became a priest in a time of general upheaval: many traditional values and institutions were being questioned, and there was widespread social and political unrest caused by unemployment and hunger. The almost absolute control of the Catholic Church in a Christian state over all areas of human life had begun to crumble under the impact of humanism and the Lutheran Reformation. Emperor and pope were engaged in the traditional power struggle for their respective territories. At the same time, imperial cities, money markets and national as well as international traders were either searching for more freedom or defending traditional privileges.[1] The long awaited reformation of religious and socio-political institutions and the reorganization of traditional society seemed inevitable. Much more than a mere reaction against abuses of the church, this reformation was to be part of a much broader movement of renewal of the Christian life. Many people expressed a desire to come closer to the Scriptures, to bring theology and spirituality together and to develop the sense of a personal responsibility towards God.[2]

As a result of their studying and travelling throughout Europe, intellectuals became the first to free themselves from the dogmatic and scholastic confines of the Catholic church. Erasmus of Rotterdam is probably the most prominent of the humanists who stood on the frontier between medieval and modern times. Although he was not a reformer himself, he greatly influenced the Reformation. He was accused of entertaining heretical notions and some of his dogmatic tenets were condemned by the Faculty of Theology of the Sorbonne, but he remained a Catholic. No one criticized the abuses and shortcomings of the clergy and religious orders of his church more effectively than he did. Melanchton called him his teacher and Zwingli appealed to his authority. Even Rothmann claimed Erasmus as a forerunner of the Anabaptist Reformation in Münster.[3]

The humanists' demand for freedom of critical thinking led to direct confrontation with the religious and political powers.[4] The Hapsburg monarchy was still trying to impose the medieval structure of a universal Catholicism in its territories by means of inquisitions and edicts, but this structure was becoming increasingly unacceptable to the humanists and the leading politicians of the imperial cities.[5] Even Erasmus, who agreed in principle with the right of the magistrates to punish heretics, pleaded for more flexibility.

Thanks to the relatively new medium of the printing press, information could now be spread all over Europe within weeks.[6] Literacy rates were increasing steadily, not because of government or church programs, but because people were themselves learning to read and write in order to read the Bible in the vernacular.[7] It was not the discovery of America or the conquest of the Aztec and Inca empires which made the headlines, but Luther's Ninety-Five Theses and his early reformation writings. Religion was at the core of everyday life. All over the Low Countries people were following with great interest the changes and renewals in church and society.

A survey done in 1514 gives us valuable insight into the demography of Holland.[8] With 31% of the population living in big cities, 21% in smaller towns and only 48% in rural areas, Holland already was highly urbanized. Industry and trade had become major factors in the Dutch economy, making it vulnerable to international, political and economic crises such as depression and inflation. Poverty, especially in the cities, was a major problem from the beginning of the sixteenth century. In 1514 the average percentage of paupers[9] in Horn, Delft, Haarlem, Gouda, Amsterdam and Leiden was 38%, with Leiden leading at 63%. Below the class of the paupers there were the beggars.

The impoverishment of the urban population increased rapidly with the decline of the textile industry in the first decades of the sixteenth century. When England produced a cheaper quality cloth for the European market after 1500 and increased export duties on quality wool[10] the Dutch industry, which was dependent on imports from the British Isles, was faced with one crisis after another. The years 1527-1530 were difficult years, but unemployment reached an all time high in 1533. When England placed a temporary embargo on the export of wool and the warehouse in Calais was temporarily closed,[11] the city council of Leiden was afraid that unemployed workers might turn to rioting and insurrection.[12] If it was already being said on the streets of Leiden in 1521 that a hundred unemployed weavers were for hire,[13] by 1533 there must have been many hundreds.[14]

Insurrection was a threat not only in Leiden, but also in Waterland, Amsterdam and Delft. The Lords of Holland wrote in this regard to the governess in Brussels that they "noticed that all the poverty stricken people as a result of the lack of breadwinning are much inclined to demand that the rich share with them, which would reduce the country to desolation."[15] Without daily work, artisans and labourers were reduced to begging. On December 1, 1530 the mayor of Leiden, Willem van Oy, opened a session of the city council by stating that because the textile trade was in such decline, severe poverty, great hunger, and grief were suffered daily by the people. A common daily prayer was, "O dear Lord, do not pass us by with the plague, because we would rather die than continue to live." Some of the poor resorted to stealing, and many textile workers were forced to leave the city.[16] Reduced to begging, they moved from town to town by the hundreds, sometimes stealing and plundering in order to survive.[17]

With economic crisis came political crisis. In 1531 Christian II of Denmark with his army of 12,000 soldiers spent some time in Holland. The city of Alkmaar was plundered. Charles V, who supported Christian, barred Dutch ships and grain barges from passing through the Sunt, the narrow channel connecting the Nordsee to the Ostsee. By the time Christian's army finally left on Dutch boats for Norway, some 8000 fishermen had lost their employment.[18] The closing of the Sunt to the Dutch, first in 1522-1523 and then in 1531-1532, caused the price of bread to rise considerably because the Netherlands depended for its grain imports on the Baltic countries.[19] Another cause of inflation was cheap silver, a result of the new technology introduced in central Europe and growing trade with Africa, that had been flooding the money market since the beginning of the century. Gold from Mexico and Peru, and later silver from Potosi and Zacatecas continued to increase the rate of inflation. As a consequence of all these factors, the price of grain tripled between 1519 and 1560.[20] With the high rate of inflation and increasing food prices, the impoverishment of the urban poor also grew. The government watched nervously as civil unrest spread. If the unemployed textile workers were to join forces with the sailors and fishermen, riots and insurrection were to be expected.[21] According to the historian Mellink, stagnation in the Dutch textile, fishing and shipping industries during the years 1532 to 1536 greatly encouraged the spread of Anabaptism.[22]

The religious issues of the day were hotly debated everywhere. Posters and libelous placards appeared in public places pillorying the abuses of the church and the clergy in general.[23] Rhetoricians and popular writers eagerly selected those ideas which supported their visions of a new society and thereby contributed, sometimes unintentionally, to the preparation of the ground for the Reformation.

Popular faith in the first decades of the sixteenth century was pious, superficial, superstitious and receptive to supernatural events. Decrees of the Roman Catholic church were still accepted without question, but when it came to the canonical law and the jurisdiction of the church, even the most pious Catholics had problems. The many privileges of the church were generally considered to be unjust. Many of the pious, however, never considered leaving the church, despite their strong anticlerical feelings. Criticism was aimed at the abuses of the clergy and the religious orders, not at the doctrines of the church.

Anticlericalism had a long tradition in the Netherlands and was prominent in the general desire for reformation, for economic as well as religious reasons.[24] One example of an economic issue that fuelled this desire came in 1517 when the magistrate of Leiden demanded an extra contribution from the clergy and members of religious orders for the restoration of the city walls. They finally agreed to give nine pennies each a year if the burghers would make regular payments as well, and if their privileges would be guaranteed.[25] The constant expansion of the property of the eleven monasteries in the city of Leiden had long been a problem. As a consequence of their expansion the number of taxable households in Leiden had diminished from 1114 in 1497 to 976 in 1502, an average decrease of more than 2% a year. In 1524 Charles V decreed that the monasteries were not to be allowed to buy or receive any houses or properties within the city walls, but the practice continued until the Reformation made most of the monasteries obsolete.[26]

In the textile industry and in food production even more than in real estate, the monasteries were unfair competitors for the burghers.[27] As early as 1453, the magistrates of The Hague intervened to prohibit the monastery of St. Elisabeth from producing any woolen cloth for the market so that the income of poor communities would not be reduced.[28] Wage work of monks and nuns, however, was not included in this injunction. In the early sixteenth century the religious order of the Beguines was the target of a protest by linen and wool weavers together with the guilds of the provinces of Holland and West Friesland. They maintained that as a consequence of the unfair competition from the beguinages they had become paupers, forced to beg for bread with their children. If the government would not take action, they would have to emigrate to other countries. The government responded immediately by prohibiting the Beguines from producing any linen or woolen cloth for the market.[29] Seldom would the church voluntarily give up any of her privileges. The political and economic power of religious institutions finally decreased during the Reformation, when the number of members of religious orders declined rapidly.[30]

The ignorance, incompetence and fanaticism of the conservative clergy often made an important negative contribution to the Reformation as well. After the condemnation of Luther by the faculty of Louvain in November 1519, the Dominicans led the rest of the conservative clergy in a fierce counter-attack on the Saxon reformer. In some places sermons were preached against Luther every Sunday. Erasmus was correct when he observed that a campaign of vilification was likely to advance the very cause people sought to injure. It was probably for this reason that in 1525 friars were forbidden to mention Luther at all in their sermons.[31]

In Leiden the city council identified the cause of Lutheran heresy as the abuses of the higher clergy and the growing number of members of religious orders from outside the city who were establishing themselves in the local monasteries. These newcomers were blamed for spreading all kinds of false doctrines.[32] In January 1525 the magistrate decided to investigate these problems and present his findings to the attorney general at the end of March.[33] The initiative was strongly supported by the Governess of the Low Countries, Margaretha of Austria. In a letter to the Count of Hoogstraten she wrote that the major cause for the growing number of Lutherans must be seen in the many abuses committed by the clergy. For this reason, she argued, Governor Hoogstraten should instruct the local city councils to make a rigorous inquiry into those abuses and report their findings to her. A general report would then be prepared and presented to the secret council of her government in the presence of the highest officials of the church.[34] When the heretic hunters from Louvain complained to Margaretha that the writings of an unlearned man like Luther had such surprising effect, she quipped: "Well then, why don't all of you, who are apparently so learned, write against this unlearned one? Will the world not believe a crowd of learned ones more than one unlearned man?"[35] The governor Hendrik van Nassau was even more blunt with the Dominican friars in Den Haag: "why don't you go and proclaim the gospel of Christ honestly and sincerely as Luther does, avoid any offence or scandal, and you will have no reason to complain about anybody."[36] The government's tacit support of Luther did not pass unnoticed by the local authorities.[37] Generally they were unwilling to undertake any action against the Lutherans as long as they gave no offence and created no public disorder.

The Frisian chronicler Peter Taborita described the general religious situation in the Low Countries around 1524 in his *Historie van Friesland*.

Luther, he wrote, had caused a lot of trouble. All Christianity had been affected by his tracts against the Pope, the clergy, indulgences, the mendicants and parents who lock their children up in monasteries at an early age. These children were now leaving religious institutions. There was great unrest among the monks and nuns. No one wanted to give alms to the mendicants and if they preached something unfamiliar, people wanted to know where it was written in Scripture. Compared to Amsterdam, where quarrels and possible riots made the situation tense, Friesland was relatively calm. To Taborita's knowledge, only two priests had left the church to become Lutherans, but he had to admit that even in Friesland many of the clergy and learned ones felt attracted to Luther because he proved his arguments so convincingly from the Scriptures.[38]

At the same time, the common people were attending Bible study groups or conventicles in greater and greater numbers. In March 1524 one of these groups, composed entirely of artisans, was surprised in Antwerp and summoned before the magistrate. The fact that no member of the clergy or scholar was leading this large group of thirty or forty men points to the presence of strong lay leaders and a high rate of literacy.[39]

The general name given to these "heretics" was now "Lutherans," but how Lutheran was the content of the faith of these dissenters? The trial of Willem Dircx, called the "Roode Cuiper," in Utrecht from July 6-13, 1525 provides us with some information. Willem was accused of being a Lutheran heretic, or a dirty Lutheran scoundrel. People had heard him say that the pope has no power to bind or to loose; that St. Peter was not a pope; that no one should honour or pray to the saints; that they ought to pray to God alone; that there was no need to go to confession; that the apostles were Christians like them, and if they had done no wrong they would not have been punished; that a priest should be married and have children before his ordination, as Paul clearly points out to Timothy; that Mary was not different from any other woman, but like a bag from which flour had been poured out; that the eucharist was nothing more than common bread; that pilgrimages where nonsense. When Willem was asked where he got his wisdom, he replied that God was giving him the same grace he had given the fishermen in Jesus' time.[40]

Forced to recant, Willem was condemned to do proper penance before he was forgiven. In his penitential sermon at the Cathedral of Utrecht, he reviewed his heresies once more, including his rejection of the oath and his belief that faith cannot exist without good works. In regard to the celibacy of the church fathers, Willem simply stated he had never seen any of them. The apostles, Willem explained, were considered to be criminals by their pagan judges, just as the Jews considered Jesus to be a breaker of the law. The mass, Willem was sure, was never mentioned in the gospels. If it is profitable before God, he did not know. All he knew about the mass was that it was good business for the priests. The closing remarks of his sermon made it clear that Willem was eluding the crucial questions by simply saying he did not know. It is not surprising then, that his sermon ended with a question: How is it possible that a grown man can be considered to be a good Christian without knowing the basic truths of the church, which even children know and believe?[41]

Willem de Cuiper was Lutheran in his rejection of the priest's mediating role, celibacy, the apostolic succession of the papacy and the binding and loosing power of the pope; in his interpretation of the martyrdom of Christ and the apostles, he was not. The rejection of Mary as being in any way different from other women was quite common among the Lutherans in the Low Countries, but that she served as a bag from which the flour has been poured out sounds very much like the later Melchiorite and Mennonite doctrine of incarnation, whose exact origin is still unknown.[42] It is also noteworthy that this point was not one of the eleven accusations against him dealt with in his public sermon of penance. Not "Lutheran" as well were his rejection of the oath and his emphasis on good works, as well as his rejection of any kind of transubstantiation. All these differences point to the fact that Willem de Cuiper was not a Lutheran but a Sacramentarian. Sacramentarianism at this stage was a heterogeneous religious movement whose major common denominator was the rejection of the Roman Catholic sacraments. A second characteristic, growing in importance, was the view that Scripture had greater authority than the doctrines and traditions of the church.

Jan de Bakker, known as Pistorius, was born in 1499 and educated in the famous Hieronymus School of the Brothers of the Common Life in Utrecht. Under the influence of such famous teachers as Hinne Rode and probably Brother Wouter, Jan soon adopted Sacramentarian views. In 1520 he was sent to Louvain with a special recommendation to Erasmus and in 1522 he was ordained in Utrecht in spite of his "evangelical-mindedness." As a priest Jan wasted no time reading the mass, but spent most of his time in Woerden teaching and preaching the gospel. In 1523 he and his friend Aert were captured for the first time for spreading heresies, but a supporter from Woerden managed to get them out of prison. Sentenced by the Emperor to make a pilgrimage to Rome, they travelled to Wittenberg to visit Luther and were back within three months. Because Woerden had now become too dangerous for them, Pistorius began to travel as an itinerant evangelist from town to town and from village to village, teaching and preaching at the many Sacramentarian conventicles that had begun to form in the Netherlands. In 1524 Pistorius renounced his ordination as a priest and secretly married Jacoba Janszdochter. His support seems to have been so strong that it needed the intervention of the government of Holland to capture him and send him to The Hague on May 19, 1525. Even on the way there his guards gave him an opportunity to escape which he refused.

Pistorius' trial lasted from July 11 until he was burned at the stake on September 15. This was reported by Gnapheus, his former friend from the Hieronymus school and a co-prisoner.[43] The main charge against Pistorius was his secret marriage, which he defended as being biblical. The official reasons for his death sentence were: (1) Jan de Bakker does not believe that the pope is the vicar of Christ. During his trial Pistorius had stated that most of the popes had been scoundrels. He believed that the entire institution of the papacy was built on worldly power and had no spiritual authority at all, and the power to bind and to loose belonged only to God.[44] (2) Jan felt free to eat meat on Fridays, because fasting was a human institution already rejected by Jesus and by Paul.[45] (3) Jan stated that a priest is free to marry, referring to Genesis and to Paul. It was better to marry than to burn, even for a priest. Celibacy he called a human regulation and not of God.[46] (4) Jan went to Wittenberg in disobedience to the decree of the emperor.[47] (5) Jan claimed that no one needed to go to confession. Whoever confessed his sins to God, repented sincerely and changed his life would be forgiven by God. Jan stated that the way the confessional was conducted in the church is a mockery that only fosters sin, because no genuine repentance and change of life is required for absolution. (6) Jan thought that the eucharist can be celebrated by any true believer who has received the gift of the Holy Spirit.

Gnapheus' report goes far beyond these official accusations. As one of his inquisitors observed, the Pistorius was a greater heretic than Luther. Jan de Bakker, it was charged, did not recognise the authority of the church's doctrines, ordinances or ceremonies unless they were supported by Scripture. This doctrine of *sola scriptura* seemed to be the centre of his faith: because the Bible was the full revelation of God's will, nothing needed to be added or explained by either the fathers or doctors of the church. The basic principles of this hermeneutic were that the Holy Spirit was sent by Jesus Christ to illuminate and to lead the believer into all truth, and that the Scripture was its own best interpreter.[48] Pistorius believed his ordination as a priest to be worthless, because he had bought it for money while, in fact, no one could be made a priest by ordination. The congregation, he believed, should follow the instructions of Paul and Peter and elect its own pastors,[49] with the entire congregation participating in the process of decision making. The genuine church was an invisible spiritual gathering of all those who believed, ruled by nothing other than the Word of God.[50] Membership in such a church was voluntary and based upon faith, commitment and a new life. The function of the church was only to proclaim the gospel; it was God who gave the growth. No one should be forced to become a Christian, or persecuted because he was not one; whoever does not want to believe should be free to remain an unbeliever.[51] The power of such a church was spiritual, and the sword with which she fought was the Word of God[52] which enabled her to admonish and rebuke, but never to persecute or use any form of compulsion or violence. The believer who fell into sin and did not repent after being admonished two or three times must be shunned according to the instructions of Paul.[53] Believers were not to be magistrates,[54] but like Paul should use their gifts and powers only for service and healing. Paul gave the literal sword to the magistrates to punish evildoers (agitators, adulterers, fornicators, drunkards and blasphemers) and to protect the good. Heretics should be admonished and punished only with the word of God, but the government and the church together are crucifying believers as the Jews did Jesus, and letting Barabbas go free.[55] Assured that his sins were forgiven, Jan did not fear the fire of the stake. In any case, his death would not be the end of the movement, because "there are many thousands in Holland, who feel and understand the same way as I do."[56]

From the additional information provided by Gnapheus, it is evident that Pistorius had gone beyond Luther. In his ecclesiology, his understanding of church discipline, his interpretation of the Lord's Supper, his rejection of any kind of violence for religious purposes and his statement that Christ prohibited his followers from participating in all government, he was neither Lutheran nor Zwinglian, but came very close to the understanding of Swiss Anabaptism.[57] This is not to suggest that Jan de Bakker was an Anabaptist, but it would explain the rumours of the presence of Anabaptism in the Netherlands before 1530. Even if we take into account that this report was edited by Gnapheus between 1525 and 1529, and thus probably reflects some of the editor's own insights,[58] it is still amazing how close Pistorius came to many of the later Anabaptist positions, especially those of Menno Simons. In his own way, Menno would repeat virtually all of Pistorius' statements. Did Menno know Jan de Bakker, or the report from Gnapheus? The sources do not say, but it is significant that such "Anabaptist" ideas were circulating among Sacramentarians in the Netherlands in the 1520s.

The Sacramentarian message was negative in its rejection of the teaching authority of the Pope and the Catholic church, the mediatory function of priests, the confessional and the eucharist. In time, its positive message became more clear: salvation for all people for all time had been accomplished by Christ's death on the cross, and participation in this salvation is possible by faith.[59] The main emphasis of the Dutch Sacramentarians, however, was not justification by faith *alone*, but faith followed by new life in accordance with the gospel. This praxis-oriented emphasis on the Christian life went back to the Modern Devotion, which certainly helped to prepare the ground for the Reformation even though its basic doctrines remained Roman Catholic. As the Reformation would do later, the Modern Devotion emphasized the preaching and reading of the gospel in the vernacular, and a turning away from the ceremonial and liturgical to a simple biblical life style which sometimes was called "evangelical-mindedness."[60] Probably because of this long tradition of Bible-oriented Christian life within the Catholic church, Pistorius along with many other evangelical priests and humanists still believed in the early 1520s that a genuine change of life within the framework of the existing church was possible.

In a writing published already in 1523, the *Summa der godliker schrifturen*, J. J. van Toorenbergen saw the baptismal vow as the starting point for a religious change which, if it were taken seriously by all Christians, would transform their individual as well as their social lives.[61] Baptism was the sign of dying to sin and resurrection to new life, as well as the promise of lay Christians, clergy and members of religious orders alike, to obey the gospel. The real difference was not between lay Christians and the clergy, but between believers and unbelievers, between obedience and disobedience to the word of God, van Toorenbergen emphasized.[62] Faith not only justified believers, but also changed their lives, because faith brings forth good works. Those who believe, begin to love, and only love can produce deeds which are pleasing to God.[63] For van Toorenbergen, if every Christian would begin to love, all of society would change. There would be enough resources for everyone to live decently. Everyone would be literate and read the Bible in the vernacular.[64] Government would use its sword with justice and compassion[65] only for the punishment of the evil and the protection of the good. Aggressive violence would be out of the question.[66] In fact, in a truly evangelical society no government would be needed, because every Christian would already be doing from the heart everything that is right.[67] Van Toorenbergen was still careful not to encourage dissent from the Catholic church: "I do not teach you that you should not keep the commandments of the holy church, but I teach you that you should know, . . . that you do not sin, if you do not keep them," because the church now decrees many things which God never commanded.[68] For him the gospel was the only norm and authority for Christian life, but writing in 1523, he still considered it possible to evangelize from within the Catholic church.

Gnapheus, in the introduction to his *A comfort and mirror for the sick* (*Een troost ende spiegel der zieken*) written in 1525, saw things very differently.[69] Responding to the wish of "many brothers,"[70] he began with a strong anticlerical statement. The clergy were not like pastors, but like wolves eager to devour the possessions of the poor, of widows and orphans, and of the rich as well.[71] Whatever they did was all for the sake of money. They carried the gospel on their sleeves and in their mouths, but not in their hearts and hands.[72] While praying long prayers for the sick, they were waiting for them to pass away in order to lay their hands on their inheritances and property.[73] They did not understand the figurative meaning of the sacrifices in the Old Testament and their fulfillment in Jesus Christ, nor did they understand that now is the time of compassion and not of sacrifices.[74] They sold the justification and peace of God to unbelievers for money.[75] If lay people admonished them, they became irritated and did not listen.[76]

Anticlericalism obviously remained at the core of Sacramentarianism. What made this document so dangerous to the Catholic church was its character of moral indignation. Gossip and slander of the clergy had existed long before the Reformation, but now the criticism had developed into a clearly defined critique based upon the standards of Scripture. The clergy had simply failed to do their job properly, and because they were quite unwilling to change anything, a polarization was inevitable.

But Gnapheus did not stop with this negative critique. He knew that to dwell on the shortcomings of the church did not help or change anything. It was time for lay people who read the Scripture and who recognized divine truth to decide for themselves how they ought to walk in the ways of the Lord, for they had been called to "follow after" (*navolchden*) him.[77] As believers they were called to do God's will[78] and to help their neighbours, like the good Samaritan.

The new programme to be carried out by committed Christians was straightforward. The rich must share with the poor, for they had received their wealth for that purpose. Those who had received wisdom must teach the unwise. Those who had worldly power were to use it in defence of the powerless, the widows and orphans. Whoever had received light must let it shine. Love of God was in the first place love for one's brothers.[79] The Christian life does not find fulfillment in material wellbeing or in ceremonies or sacraments. Rather, it is life in Spirit and in truth, in love and compassion, in peace and tranquility in the Lord.[80]

Gnapheus' new program did not limit itself to individual Christians. He continued with the presentation of a platform for an evangelical town. All the money now given to the church and its different institutions was to be deposited into a community fund. There was no doubt in Gnapheus' mind that this money would be enough to solve all the immediate and long term problems of the evangelical town such as poverty, illiteracy, unemployment, mendicancy, prostitution of the poor and idleness. In the hands of honest deacons the money would serve the purpose for which it was given. All this would be possible in a Christian society if the love of virtue and compassion would come from the heart.[81] But even Gnapheus was realistic enough to admit that the strongest opponent of such an evangelical society would be the church, especially the mendicants.

The 1557 revised edition of *A comfort and mirror for the sick* has been greatly altered. In it, the initiative for the building of an evangelical society had been taken away from the laity and given to the God-ordained government.[82] Lay people were individual Christians who practiced charity and love for their neighbours. The kingdom of God was turned inwards: God's kingdom was a spiritual and inward kingdom which did not come about by the outward observance of time, place, person, holy days, hymns or candlelight. The kingdom of God was within each believer as righteousness, truth, holiness, peace and joy in the Holy Spirit.[83]

After the trials of 1525 most of the prominent Sacramentarian leaders disappeared, either going underground or leaving the country.[84] But the growing persecutions which resulted from ever stricter sanctions against leaders did not stop the spread of sacramentarianism. Between 1525 and 1530 the movement penetrated many towns and villages, and the number of conventicles, now mostly led by lay people, continued to increase. By 1530 the reformation of the Netherlands had become a movement of the common people[85] who read the Bible with the faith of children, taking everything literally.[86] When they compared the apocalyptical visions of the end times with contemporary circumstances, they came to the conclusion that the end times had already begun. At the same time, the movement became more aggressive in its protest against the moral misconduct and corruption of the clergy. The posting of critical satires and lampoons on church doors or confessionals was often used as a means of public protest.[87]

Women played a prominent role early in the Sacramentarian movement. It appears to have been three women who attacked the houses of some of the distinguished burghers of Leiden as well as those of the pastor of St. Peter, smearing the doors with dirt and smashing the windowpanes.[88] In this time of lay leadership, charismatic gifts were given a more significant place. On July 8, 1529, an unnamed labourer was leader of a conventicle in Veere at the house of Cornelis de Cuyper. One of the participants confessed later at her trial that this preacher was certainly filled with the Holy Spirit. Another stated that one could not listen to the words of this man without feeling blessed, and he was willing to lose his wife, house and everything else just for the sake of hearing him.[89] Two important shifts are evident in this report: Sacramentarians were gathering not only to read the Bible together, but also to listen to spirit-filled lay leaders; and requirements for leadership included not only knowledge of the Scripture, but also charismatic gifts. Although we do not have enough evidence to prove that this was a general development within the Sacramentarian movement, it is an early indication of a trend which dominated the decade of the thirties.

Another indication that Sacramentarianism was becoming more sectarian is that it was reported in Leiden that the number of participants in conventicles was increasing. According to official reports, at their gatherings the Holy Scripture was read and interpreted in the following way: "One of the people had a big book on his lap. He preached from it and gave interpretations in accordance with their appetites."[90] Even if this report is a subjective one, the development of the movement in succeeding years proves it to be correct. Once unqualified charismatic lay leaders took control of the movement, they certainly were able to find in Scripture whatever they needed to justify the satisfaction of their "appetites."

The Sacramentarians in the Netherlands did not become Lutherans, although Luther was well known in the Low Countries.[91] The central theme of his Reformation, justification by faith alone, did not satisfy the Sacramentarian emphasis on Christian life and praxis and their expectation of a radical reformation of the entire society. Duke observes that "given the cardinal importance of justification by faith alone in Reformation theology, there are disconcertingly few explicit references to it" in the Low Countries.[92] The historians de Hoop Scheffer,[93] Kuehler,[94] Mellink,[95] and Duke agree that Sacramentarianism eventually merged with Anabaptism.[96] As Duke notes, "Long before 1530, heresy had penetrated to the grassroots of society and shown, on occasions, a disposition to violence, but as the decade went on dissent took a more popular and aggressive note, as if in preparation for Anabaptism."[97] Deppermann comes to the conclusion that the Melchiorite message of the early thirties found its most important foothold in the Netherlands in lay oriented Bible study groups or conventicles.[98]

Menno Simons was ordained a priest in a time of general unrest, a time of fundamental social, political and religious transitions. Most of the radicals of the 1520s, including Erasmus, still believed a reformation of all areas of life was possible from within the existing structures. In the 1540s, Menno issued a call for the establishment of a Christian society led by a Christian government. As can be seen by surveying the Dutch historical and intellectual landscape of the first two decades of the sixteenth century, Menno's call was not really new, but rather mirrored similar calls being made by reform-minded contemporaries. Pistorius, the *Summa der godliker sriptuuren*, W. Gnapheus and other Christian Humanists had already developed similar visions and even platforms for the establishment of a Christian society in the 1520s.

If there where thousands of Christians who thought as Pistorius thought, as he claimed at his trial in 1525, was Menno Simons one of them, or was he at least influenced by such people? This would seem to be a logical conclusion, particularly since his early actions, such as his questioning the doctrine of transubstantiation from the beginning of his priestly ministry, suggest a strong Sacramentarian influence. Menno claimed, much later in his life, that only his desire for money and fame kept him in the Catholic church until 1536, but a plausible hypothesis can be made that as a Catholic priest, Menno shared with other evangelical priests and humanists the expectation of a reformation from within. His earliest writings, as we will see, confirm this hypothesis.

When Menno left the Catholic church, he accepted baptism at the hands of Melchiorites, thus joining the baptizing movement at the worst possible time, just after the collapse of the Münsterite kingdom. What explanation can be given for this? Was Menno perhaps already committed to aspects of the movement as a fellow member of the covenant? What, in fact, was Menno's relationship to Münster and the Münsterites, given that he continued to call them his "dear brothers and sisters, who erred just a little"? In chapter two we will explore these questions by examining Menno's earliest writings in detail.

CHAPTER TWO

MENNO AND MÜNSTER:
A VISION OF THE NEW JERUSALEM

As a Roman Catholic priest, Menno Simons shared many of the reforming expectations of his contemporaries. He was, however, first of all interested in his career and the security of his office. Sacramentarian ideas and the early writings of Luther forced him to study the Scriptures seriously and he became quite an effective "evangelical priest," but like many others he was able to spiritualize his new understanding of the Lord's Supper and of baptism while continuing to celebrate the Eucharist and to baptize children into the Catholic church.

Menno's career as an evangelical priest and his growing relationship to the Melchiorite "covenanters" has remained in the shadows, even though it is known that he established contact with Melchiorites and Münsterites while serving as a priest. A careful analysis of Menno's earliest writings sheds light on the early transitions Menno experienced. There is strong circumstantial evidence, first of all, that Menno may have been a baptized "covenanter" while still serving as a priest. In the second place, the evidence of Menno's early writing places Menno much closer to the events in Münster than is sometimes assumed. The messianic kingship of Jan van Leiden and the apocalyptic crusade of the Anabaptist kingdom of Münster against the unbelievers were events that forced Menno to develop his own understanding first of the kingship of Christ and of his kingdom, and then of the anticipation of the New Jerusalem in the community of regenerated believers.

When did Menno join the Covenanters?

The time of Menno's baptism has always been a subject of speculation. It has been assumed that he was baptized by Obbe Philips after his departure from the Catholic Church in January 1536. This assumption is supported by tradition, but has no other support in the sources.

Menno himself makes only one explicit reference to his baptism. It comes a long time after the event, in 1544 in the exposition of the doctrine of incarnation for John a Lasco.[1] There he writes, "Yes, I was often troubled at heart, even after my baptism, (so much so) that many a day I abstained from food and drink because of the great anxiety of my soul ..."[2] According to Menno, he learned about the Melchiorite doctrine of incarnation from "the brothers" (*den Broederen*) and struggled with it for days, weeks and months before and after his baptism. In fact, Menno must have been confronted with the Melchiorite doctrine of incarnation from the time he first began to oppose the Münsterites with mouth and pen, maybe even earlier, but certainly not later than spring or early summer of 1534.[3]

The quoted text from 1544 is vague enough with regard to time, so that different readings are possible. Menno says that he was shocked when he heard about this doctrine from the brethren for the first time, but perhaps this happened already in 1534, and given the slowness of the process of Menno's formation of theological concepts, he may still have had to struggle with it when he was baptized in 1536. This is the traditional interpretation of events, that places Menno's baptism after his departure from the priesthood.

There are a series of points that can be brought against this reading of the evidence.

 a. The quoted text suggests a period of months, not years, suggesting that Menno's baptism must be placed close to the time that he learned about the Melchiorite doctrine of incarnation.
 b. Menno learned about the Melchiorite doctrine from "the brethren," opening the possibility that he might have been one of them already.
 c. Menno must have become acquainted with Melchiorite incarnational doctrine no later than early 1534, since it was one of the key doctrines upon which the Münsterite kingdom was built. In 1551 Menno claimed to have opposed the Münsterites for more than seventeen years, thus from 1534 on.[4] His analysis of the internal development of the Münsterite kingdom in his *Fundament-book*,[5] as we will see below, reveals a much closer relationship to Münster than Menno was willing to admit in his later writings.
 d. In his debate with Martin Micron in 1554, Menno states: "Already during my time in the papacy I came to understand that Christ, the Son of God, could not be a man of our human flesh."[6] Thus it appears that he became acquainted with the Melchiorite doctrine of incarnation while still a Catholic priest.
 e. The Melchiorite incarnational doctrine became the key to Menno's radical understanding of regeneration, as he described it in his

early writing on *Spiritual Resurrection*.[7] The unbalanced use of Scripture, the apocalyptic language and imagery, and the non-committal spiritualism of that writing argue that this tract was written before the *Blasphemy of John van Leiden*, most probably in the summer of 1534. When Menno wrote the *Spiritual Resurrection*, he obviously no longer had problems with the Melchiorite incarnational doctrine.

f. Judging from the contents of the tract, the writer of the *Spiritual Resurrection* must already have received the sign of Thau himself.

g. Menno's confession of faith dates from 1534. According to his tract *A Pathetic Supplication to all Magistrates* of 1551,[8] he opposed the Münsterites from the time of his conversion, for more than seventeen years.[9] Assuming that this dating is correct, Menno made his confession of faith in 1534, and may also have been baptized at that time, in the same process.

h. Assuming an early confession and baptism does not necessarily contradict the autobiographical presentation of his conversion in the "Autobiography" (*Uitgangh*). Although he confessed the name of the Lord early, he still remained in the security of the Catholic Church as an "evangelical preacher" and spiritual Christian. When, after Oldeklooster, this living in two worlds was no longer possible, he finally left the priesthood and was "converted in a new way..."[10] The emphasis in Menno's statement is not on conversion as such, but on the "new way" or "new sense" in which he was converted. A possible interpretation is to conclude that Menno already was a born-again Christian, but with his departure from the Catholic Church, his conversion received a deeper meaning and finally was complete.

i. In the *Spiritual Resurrection* Menno refers to baptism as the sign of Thau. Although he was very careful not to use this dangerous "Münsterite" metaphor in his later writings, in his *A Kind Admonition* from 1558 he states that because we have been born again, we have become brothers and sisters of Christ, recreated into the image of God, and "So we have been marked on our foreheads with the sign of Thau. Ezekiel 9."[11]

j. As Vos states, Menno recognized the Münsterite baptism with the sign of Thau as valid.[12]

k. Menno never denied having been baptized with the same baptism as the Münsterites. As a matter of fact, in the revised edition of the *Fundament-book* (1554/55) he states: "We do confess, dear Lords, that some of the false prophets have been baptized externally in

l. G. Nicolai states that Obbe Philips baptized Menno after the Anabaptist riots in Groningen and the taking over of Oldeklooster, thus in the spring of 1535.[14]

m. From the point of Menno's theological consistency, baptism in 1534 or 1535 must be considered a possibility because baptism as such did not have major ecclesiological implications for him. In Menno's early understanding, baptism was the sign of an individual covenant with God, but not of believers with one another.

n. Given the importance of believers' baptism in Menno's theology, it is strange that he never willingly gave away any information about his own baptism. If he was baptized already in 1534 or 1535 with the apocalyptic sign of Thau, this secrecy would be understandable.

Although the evidence gathered here is not indisputable or conclusive regarding Menno's early baptism in 1534 or 1535, it is the best evidence available. An examination of Menno's early writings and the influence of Melchiorite teaching on his own thought suggests, as will be seen below, that an early, rather than a late dating of Menno's joining the "covenanters" by baptism is a strong possibility.

Menno and the Münsterites: the *Blasphemy of Jan van Leiden*

The authorship of the Blasphemy

The tract against the *Blasphemy of Jan van Leiden*, attributed to Menno Simons, has raised many questions for scholars. Sepp was the first to question its authenticity on the grounds that it was first printed in 1627, and that no reference was ever made to it either by Menno himself or by his enemies.[15] In what follows we will review the evidence for and against Menno's authorship, turning in the end to the enduring question: If Menno really wrote the *Blasphemy*, why did he never use it to defend himself against the accusation of being a Münsterite?[16]

De Hoop Scheffer[17] countered Sepp's arguments, and maintained Menno's authorship of the tract. First of all, he asserted, the language identifies the author as Frisian. In 1535 there was only one Frisian who had the theological education and scriptural knowledge required to write such a tract, and who also called himself a covenanter, and that was Menno Simons. Furthermore, the style is the same as that of Menno's later writings: the *Fundament-book*, the *Meditation*, the *Spiritual Resurrection*, and the *New Creature*. Like Menno, the author of the *Blasphemy* shares the same expectations as the Münsterites except for his rejection of physical violence as the means by which to realize the kingdom and his rejection of polygamy. Moreover, tradition identified Menno as the author and the publishers of 1627, pious "Mennonites" who had known Menno's daughter,[18] recognized Menno's handwriting and did not question the authenticity of the tract. When he wrote this tract, Menno was unable to reveal his true identity because he was still the officiating priest in Witmarsum. The tract probably circulated only as a manuscript and remained unpublished after the government placard of spring 1535 imposed capital punishment on the publication of any heretical literature. Finally, de Hoop Scheffer argues, Menno appeared to make two allusions to this tract in the 1550s, both in his *Reply to Gellius Faber*[19] and in his *Reply to False Accusations*,[20] where he wrote that he had been fighting against the Münsterites from their earliest beginning to the end, in public and in secret, verbally and in writing. Cramer was not completely convinced by de Hoop Scheffer's arguments, but Frerichs supported his position.[21]

The historian Karel Vos came to the same conclusions as de Hoop Scheffer.[22] Vos considered the interesting possibility that the writing was a forgery dating from around 1620, but rejected the possibility. The language of the *Blasphemy* is identical to that of the early writings of Menno, but because these earlier writings were not known in the seventeenth century, no one could have imitated them. Starting from the assumption that the *Blasphemy* was written against Rothmann's *Van der Wrake (On Vengeance)* Vos argues that by 1620 it would have been impossible for anyone to write a refutation of Rothmann's pamphlet, because it had been completely forgotten by that time. Vos further confirmed the similarity of the language and style of the *Blasphemy* to that of the early writings of Menno Simons, but unlike de Hoop Scheffer, he assumed that the *Blasphemy* was published in 1535-36, possibly in Emden. He surmised that like the first print of Rothmann's *Van der Wrake*, the print of the *Blasphemy* was lost completely, except for a handwritten copy which ended up in Hoorn and was then printed with the annotation "Never Published Before."

Kühler[23] agreed with Scheffer and Vos that Menno wrote the *Blasphemy* in response to Rothmann's *Van der Wrake*. He maintained that although Menno had refuted Jan van Geelen publicly, he was losing his own parishioners to the Münsterite kingdom because of his ambiguous position. In his heart he already was a covenanter, but publicly he continued in his secure position as a Catholic priest. In order to deal with the mounting pressure he wrote his *Blasphemy*, but never had it published. When the kingdom of Münster collapsed a short time later, the need for its publication also disappeared. Kühler concluded that the manuscript was discovered later among the papers held by Menno's daughter and was subsequently published for the first time in 1627.

Modern scholars have not been entirely convinced by the above arguments. I. B. Horst[24] concluded that "internal evidence appears to substantiate Menno's authorship, but the arguments on this ground are not fully convincing." Krahn stated that Menno wrote his *Blasphemy* after Oldeklooster, thus after April 7, 1535, but never had it published.[25] The problem for Bornhaeuser was the same as for Sepp: if Menno was the author of the *Blasphemy*, why did he never use it in his own defence against the accusation that he was a Münsterite himself?[26] As we will see below, there is a plausible answer to this question that emerges from an analysis of the text itself.

There is one further body of evidence that speaks to the question of Menno's authorship of the *Blasphemy*, and that is a comparison of the Scripture references in the *Blasphemy* with uses in Menno's later authenticated writings. In fact, when we compare the Scripture references cited in the *Blasphemy* with the references used in the *Meditation*, the *New Birth* and the two editions of the *Fundament-book*,[27] where Menno makes many of the same statements in condensed form, the similarities in the content of the arguments and the quotations are significant, and can hardly be called accidental (see the Appendix below). Of the eighteen key references used to support the universal kingship of Jesus Christ against the pretended messianic kingship of Jan van Leiden in the first edition of the *Fundament-book*, ten were used in the *Blasphemy*. Of the eleven such references in the revised edition of the *Fundament-book*, eight were quoted in the *Blasphemy* and eight in the first edition. The fact that there are three references which occur only in the *Blasphemy* and in the revised edition suggests that Menno used the *Blasphemy* as a source for both editions.

The Scripture references used by Menno to support his arguments against the use of the sword show a similar pattern. Five of the eight references in the *Blasphemy* reappear in the first edition of the *Fundament-book*, and three of those five appear again in the revised edition. But when we compare the references of the first edition with those of the second, we find that five of the eight quotations in the second edition are the same as those in the first, and three[28] had not been used before at all. It appears that when he was discussing the problem of the sword in preparing the second edition, Menno sought out new quotations because the problem of violence was still present in 1554-55, whereas the Münsterite kingdom had become history by then.

The parallel biblical citations thus lend support to the conclusion that Menno Simons was in fact the author of the *Blasphemy* and that de Hoop Scheffer's thesis is correct, as supported by Vos and Kühler. When it is granted that Menno was the author of the *Blasphemy*, the conclusion is inescapable that he shared very many, if not most of the Münsterites' expectations. The question remains: if he agreed with the basic Münsterites programme, why did he oppose the Münsterites in this tract? A close examination of the *Blasphemy*, following the assumption that Menno wrote the tract, provides the answer.

Menno and the Münsterites: evidence from the Blasphemy

After Jan van Leiden arrived in Münster on January 13, 1534 every new development in the city became more and more determined by the apocalyptic anticipation of the New Jerusalem. The key actors, Melchior Hoffman as Elijah and Jan Matthijsz as Enoch, were present and the stage was set for the apocalyptic drama. Signs in the sky, prophetic visions and new revelations, and the taking over of Münster by the Anabaptists all seemed to confirm that the End Times had already begun. The covenanters, baptized with the sign of Thau on their foreheads, moved to the New Jerusalem by the thousands in order to escape the last day of judgment expected on Easter 1534. In the meantime, the leaders of Münster worked toward the restitution of God's people by instituting community of goods, rigorously implementing the true values and norms of the kingdom of God, and organizing a new society based on justice and righteousness.

The siege of the bishop was seen by the Münsterites as the final apocalyptic confrontation between the evil powers of the fallen world and God's new creation. When the ultimate apocalyptic event, the second coming of Christ, did not happen on Easter as he had predicted, Jan Matthijsz committed military suicide. It was Jan van Leiden's thankless task to bridge the chronological gap between the beginning of the End Times and their final consummation with new revelations—and mass-entertainments—until the Münsterite kingdom finally collapsed. What had begun as a spontaneous anticipation of the New Jerusalem, inspired by visions and miracles, ended as one of the most derided and tragic events in the history of Christianity.

Menno did share with the early Münsterites their doctrines of incarnation, the Lord's Supper, believers' baptism, nonviolence[29] and their eschatological expectation, which in Münster soon became apocalyptic. He did not object to the taking over of Münster by the Anabaptists through legal elections. Even the defence of the city against the siege of the bishop might have been acceptable to him[30] as a function of a legitimate government. What he could not support, however, was the proclamation of Münster as the New Jerusalem where the 144,000 elect, marked with the sign of Thau, should gather to start the conquest of the entire world in preparation for the coming millennium. Menno's view of the End Times in his *Blasphemy* is clearly amillennial. Against the Münsterite claim that they had been called to punish evildoers before the kingdom could be handed over to Christ, Menno states that the kingdom has been given to Christ *already*. When Christ returns, it will be for the final judgement of believers and unbelievers:

Then the faithful servants shall enter into the kingdom of their Lord; then the wicked will be punished, and all whose names are not found written in the book of life will be cast into the lake of fire . . . .[31]

After Münster was delivered miraculously into the hands of the Anabaptists, all the covenanters were summoned to meet at Bergklooster near Hasselt for the exodus to the New Jerusalem.[32] The response was overwhelming, alarming the magistrates of the cities and the central government,[33] whose quick action and massive apprehension of the covenanters prevented most of them from ever reaching Münster.[34] An attempt by the covenanters to take over Amsterdam in March 1534 failed,[35] and three of the Münsterite leaders were captured and executed with four others on March 26, 1534. Among them were Willem de Kuiper and Bartholomeus Boekbinder, who baptized and later ordained Obbe and Dirk Philips as elders of the Anabaptists.

While this was going on, Menno was still functioning as a parish priest. It appears that he continued to oppose the Münsterites, without much success. Excited by tales of miracles and signs from heaven and by reports of political and military victories of the covenanters in the New Jerusalem, people were unwilling to argue with or even to listen to someone like Menno. Although the promised deliverance of the besieged New Jerusalem did not come about on Easter and Jan Matthijsz' single handed attack on the army of the Bishop cost him his life, the kingdom of Münster continued under the leadership of Jan van Leiden.

Internal evidence indicates that Menno wrote his tract against the *Blasphemy of Jan van Leiden* after the proclamation of Jan van Leiden as the messianic King David of the New Jerusalem on the 31st of August, 1534.[36] Van Leiden's claim to be the "joyous king of all, the joy of the disconsolate" was unacceptable to Menno, and he repeats this sentence five times at the beginning of his tract.[37] The joy of the dawning kingdom of righteousness was a prominent theme of the New Jerusalem and the messianic kingship of Jan van Leiden,[38] so we can assume that it was used as a propaganda slogan in the Netherlands as well.[39] It appears that it was this political goal, summarized in this new political slogan of King David aimed at bringing more covenanters into the troubled New Jerusalem,[40] which caused Menno to take up his pen. [41]

Menno himself gives the reasons for writing his response in the beginning of his tract. [42] He says that he can no longer tolerate the Münsterite deceit. The Münsterites were avoiding any personal and public debate with him, and they had been unable to defend their heresy[43] with references from Scripture.[44] Thus it appears that Menno must have written his *Blasphemy* after Jan van Leiden's proclamation as King David (August 31, 1534) but before the publication of Bernhard Rothmann's *Restitution* (October 1534) and Concerning Vengeance (*Van der Wrake*, December 1534). A careful reading of the *Blasphemy* will provide more evidence for this conclusion.

Menno's purpose for writing against Jan van Leiden is clear. Menno argues on the basis of scriptural evidence that Christ was and is the only Messiah, the fulfillment of the promises of the Old Testament. The false teachers of Münster are deserting the pure doctrine of Christ, leaving their master behind and forgetting their covenant with God.[45] This covenant, which finds its fulfillment in love coming from a pure heart, a good conscience and a sincere faith, is being replaced in Münster by a new kind of pharisaic legalism which for Menno, as an evangelical priest and a spiritual Christian, was unacceptable. In the same way these false teachers had forgotten their baptism upon the cross of Christ because they had been seduced by the Babylonian harlot to the use of the sword.[46] It is now time for a Jeremiah to reprove the deceivers of the people and to burn the stubble of the false teachers with the fire of the Word of God.[47]

Continuing his scriptural arguments, Menno insists that Christ is the true King over all the earth and over his church. Since this is true, how can Jan van Leiden call himself "a joyous king over all, the joy of the disconsolate?"[48] Christ alone is our joy and salvation.[49] When Jan van Leiden claims to be the messianic King David of whom all the prophets testify,[50] he denies that Christ is the promised Messiah.[51] A greater Antichrist cannot arise, Menno concludes, than he who poses as the promised David. The church of Christ confesses no other King and Lord than Christ,[52] her only true shepherd,[53] the anointed David[54] who will remain forever.

In the *Blasphemy*, Menno already opposed the use of the sword. When the Münsterites supported violence by alluding to the armour of David, he argued, they should not forget that the Old Testament figure is to be applied to the truth of the New Testament, and that the flesh is to be understood as referring to the flesh; for the figure must reflect the truth, the image must reflect the being and the letter must reflect the Spirit.[55] Using this basic hermeneutic principle, it is easy to understand that Christians should fight only with the Word of God, which is *like* a two-edged sword (Rev. 2:16), but is not a physical sword. Christ himself never used any other weapon and neither should his followers, because they are to be like him.[56]

Referring to the apocalyptic crusade being preached in Münster, Menno argues scripturally that God has never used his people to punish his enemies. It is not by Christians that the Babylonian harlot will be destroyed (Rev. 16:17).[57] Before the last judgement Christ must return again as Scripture clearly testifies, but no one knows when this will happen. Jan van Leiden can never be the David who is preparing for the peaceful kingdom of Christ by destroying his enemies, because according to Scripture the messianic kingdom will be given to Christ by the Ancient of Days, not by Jan van Leiden (Dan. 17:15). The parable of the weeds is also misinterpreted by the Münsterites: it is not the covenanters, but rather the angels of God who will gather and burn the wicked ones after Christ's return.[58]

In his final appeal of the *Blasphemy*, Menno once more exhorts the Münsterites to take Scripture seriously. All that Christians need to do is to trust in the Lord and not in horses and swords (Isaiah 30:15). They have crossed the Red Sea, so why are they looking back to Egypt? Christ did not conquer his kingdom with the sword, but entered it through much suffering.[59] The imagery Menno used here was in part still apocalyptic, just as it still was in the *Spiritual Resurrection*. Menno quotes the book of Revelation fourteen times, but the framework of his theological discourse is now based upon Matthew (twenty-four references), Luke (sixteen references), John (twenty references) and Hebrews (fourteen references).

When was the blasphemy written?

As we have seen above, a general scholarly conclusion has been that Menno wrote his *Blasphemy* against Rothmann's *Van der Wrake*, probably after Oldeklooster.[60] If this were true, it would significantly shift the date of Menno's composition of the *Blasphemy*. In Vos' judgement, Menno's refutation follows Rothmann's *Van der Wrake* step by step.[61] But in fact, although Vos read Menno's *Blasphemy* very carefully, he never did compare it point by point with *Van der Wrake*. A careful reading of both tracts together soon makes it evident that Vos' thesis is very unlikely. In his supposed refutation Menno fails to mention the main subject of Rothmann's tract, namely the quest for vengeance. Even if Menno had been writing to counter the Münsterite claim that God wished to use them for the punishment of the wicked,[62] there is a wide gap between the "justified punishment" Menno is arguing against and the "relentless vengeance" or "vengeance with a double measure" advocated by Rothmann in *Van der Wrake*.[63] Furthermore, there is no attempt on Menno's part to argue against Rothmann's central concept of restitution. Inaugurated in Münster in February 1534[64] and based on new revelations that superseded the gospel of the suffering Christ,[65] restitution, according to Rothmann, included a new historical timetable.[66] The time of suffering and apostasy was now over, and the new time of restitution under the leadership of Jan van Leiden was dawning.[67] Apparently Menno knew nothing of this timetable, because he did not mention it, as he also failed to mention vengeance.

To the contrary, the central argument in the *Blasphemy* is directed against the Münsterites' claim that Jan van Leiden is the promised David, a joyous king over all, the joy of the disconsolate. This claim had clear messianic overtones[68] which Menno could not tolerate. If Menno had written his *Blasphemy* against Rothmann's *Restitution* and *Van der Wrake*, he would have been missing the point of those writings altogether. In those writings Rothmann explained that Jan van Leiden could not be David/Christ, because it is not David but Solomon who is the image of Christ.[69] Rothmann also was aware that the parable of the weeds (Matt. 13,30)[70] was interpreted by some to mean that it would not be the Münsterites, but God himself coming down from heaven with his angels who would take revenge on the unbelievers.[71]

In none of his works did Menno ever mention Rothmann or the titles of any of his writings, although in his later polemic writings as well as in the *Blasphemy* Menno constantly addresses his opponent by name.[72] There seems to be no doubt in Menno's mind that Jan van Leiden is the only one to be blamed for the new developments in Münster.[73] Furthermore, nowhere in the entire *Blasphemy* does Menno quote directly from *Van der Wrake*, nor does he refute in detail any of Rothmann's arguments. Considering the tendentious way Menno later refutes every argument and quotes every point made by opponents in his polemic writings against Martin Micron or Gellius Faber, this is an inconsistency that is hard to explain, if we are to assume that Menno is writing against *Van der Wrake*. Either Menno was not the author of the *Blasphemy*, or he did not know Rothmann's *Van der Wrake* at all, and it appears that the latter conclusion is the one warranted.[74]

Through his personal contacts with the leaders of the early Münsterite kingdom and with the members of his own parish who joined the New Jerusalem, Menno must have been very well informed about the ideological and theological developments in Münster.[75] As someone with inside information who called himself a covenanter, but who maintained a critical distance from Münster, there is hardly anything in the *Blasphemy* that Menno could not have known by early September or October 1534. Since the *Blasphemy* is clearly not a refutation of Rothmann's *Van der Wrake*, the conclusion is justified that Menno wrote this tract against Jan van Leiden's self proclaimed messianic kingship in the second half of 1534.

The use of Scripture references also suggests that Menno was not attempting to refute Rothmann's arguments in *Van der Wrake*. Rothmann's use of Scripture is sophisticated, selective and to the point. He introduces the theme of vengeance with Psalm 149:6-9.[76] From Acts 3:20-23 he concludes that Christ is now in heaven and will remain there until the creation of a new heaven and a new earth. In the meantime the revelation of Jeremiah 30 is being fulfilled: God has raised from among us a prophet to whom we now must listen, Jan van Leiden. Using Jeremiah 30:18-24, he then argues that the true Israel is now being restored in Münster under the leadership of a prophet who has come very close to the Lord. This, then, must also be the time of God's vengeance[77] on his enemies. The yoke of slavery (Jer. 30:8-9) has been broken from the necks of the true Israelites and covenanters in Münster. Now they serve only the Lord and their King David. Jan van Leiden is not the Christ,[78] for Christ's kingdom is not of this world (John 18:36). Rather, Jan van Leiden is the David who must come to take vengeance on the wicked before the Christ can establish his everlasting kingdom of peace.[79] Only when the time of vengeance is over will the kingdom of God be established.

The key references in *Van der Wrake* are Psalm 149, Jeremiah 30, Acts 3, and 2 Peter 3. They are all used to legitimize the role of Jan van Leiden as prophet and King David over the new Israel, to support the doctrine of restitution and to justify vengeance on unbelievers. Rothmann does not claim a messianic role for Jan van Leiden, nor does he claim that Münster is already the everlasting kingdom of peace. But Münster is the beginning of the restorations that will occur in the End Times, based on new revelations that supersede all revelations of the Old and New Testaments.

It is well known that Menno used Scripture as much as possible to make his points, so it is significant that he does not refer directly to any of Rothmann's quotations or interpretations except for Jeremiah 30:8.[80] For Rothmann, this text proves that Jan van Leiden is the promised

David, whereas for Menno it applies to Christ.[81] Menno has no key references on which to build his arguments as Rothmann does. What he tries to prove in his *Blasphemy* is that Christ is the promised David who is already the Lord of heaven and earth, that in claiming to be "the joyous king over all" Jan van Leiden is putting himself above Christ, that we now live in the time of the cross of Christ until his second coming, and that the punishment of the wicked will be carried out by God's angels on the day of judgment.

If Menno did read Rothmann's *Van der Wrake* before writing his *Blasphemy*, we can only conclude that he missed Rothmann's major point when he argued against the pretended messianic kingship of Jan van Leiden. Rothmann is very clear throughout the entire document that although Jan van Leiden has been chosen by God from among them as prophet and ruler to prepare the way for the coming messianic kingdom of peace, and has been seen by some as David/Christ,[82] he is not the messiah. Menno's *Blasphemy* makes a convincing argument against the popular conception of Jan van Leiden's role,[83] but it is not a refutation of Rothmann's *Van der Wrake*.

Menno and the Münsterites: Menno's baptism

In the *Blasphemy* Menno identifies himself with the Münsterites. Addressing all true brothers and fellow members of the covenant,[84] he constantly uses the first person plural pronoun "us": God has called "us" out of the darkness into the light; Jesus Christ must keep "us" upon the right way; Satan should not deceive "us"; no bitterness must spring up among "us"; it must be that sects spring up among "us."[85] This "us" implies that Menno identified himself fully with the true brothers and fellow members of the covenant, sharing their understanding of faith and life before the false teachers arose from among them, before the Münsterite kingdom under the leadership of Jan van Leiden was established. The evidence points to Menno as a covenanter who might even have been baptized, as Vos suggests.[86]

This hypothesis does not, however, answer all our questions. Why did Menno not address the urgent question of polygamy, the greatest scandal of the New Jerusalem, which was introduced in July of 1534?[87] Did he not believe the rumours?[88] He may have considered them slander, a most effective weapon in the time of the Reformation which Menno himself learned to use masterfully, as we will see later. That information about this scandalous institution[89] could have been kept within the walls of Münster for very long is unlikely, but we must remember that polygamy was only defended officially for the first time by Rothmann in his *Restitution* of November 1534. There is also a clear statement in *Van der Wrake* that some aspects of the new freedom in the New Jerusalem cannot be released to outsiders.[90] When Menno in his *Fundament-book* called the Münsterites his "dear sisters and brothers" who "simply erred a little," he considered their error to be not polygamy, but the use of the sword to protect their faith.[91] Marriage did become a problem in Münster, but in 1539-40 Menno was still reluctant to name polygamy as the offence. Perhaps Menno did not believe all the rumours, or perhaps polygamy was not the general practice in Münster. All Münsterites, especially the "dear sisters and brothers of Menno," may not have been involved.

Other issues that the *Blasphemy* leaves unaddressed are the taking over of the city by the Anabaptists, the "magisterial reformation" of all its burghers on penalty of expulsion, and the defense of the city against the siege of the bishop. From Menno's later writings, it is evident that he was open to the possibility of a Christian government that would carry the sword for the punishment of the evil and the protection of the good (Rom. 13), and possibly also for the defense of its subjects against illegal aggression.[92] When it comes to matters of faith, however, Menno maintained throughout that Christians should fight only with the double edged sword, the Word of God.

Conclusion

When we conclude, as it appears that we must, that the Blasphemy was written by Menno Simons, the evidence leads to the conclusion that he called himself a "covenanter" as early as 1534. He shared with the early Münsterites their belief in the baptism of adults[93] and most of their doctrines and expectations. Being very well informed, through private and public debates with the early Münsterite leaders and confrontation with his own parishioners who had joined the Münsterites, Menno became suspicious as soon as the New Jerusalem began to be built by human will and force. Apparently he had no objections to the taking over of Münster by the Anabaptists through legal elections, miracles and charismatic actions, given his silence on these matters. But the aggressive use of the sword and the messianic kingship of Jan van Leiden made Menno the most outspoken leader of a growing opposition to the Münsterites in the Netherlands. Menno insisted that God's kingdom, the New Jerusalem, could be anticipated only by service and suffering love. Its fullness would be achieved only after the second coming of Christ in a new heaven and a new earth. This did not mean for Menno that the covenanters should not aim at the restoration of the entire society, as long as the right means were used, but when false teachers and prophets, motivated by ambition, greed and lust, legitimised the use of the sword for this purpose, Menno opposed them with mouth and pen.

It seems clear that Menno did not know about polygamy, vengeance, new revelations and the new time table when he wrote the *Blasphemy*. He wrote against the blasphemous kingship of Jan van Leiden, the aggressive use of the sword, and the claim that God wanted to use the Münsterites for the punishment of the wicked. The *Blasphemy*, written after Jan van Leiden's proclamation as "joyous king over all," but before Rothmann's *Restitution* and *Van der Wrake*—thus in fall of 1534—is one of Menno's best pieces of polemic writing, in which he used the entire Scripture to make his point.

Rothmann's use of Scripture was eclectic and very sophisticated, but in order to defend and to legitimise the new freedom of polygamy, vengeance and the kingship of Jan van Leiden, he had to refer to a new time table and to new revelations which superseded the Old and the New Testaments. Rothmann had to justify polygamy as part of the freedom of the New Jerusalem and vengeance as preparation for the coming of Christ, defending both as new revelations. King David was the promised leader and prophet of the End Times. God had called him from among the Münsterites. King David is not David/Christ, because Scripture is very clear that Christ will not rule in this world, but rather the one which is to come. For the time being, Rothmann argued, God is using his chosen people, the new Israel, for punishment and vengeance upon the unbelievers. Münster, he insisted, is not the coming kingdom of peace, but rather God's kingdom of wrath.

There is no evidence in Menno's *Blasphemy* and later writings that he ever read Rothman's *Restitution* or *Van der Wrake*.[94] Judging from what Menno wrote, Jan van Leiden was the sole instigator of the Münsterite kingdom, and it was only against him that he was writing. Menno's assessment of Jan van Leiden's messianic kingship had not changed by 1539-40[95] or by 1554-55, the dates of the first and second editions, respectively, of his *Fundament-book*. In the 1539-40 edition, Menno was reluctant to give any names away, but in the second edition of 1554-55 he did not hesitate to name Jan van Leiden as the instigator of the Münsterite kingdom.[96] The central argument from the *Blasphemy* is repeated in condensed form in both editions of the *Fundament-book*. Defining Jan van Leiden's pretended kingship as *"na den geest"* (of the Spirit) is seen as being in competition with the spiritual kingship of Jesus Christ. To illustrate his point, Menno used the example of Adonijah (1 Kings 1:1-27) who proclaimed himself king of Israel in the place of Solomon.

Thus Menno never did revise his negative assessment of the messianic kingship of Jan van Leiden. Together with other evidence, especially the overlapping use of Scripture references, it confirms our assumption of Menno's authorship of the *Blasphemy*, and his unawareness of Rothmann's *Restitution* and *Van der Wrake*.

There is no evidence that the *Blasphemy* was ever published in the sixteenth century, but the fact that the *Blasphemy* provides us with the sound biblical arguments that Menno was using in his preaching and in his debates with the Münsterites and against the "messianic" kingship of Jan van Leiden makes the question of whether the *Blasphemy* was published in 1534 or later a secondary one. The answer to the question of why Menno never made any reference to the *Blasphemy* is obvious: it was too compromising and too dangerous, because it revealed his own closeness to the basic teachings of the Münsterites.

Menno and Münster in light of the *Meditation on the Twenty-Fifth Psalm*

The *Meditation on the Twenty-Fifth Psalm* is Menno's first published response to the Münsterite debacle. It was first published in 1539, but appears to have been written well before that date. One of the basic questions of this prayer of confession[97] is: "Why do they hate me? Is it because I defend the order of Christ and his apostles as true and right?"[98] It seemed to Menno that as long as he had served the world as a Catholic priest and an evangelical preacher he had received honour and gratitude, but ever since he had left the church and committed his life fully to the service of the Lord, he had been slandered and abused by everyone.[99] The much-honoured evangelical preacher was in serious danger of collapsing under the heavy weight of the cross of Christ.[100] Scoffed at by the learned preachers and theologians and shunned by his former friends, Menno felt like a lost sheep in the wilderness. Because he had unexpectedly become identified with the much hated and persecuted Anabaptists, he was misunderstood by friends and foes. His enemies accused him of libertinism and insurrection, while the Münsterites and Melchiorites considered him to be a quietist and a legalist. In the post-biblical era of the apocalyptic dawn of the kingdom of God, Menno's continual insistence on *sola scriptura* in his writings, and presumably in his debates with the Münsterite delegations, must have been perceived as a return to Judaism and legalism.[101]

It is understandable that under the circumstances of the time, Menno was very careful not to make any direct reference to Münster. He spoke about those who had escaped from Sodom, Egypt and Babylon and submitted to the cross of Christ, only to be seduced by the false prophets as easily as if they had never learned to know the Word of the Lord. Their error now was a thousand times worse than it had been before. No matter how far-fetched their new doctrines may have been, they still defended themselves with the Word of the Lord.[102] This was typically Satan's way of seduction: wherever Christ comes, the devil will soon arrive as well, as Menno knew from his own recent experience. Appearing as an angel of light, Satan changed the spiritual meaning of Scripture and made it subservient to the selfish ambitions of false teachers,[103] so that they easily managed to justify the use of the sword.[104] Even scandalous polygamy could be excused in this way and justified by the example of the Old Testament patriarchs.[105] Seduced by Satan, the false teachers proclaimed a human king and a visible kingdom. But as we have seen with our own eyes, Menno wrote, whatever the Lord has not planned must come to an end in disgrace.[106] Against the Münsterite teaching that Christ now rules only in heaven,[107] Menno argued that all power in heaven and on earth had already been given to Christ, quoting from Matthew 28:19 and Ephesians 1:21.

In his interpretation of Ephesians 1:22 Menno implicitly describes the contemporary situation after Münster, using metaphors from the Old Testament. Israel is scattered and straying like sheep without a shepherd. The children of Abraham and Jacob are returning to the slavery of Egypt. Jerusalem, the lovely vision of peace, has been changed into an inhuman guzzler of innocent blood with no king, no citizens, and no walls. The temple of the Lord, which should be a place of true worship, has become the unchaste bed of the adulterous Jezebel; the bride of the Lord, adorned with many presents, has become a disgraceful harlot. Menno laments with Esdras the destruction of the sanctuary of the Lord and prays with John for faithful laborers to work in the harvest and for wise builders to lay a good foundation for the new house of the Lord, which is to become a light for the nations.[108]

The entire discourse in the *Meditation* reveals Menno to be a *bondgenoot*, that is a covenanter, a member of the covenant of the people of the New Jerusalem. It is this covenant with the Lord that really matters to him.[109] Baptism, mentioned as the sign of the covenant, has no validity in itself and the local congregation as such has no importance either. The concepts which dominate Menno's theological argumentation at this point are the people of God, Israel, the temple of the Lord, the New Jerusalem, Egypt and the Babylonian harlot. The metaphors and themes of the *Meditation* are the same as those of the *Blasphemy*.

Münster from the Perspective of the
Fundament-book, 1539-1540 and 1554/55[110]

When Menno wrote his *Fundament-book* (Foundation of Christian Doctrine), less than five years after the collapse of Münster, he was in the process of becoming the new leader of the Anabaptist movement in the Netherlands and northwestern Germany.[111] Recent research has shown that David Joris assumed the leadership of the Anabaptists in Bocholt in 1536 and was able to maintain it for at least the rest of the decade.[112] From the 1540's on, however, the *Fundament-book* became the guideline of life and faith for the emerging peaceful Mennonites, going through 23 new editions and reprints between 1539 and 1869.[113] Menno himself was in charge of the second edition of 1554-55, which proved to be a major revision of the original text,[114] even though Menno insisted he had not changed the content of the first edition, but only corrected printing errors and added explanations to the text wherever the argument needed clarification.[115]

Meihuizen's conclusion in the introduction to the 1967 critical edition of the original text actually simplifies the complex relationship between the original text and later revisions. He states that whoever reads the relevant passages objectively will soon discover that even though Menno originally held the same view of baptism as the Münsterites, he actually abhorred Münsterite practices.[116] In fact, Menno shared not only the Münsterite view of baptism, but most of their other doctrines as well. He rejected only their claim that Münster was the New Jerusalem, their assumption that Jan van Leiden was the third David, their practice of polygamy and their acceptance of the use of the sword.[117] In the preface to the 1539-40 edition Menno himself refers to a common past with the Münsterites:

> ... we find that Satan can transform himself into an angel of light, and sow those objectionable tares among the Lord's desirable wheat, such as sword, marriage, external kingdom of Christ, idolatry, deceit and other heresies on account of which the children of God today are being slandered and have to suffer much.[118]

The rephrasing of this paragraph in the revised edition of 1554-55 is revealing. The "we" of the first edition has been omitted, "marriage" has been replaced with "multitude of wives," "external Kingdom of Christ" is now "external kingdom and king," and the "children of God" are now the "innocent" who have to suffer much.[119] The trend of this revision is clear. In the first edition Menno is writing to prove to magistrates, preachers and scholars as well as to the common people that his doctrine is biblical and that most of the Münsterites "simply erred a little";[120] in 1554-55 he wants to disassociate himself and his followers as much as possible from the Münsterite kingdom.

In 1539 there was no doubt in Menno's mind that the majority of the misled Münsterites, like himself and his followers, were God's children even though tares had been sown among them. Although the Münsterites developed only the external appearance of the kingdom and not the more important internal change of life, he does call Münster the kingdom of Christ. Menno admits that marriage became a problem in Münster, but he does not call their practices polygamy. It is only when writing about baptism that Menno becomes explicit about Münsterite marriage practices. The motivation for baptism, he says, should never be the desire that he imputes to the Münsterites to fight and combat, to have two or three wives, or to gain great glory upon this earth.[121] In the 1554-55 revision, fighting and polygamy are still rejected as an adequate motivation for baptism, but in addition any expected glory here on earth or any kingdom in this world are also rejected.[122] Even in 1558 he calls the true believers in Münster God's children. They simply were the innocent who had to suffer much.

How much the baptism of believers was associated with the Münsterite kingdom by Menno's contemporaries is evident from the following statement from the 1539 edition:

> I know well that we will be confronted with king, marriage, sword, external kingdom, murder, robbery and similar heresies, which cursed ungodly dealings and devilish heresies they say come out of baptism....[123]

In the first edition Menno avoids the name of Münster and everything involved with it as much as possible, referring only to "secret sedition, insurrection and treason, which ... has been seen and heard about too much in some places."[124] In 1558 he has no inhibitions about calling it by its name. Münster, along with other events of rebellion, is now being used by the learned theologians and preachers to justify the bloodshed authorized by the magistrates.[125]

Describing the false teachers of the Münsterites in the first edition of 1539, Menno had no problem appropriating the description of 1 John 2:19 that "the false prophets went out from us, but they were not from us. For if they belonged to us, they would have remained with us." The fact that the false prophets came from among the covenanters did not disturb Menno at this point. Did not the Lord warn his disciples in Matthew 24:24 that false prophets would appear and perform great signs and miracles in order to seduce the believers? Jesus was not warning blind Jews or unbelieving sinners, but those who were sincerely searching for the truth.[126] Under the pretence of holiness, Menno explains, the devil appeared in Münster as an angel of light whom many did not recognize, and consequently they erred and fell away.[127] This does not imply that the truth became a lie, or that the good angels must pay for Lucifer's fall. What harm was done to the eleven because Judas was a thief and a traitor? If there are wretched servants among the good servants, does that injure the pious and honest ones? What harm was done to the pure doctrine of the apostles by the many damnable sects which arose even in their time, and who called the name of Christ?[128] None of those pernicious sects had been able to change the truth of the gospel of Jesus Christ.[129] Yes, Menno admits, the false prophets of Münster did come from among us. Because some of the leaders had not been careful enough, they had not recognized Satan in his disguise as an angel of light and so they had stumbled—but this was to be expected because wherever people sincerely search for the truth false prophets will also arise.[130] The fact that this happened in Münster did not necessarily speak against the Anabaptists; it might even prove the correctness of their teaching and life. Satan was not interested in unbelievers and sinners, who already belonged to him, but rather was interested in the downfall of true Christians.

In the 1554-55 revision of the *Fundament-book* Menno no longer admitted that the false prophets of Münster "came from among" the true believers. Now he quoted only the second part of 1 John 2:19: "but they were not of us, for had they been of us, as John says, they would no doubt have continued with us."[131] Even though he still acknowledges that the Münsterites were baptized with the same baptism, they were like Menno's followers only in appearance.[132] Again Menno refers to the craftiness and subtlety of the devil; the difference is that now he says that not just "a few" but "many" have stumbled and landed on the crooked path of deceit.[133] Although in 1539 he was willing to admit a common origin for the Mennonites and the Münsterites, in 1554-55 he tried very hard to demonstrate that the Münsterites had been different from the beginning. He remained consistent only in his statement on baptism: Münster was not and could not be the consequence of believers' baptism, because water cannot make people either evil or good.[134]

Addressing the "corrupt sects" in his earliest *Fundament-book*, Menno admits that he did meet with some of their leaders in order to win their souls, but he admits that he did not succeed.[135] Although he refuted their doctrine with the Word of God, they did not really care because their deceiving pretence was more important to them than the open and plain gospel of Jesus Christ. The identity of these Münsterite leaders and princes, whom Menno met[136] is still controversial.[137] The following quotation contains the famous paragraph which has been referred to by Menno's friends and foes alike:

> There is no question in my mind that our dear brothers, who formerly misbehaved a little against the Lord since they wanted to defend their faith with arms, have a gracious God, because they were not infected, I hope, with these above-mentioned heresies. They did not seek anything other than Christ Jesus and eternal life. For this reason they gave up house, garden, land, sand, father, mother, wife, child and also their own life. . . . It is no wonder that they were seduced at this time, because they did not yet have the discernment of the spirits. The honest and the pious I call my sisters and brothers. They failed because of their ignorance. But the insincere, who did not seek God with pure and clean hearts although they were called sisters and brothers, and the princes of the seduction as in Münster and Amsterdam, I leave in the hand of the Lord. . . .[138]

This paragraph shows that Menno was much more aware of the internal development of the Münsterite kingdom than he was later willing to admit.

Research has demonstrated Menno's analysis of the situation in Münster to be correct. Most of the burghers of Münster and the great majority of those who joined them from the Netherlands and from northwestern Germany did not know what was going to happen. Once Münster became Anabaptist and the bishop began the siege, the internal political and economic development of the city was shaped by apocalyptic expectations, charismatic ecstasies, miracles, the consequences of scarcity and hunger and the will to survive.[139] In many ways the leaders of the Münsterite debacle were as much the victims of special circumstances as their followers.[140] In 1539 Menno was still honest enough to call those victims of the Anabaptist kingdom of Münster, most of whom became involved unknowingly, his "dear sisters and brothers."

The long paragraph cited above was completely omitted in the 1554-55 revision of the *Fundament-book*, for several reasons. The consequences of the Münsterite kingdom were so devastating for the Anabaptist movement that a radical disassociation from Münster had become a simple condition for survival. The persecuting magistrates and churches were unable to differentiate between the false prophets and their innocent followers. Besides, by 1554-55 the Münsterite movement had disappeared and there was no need to include this compromising paragraph in the revised edition. Menno now used the term "Münsterite" in an entirely negative sense, as a name for followers of an evil-inspired and abominable heresy, with whom Menno and his followers had never had anything in common.

In conclusion we can observe that in 1539/40 a genetic connection with the Münsterites was taken for granted by Menno. The fact that false teachers and prophets arose from "among them," just as in the time of the apostles and the early Church, served Menno as an argument to prove the rightness of their teaching and life. The majority of the Anabaptists became involved in the Münsterite errors unknowingly, an assessment confirmed by modern research. In 1539/40 Menno still called the majority of the Münsterites his dear sisters and brothers. They had erred a little by using the sword for the defence of their faith; baptism was not the reason for the Münsterite errors as the critics generally assumed, because water as such did not change anything.

By 1554/55, however, Menno had submitted to the entirely negative use of the term Münsterite, as a name for an evil-inspired and abominable heresy. With such Münsterites Menno and his followers had never had, and still had nothing in common.

Menno's Indiscriminate "No" to Münster and the Münsterites in his Later Writings

There are very few references to Münster in the later writings of Menno Simons. In his *Why I do not Cease Teaching and Writing* (1539), Menno uses scriptural proofs to explain to the general public how idolatry, ambition, selfishness, greed and lust have resulted in the many failures of the church. By misusing the Word of God, false prophets such as the pope in Rome and Jan van Leiden had seduced simple souls for their own benefit.[141] Here Jan van Leiden has certainly been promoted into prominent company. But Menno believes that it is this basic desire for power, this ambition and greed, which causes people to stumble and to become false teachers and prophets, whether they be Jan van Leiden or the pope in Rome. In Menno's understanding of history this is not a recent phenomenon but something that has always happened.

Menno did not change his basic understanding of the debacle in Münster. Wherever the Word of God is proclaimed and lived, false prophets will arise who try to use the gospel for their own benefit, as they did in biblical times and have done throughout church history. Jan van Leiden was just one more example of this basic principle. Menno's readers were called upon to recognize this and to rely only upon the written word of God,[142] checking even Menno's own teaching, although he considered it to be identical with Scripture.[143] Menno was not claiming to be a third David or a prophet as some had falsely claimed to be.[144] Menno felt much more like a Jeremiah, tempted to give up his ministry,[145] but who would then preach the pure Word of God and call for repentance?

By the time he wrote his *Reply to False Accusations* in 1551, Menno's attitude had changed drastically in regard to Münster. He and his followers were still being called Münsterites,[146] accused of being ready to disobey the government,[147] insurrectionists just waiting for the time and opportunity to take over cities and lands.[148] They were accused of practising community of goods[149] and of sharing wives in common,[150] of being unforgiving perfectionists,[151] a godless sect possessed by the devil,[152] clandestine sneakers who did not dare to come out into the open[153] even though they claimed to have the truth.

Menno's response to these accusations was vehement: no, we have never had and never will have anything in common with the Münsterites and their practices,[154] and he challenged any one to prove that he had ever agreed with the Münsterites on these points.[155] At first reading it seems as if Menno is denying any kind of common ground with the Münsterites, but in fact he limits his statement by saying that he and his followers have nothing in common with the Münsterites in regard to the doctrines and practices concerning king, sword, insurrection, vengeance, polygamy or the external kingdom of Christ on earth. Menno does admit a common baptismal practice, but he considers baptism with water to be only an external sign. What really matters is the baptism with the Holy Spirit which transforms heart and mind.[156] As for the rest, Menno testifies and confesses before God and the entire world that he and his followers detest the Münsterite heresies.[157] What Menno does not mention is that he shared with the early Münsterites not only their practice of baptism, but also their doctrines of the incarnation and of the Lord's Supper, their early rejection of violence for the propagation of the kingdom of God, their belief in the possibility of a Christian government and their eschatological expectation.

Menno now states that "from the beginning until the present moment I have opposed them diligently and earnestly, both privately and in public, with mouth and pen, for over seventeen years."[158] If the *Reply to False Accusations* was printed in 1551,[159] then Menno must have been opposing the Münsterites from 1534 on, not only verbally but also in writing:

> Beloved reader, take it for the best that I have been writing for some seventeen years, fearing the Word of the Lord in my weakness and serving my neighbor... I have ... carried his cross ... and given account in good conscience of his holy, worthy Word, will and ordinance with mouth, writings, life and death as much as was in me.[160]

If Menno's "seventeen" really was that number, his statement supports the earlier conclusion that Menno wrote his *Blasphemy* in 1534 and not in 1535.

Menno's reference to increased persecutions[161] while he is writing his *Reply* can help us to establish the date it was written. In 1550 Charles V made a final attempt to resolve the problem of Protestantism in his patrimonial provinces by simply trying to eliminate it with his so called "Blood Placard."[162] Increased persecution was the immediate consequence. Decavele's graphs show that persecution was intense in 1551 when 15 executions took place compared to none in 1550 and only 2 in 1552.[163] The number of executions in 1551 corroborates Menno's comments.[164]

The date of writing of this tract is important because it also relates to Menno's confession of faith. Referring to his opposition to the Münsterites for more than seventeen years, Menno describes it as continuing "ever since according to my ability I confessed the Word of the Lord and knew and sought His holy name."[165] The second reference to his confession of faith in this tract is even more crucial. Defending himself against accusations of insurrection and the desire to take over cities and lands, Menno states:

> For we may with clear consciences appear before the world and truthfully maintain that we from the time of our confession until the present moment have harmed no one, have desired no one's property, much less laid hands on it.[166]

Confession in these references can mean only one thing: the turning point in Menno's life, the time when he became a confessing Christian. Thus from 1534 on Menno must have been a "confessing" Christian. If confession of faith was connected to baptism, as it usually was, then Vos' hypothesis that Menno was baptized already in 1534 receives some support.

If Menno already was a confessing Christian in 1534 who considered himself a covenanter, was he then a Münsterite as well? The answer depends on the definition of the word "Münsterite" and to the time in the internal development of the Anabaptist kingdom of Münster to which one refers. Comparing the basic theological tenets of faith of the early Münsterites and the covenanters with those of Menno, he can be called a Münsterite as well. But when it comes to the later doctrinal developments of "king, sword, rebellion, retaliation, vengeance, polygamy and external kingdom," there is no reason to doubt Menno's statement that he never agreed with the Münsterites on those articles.

The *Supplication to all Magistrates* (ca. 1552) is at least in part Menno's response to the "Blood Placard" of 1550. Appealing to the magistrates to halt the bloodshed, Menno now denies any relationship whatsoever to the Münsterites: "We have from the inception of our teaching and doctrine disapproved of any heresy and Münsterite erring."[167] He continued,

> It is one of the greatest injustices of our time that for the matter of baptism we are being punished with those of Münster who, contrary to the Word of God and every evangelical Scripture, also contrary to proper policies, set up a new kingdom, incited turmoil and introduced polygamy, matters which we oppose, condemn and censure, as is evident from all our acts and public activities.[168]

In the same year Menno wrote his *Brief Defence to All Theologians* addressed to the theologians of the German nation. Menno now accused the clergy of the state churches as being responsible for the severe persecutions:

> It appears that many of you cry very angrily at us ... and move and stir up the magistrates (of which, no doubt, some are reasonable and honest) to persecution... You warn everyone against us saying we are like-minded with those of Münster, that we wish to capture cities and lands, if only we could.[169]

In this writing, Menno does not even try to define the Münsterite heresies in order to differentiate the true covenanters from the false ones, or the misled sisters and brothers from the false prophets. He simply states that the great Lord Almighty knows that he and his followers are innocent of all these abominations and excesses.[170]

Menno first calls the Münsterites a "sect" in his *Reply to Gellius Faber*, written in 1554.[171] In that writing he maintains that he opposed them by preaching and exhortation, but his admonitions were ineffective because he himself was doing what he knew was not right.[172] He defends his own call and ordination as follows:

> In this way, my reader, I was not called by the Münsterites or any other seditious sect as it is falsely reported concerning me, but I have been called, though unworthy, to this office by the people who had subjected themselves to Christ and His Word.[173]

References in *The Cross of the Saints* (1554-55)[174] to the Münsterites do not reflect any changed opinions or new insights, and by the time Menno wrote his *Instruction on Excommunication* in 1558, he no longer needed to defend himself against the accusation of being a Münsterite.

> It is more than evident that if we had not been zealous in this matter these days, we would be considered and called by every man the companions of the sect of Münster and all perverted sects. Now, however, thank God for His Grace, by the proper use of this means of the sacred ban, it is well known among many thousands of honourable, reasonable persons, in different principalities, cities, and countries, that we are innocent of and free from all godless abominations and all perverted sects, as we also make known and announce very deliberately to the whole world.[175]

By 1558 there finally was relief for the "Mennonites." Their rigorous application of the "sacred ban" had cleared them in the eyes of many thousands of honourable, reasonable persons from any suspicion of being Münsterites. Weeding the tares from within and relentless persecution from without had reduced the people of the New Jerusalem to a suffering minority from which any trace of rebellion had disappeared.

We can observe in conclusion that in the early 1540s, Menno's early explanation of the Münsterite debacle hadn't changed much: false teachers and prophets have and always will try to misuse the Word of God for their own benefit. However, by the 1550s, disassociation became essential for survival. By specifying Münsterite heresies, Menno now could honestly state that he and his followers never had had any part in it. Only an insider would notice Menno's modification of the generally accepted definition for Münsterites. Eventually, Menno stopped trying to differentiate between the seducers and the seduced, the right and the false doctrines of the Münsterites. He simply stated outright that he and his followers were not and never had been Münsterites.

CHAPTER THREE

The Heavenly Jerusalem has Descended Upon This Earth

As we have seen in the foregoing chapter, Menno Simons was closely connected to the Melchiorite and Münsterite movement while he was still a practicing Roman Catholic priest in Witmarsum, and may even have received baptism in a spiritualized Melchiorite sense while still a priest. It is not surprising that as the Münster disaster faded into the historical past, Menno increasingly distanced himself from it, and eventually disassociated himself from it altogether—particularly since "Münsterite" became synonymous in the public mind with "fanatical heresy." A careful chronological reading and analysis of Menno's early writings and later editions demonstrates not only Menno's original connections and sympathies to the Münsterite movement, but also the deliberate re-writing of that history as time passed. In this chapter we will examine how three central Melchiorite and Münsterite teachings appear and function in Menno Simons' early and later writings.

There is no surer "DNA evidence" of Melchiorite doctrinal influence than the appearance of Hoffman's incarnational doctrine, namely that Christ brought heavenly flesh with him, and was born "in" Mary, but not "of" Mary. This incarnational doctrine cleared the way for the expectation that the "heavenly seed" of Christ's divine nature would be born in believers, by the Holy Spirit. True believers were to be marked by a regenerative, spiritual new birth. This new birth, in turn, would result in new lives, reflecting the newly-born divine nature in believers. Sinful impulses were capable of being overcome, thanks to the spiritual power now born within.

A careful reading of Menno's early writings and later editorial emendations of those writings will reveal the extent to which Menno accepted these central Melchiorite teachings on incarnation, regeneration, and new life, and also how Menno began to develop and change these teachings over time. Particularly evident is the emerging importance of ecclesiology in Menno's maturing thought: the New Jerusalem increasingly assumed concrete form, surrounded by better-defined and more secure walls.

"The Word became Flesh":
The stepping stone to the New Jerusalem

Incarnation: Melchior Hoffman and Münster

The medieval view of the virgin birth resulted from the concept of original sin, considered to be transmitted from parents to children through bodily procreation. In medieval orthodox theology, only a totally blameless lamb would be a good enough sacrifice to atone for the sins of humanity, but in order to have a sinless nature, Jesus had to have a sinless origin. It was not enough to say that Jesus was conceived by the Holy Spirit; Mary also had to be freed from original sin, a requirement answered by the doctrine of the Immaculate Conception.

Melchior Hoffman and his Münsterite followers, as well as the later Mennonites, shared the Catholic doctrine of the sinfulness and complete lostness of humankind.[1] In contrast to Catholic orthodoxy, however, they did not focus their attention on the death of the sacrificial lamb, but rather on the incarnation of the Word of God. "The Word became flesh" became the centre of Melchiorite and especially of Münsterite theology. The incarnation of the deity, more than the sacrificial death of the Son of God, was considered the crucial act of salvation.

To safeguard the Word of God from any contamination by sinful human flesh, Melchior Hoffman had developed the doctrine of the "celestial flesh" of Christ.[2] According to this doctrine, Christ was conceived by the Holy Spirit and became flesh *in* Mary, but he did not receive his flesh *from* her. Hoffman used the analogy of the pearl and the oyster to explain the incarnation of Christ in Mary.[3]

> The Eternal Word, which was true heavenly dew, in an unsensual and incomprehensible way but through the Holy Spirit, fell from the mouth of God into the wild mussel of the Virgin Mary, and in her became a bodily Word and spiritual pearl.[4]

Consequently, Mary's human nature was no longer theologically significant. Christ, according to Hoffman, was an entirely new creation. In his biological presuppositions Hoffman stood, no doubt quite unconsciously, in the Aristotelian-Thomist line, which considered only the male seed to be formative.[5]

Because we have no clear documentation for the origin of this Melchiorite celestial flesh doctrine, Williams suggests that

> it seems more plausible to account for the widespread and variegated outcropping of the celestial-flesh doctrine in the sixteenth century as an effort to restate the Christological problem in the language of Eucharistic piety, experientially much more real

than the philosophical terms employed a millennium or more earlier...."[6]

Williams does not refer to the common Sacramentarian rejection of Mary as mediator and *Theotokos* ("Mother of God"), and the Sacramentarian description of Mary as "an empty flour-bag," but the Sacramentarian attitude towards Mary seems to have anticipated the later, explicit Melchiorite doctrine of the celestial flesh of Christ.[7]

The purpose of the celestial flesh doctrine of Hoffman was to prove that Christ, as an entirely new creation, had no part in the corruption of the human flesh of Mary. If Jesus had taken on the flesh of Mary he would have had Adamic flesh, which could neither have saved humankind nor have served as food for eternal life. Hoffman contended for the heavenly origin of the second Adam (1 Cor. 15:47).[8] As the Son begotten by the Father, Christ is the true Melchizedek, without earthly father or mother (Heb. 5:10; 6:20; ch.7). In this sense Mary was no more a true parent of Jesus than was Joseph.[9] Only as the Son of God who came from heaven as the second Adam was Christ able to redeem humankind from death and remove all sin. Just as all descendants of Adam are cursed, so all descendants of the second Adam and his spiritual Eve, the bride of the Lord Jesus Christ which is the church, are redeemed.[10] Thus salvation in Christ is universal in the same way as the consequences of Adam's fall were universal.

To appropriate salvation, the believer must make a covenant with Jesus Christ that, for Hoffman, resembled a marriage relationship. It was voluntary and happened by faith in God's promises, which are already fulfilled in Christ.[11] Salvation and sanctification went hand in hand in Hoffman's thinking: through a continuing process of dying to sin, believers were transformed, step by step, into the likeness of the sinless Christ. But temptation and the possibility of falling into sin again, with death as the consequence, remained with believers as long as they lived.[12]

The Melchiorite doctrine of incarnation changed the generally negative content of Sacramentarian faith into an exciting possibility for new life.[13] Salvation was no longer mediated by the church through the careful administration of the sacraments. It was through faith in the incarnate Word and a new covenantal relationship with God that redemption was achieved, a redemption which was not only spiritual but also social and political. Because the Word of God had become flesh and lived among believers, all areas of human life were transformed.

We have no clear evidence as to when Hoffman's doctrine of incarnation spread throughout the Netherlands. It most likely was part of his message from the time he began teaching in 1530. Next to the baptism of adults, this doctrine became the most distinctive characteristic of Dutch Anabaptism,[14] and it was well known among the thousands who participated in the exodus to Münster in March 1534.[15] This doctrine already played a prominent role in the Christology developed by Bernhard Rothmann in his *Confession of Faith* in early 1534.[16] According to the eyewitness Gresbeck,[17] a coin with the inscription, *dat wort wirt fleisch* was handed out to all those who were baptized, both men and women, after the Anabaptists took over the city of Münster in February 1534.[18] In his confession[19] Johan Klopris confirmed Gresbeck's report that all those who entered or left Münster had to wear this sign, which he describes as a patch of cloth with a piece of silver sewn on it with the letters DWWF.[20] This sign was to protect the covenanters as well as to identify them. Once the apocalyptic crusade against the unbelievers began, only those marked with this sign would be spared.[21] In September 1534 the new Münsterite coins received the inscription: Et Si Dat Imadt vpt Nie Gebare Werde, so Mach he Gades Rike Nicht Schei. Ein Her, ei Gelo, Ein Doep; Dat Wort is Fleisch Gworden V Wa VN VNS: "Unless a man is born again, he cannot enter the kingdom of God. One Lord, one faith, one baptism. The word became flesh and lives among us."[22]

For Rothmann this doctrine had important moral consequences: since Jesus gave his life for the forgiveness of their sins, believers were called to live clean and spotless lives.[23] Because Christ as the incarnate Word of God, conceived by the Holy Spirit and becoming flesh in Mary, now lived in believers, they were required to follow his example even if it meant suffering. Faith in Christ's sacrifice was not enough for sinners to enter the kingdom of God; they needed to personally recognize Jesus Christ as their saviour and follow him in order to become like him.[24] Upon this faith believers could be baptized.[25] Cleansed from the contamination of this world, they entered into a new covenantal relationship with God and fellow believers, in which there was no room for backsliders.[26] Members of this new community of the covenant would rather have died than tolerate any infraction against the will of God.[27]

Life in Münster was already life in the New Jerusalem, at least according to Rothmann:

> We already have the community of love, as is proper and right and the Scripture announces, and the articles of Christian faith also imply, . . . so that we can say with David in Psalm 32 [133:1]: How good and pleasant it is when brothers live together in unity.[28]

Utopia had become topia in Münster.[29] The pure Word of God had become flesh and still lived among them.[30] Faith, obedience, and a new covenantal relationship with God and with each other had made Münster into the new city of God. Through brotherly love, community of goods, perfectionism and rigorous discipline, the kingdom of God was anticipated. In his *Restitution*, Rothmann listed additional characteristics of life in the New Jerusalem: there is oneness of heart and mind in the worship of God through Jesus Christ; all believers were serving each other in different ways; justice had been established in the sense that every exploitative activity had ceased.[31] Rothmann believed that what was happening in Münster could have happened all over the world, if people would repent before God and live their lives in brotherly love and community.[32]

In the closing paragraph of the *Confession of Faith*, Rothmann gave a brief overview of the crucial events in Münster during the last months.[33] After he and his fellow preachers were freed from the Babylonian captivity and committed their lives fully to the service of the Lord, the bishop tried to force them out of the city, but he did not succeed. Although he had promised them tolerance in questions of faith, one of the citizens of Münster was caught in Dulm and executed. On November 5, 1533 the papists demanded the extradition of the evangelical preachers from Münster so that they could be hanged, but God again did not allow this to happen. On February 9, 1534 the papists armed themselves in order to regain control of the city. When the Anabaptists gathered at the market place to pray, the enemies opened the gates for the army of the bishop, but signs and miracles occurred. According to Rothmann, without direct intervention on the part of the Anabaptists, God had defeated their enemies and threw them out of the city. Now they were trying to regain it from outside. Rothmann did not know what was about to happen, but the Anabaptists were trusting in God's deliverance.

Much more than a chronological report, this paragraph is the presentation of historical evidence meant to demonstrate that God had given Münster into the hands of the covenanters. With miracles and signs he delivered them from the hands of their enemies time and again, requiring nothing from them but to be faithful and trust in the Lord. The question of violence in defence of the New Jerusalem was not even mentioned; it obviously was an accepted fact which needed no further justification. On the contrary, "the more they increase the siege, the more confident we are, knowing that God will not forsake the righteous,"[34] Rothmann wrote with confidence. In any event, it was only a question of time until God would awake and prove that he alone was the Lord and judge of the earth, and then even the powerful would receive their deserved punishment. Rothmann stated that he knew more about when this time would come, but was reluctant to give more information.³⁵ In the summons to the Dutch covenanters the date for the second coming of Christ was set for Easter, April 5, 1534.

The apocalyptic expectation (actually the perception that the End Times had already begun) made it easier to make a radical commitment to the New Jerusalem. Because the second coming of the Lord was believed to be only weeks away, not only the persecuted, the poor and the unemployed, but also many of the well-to-do³⁶ sold their property and joined the exodus to the New Jerusalem in order to save their lives. Besides, all those who had been baptized upon their faith were legally outlaws who would lose life and property whenever and wherever they were discovered. Münster, with its Anabaptist government, became a city of refuge for these persecuted covenanters. In the third place, we should not underestimate the appeal of believers' baptism, brotherly love, community of goods and Christian discipline. In many ways the early Münster met all the criteria for the "evangelical town" hoped for by the Sacramentarians and the Melchiorites. Lastly, there was a general fear of the "last day of judgment." If Christ was to come on Easter, and only those who reached Münster would be saved from the worldwide punishment of unbelievers on the "last day of judgment," who would want to stay behind?³⁷ So people left for Münster from all over the Netherlands and Westphalia by the thousands,³⁸ even if not all of them had yet been baptized with the sign of Thau, the seal of the 144,000 elect.³⁹

When Easter 1534 passed without the return of the Lord, Jan Matthijsz faced the army of the bishop almost single-handed. He had no choice. In order to preserve his credibility as the prophetic messenger of the end times, he tried to force the promised miraculous delivery of the New Jerusalem by attacking the army of the bishop, and lost his life in the attempt.⁴⁰

It was not until the "prophetic" and later the "royal" leadership of Jan van Leiden that Münster became a "Davidic theocracy" in charge of the apocalyptic crusade against the unbelievers,⁴¹ but even then the Melchiorite doctrine of incarnation remained essential to the New Jerusalem. John 1:14 reappeared together with John 3:5 as the inscription on the new Münsterite coins of September 1534: "Unless a man is born again, he can not enter the kingdom of God. One Lord, one faith, one baptism. The Word became flesh and lives among us."

Menno's Doctrine of the "Celestial Flesh"

Menno Simons accepted the Melchiorite incarnation doctrine early, and defended it to the end of his life. During his debate with Martin Mikron in Wismar in February 1554, Menno stated that he had become aware of the Melchiorite doctrine of incarnation while he was still with the papacy.[42] He learned of it while opposing the Münsterites in his own parish of Witmarsum and debating with their leaders, probably in early 1534. At this time he may already have become a covenanter himself, because he says that the doctrine of the heavenly flesh was brought to his attention by his "brothers."[43] Menno anxiously considered the mystery of the heavenly flesh for some time,[44] even discussing the matter with some of the reformed preachers, but he found them to be misinterpreting this text in light of the rest of Scripture. Finally Menno was forced to recognize the doctrine of the heavenly flesh as biblical truth and was, he says, refreshed and comforted in his heart.

In his later office as elder, Menno was reticent about preaching and teaching this doctrine, especially in his writings. In the *Fundamentbook* it appears only implicitly.[45] When Menno had a disputation with reformed preachers in Emden in 1544, he acceded to their request and reluctantly sent a written summary of his doctrine of incarnation to Jan a Lasco, although he stated:

I repeat, this is my confession for those who demanded the revelation of my faith and my feelings in regard to this article. I never teach this article in my general exhortations to the brothers and devotees so precisely and profoundly and never have done it so profoundly before.[46]

This written response to a Lasco was later published against his will.[47] In his own words, Menno believed that

This eternal Word of God has become flesh. It was in the beginning with God and was God (John 1:2). Conceived (I say) and come forth of the Holy Spirit (Matt. 1:18); nourished and fed in Mary, as a natural child is by its mother; a true Son of God and a true son of man, born of her, truly flesh and blood. He was afflicted, hungry, thirsty, subject to suffering and death, according to the flesh; immortal according to the Spirit, like us in all things, sin excepted Heb. 2:9. Truly God and man, man and God. He was not divided nor separated as being half heavenly and half earthly, half of the seed of man and half of God, ... but an unmixed, whole Christ, namely, spirit, soul, and body, of which, according to Paul, all men are constituted.[48]

It was this same Word of God which in the flesh of Jesus Christ died for our sins on the cross, arose from the dead, ascended into heaven and is seated at the right hand of God. By his righteousness and obedience he paid for our sins and fulfilled the eternal righteousness of God.[49]

In his *Reply to Gellius Faber* of 1554, Menno again based his Christology on the Melchiorite doctrine of incarnation. It was the wholeness of Christ which was of foremost concern to him. He and his followers preached and confessed a whole Christ, both in accordance with his deity and in accordance with his humanity.[50] On the contrary, the learned ones with their deceiving glosses and reasoning made of the Son of God a composite, impure and impossible Christ, who assumed the human nature of our flesh and was born of the natural seed of a woman.[51] But, Menno argued, if Jesus was the natural fruit of the flesh and blood of Mary, then the eternal Word of God could only dwell in him, and so when he was crucified it was the man Christ Jesus who died, but the Word remained whole and intact.

In Menno's understanding, the logical consequence of the "reasoning of the learned ones" (who held to an orthodox doctrine of incarnation) was, in the first place, that Christ was unclean and sinful, who was tempted by his own flesh and died in recompense for his own sin, and not as an act of grace.[52] The death of such a Christ would achieve no more than the suffering of a common saint.[53] In the second place, the learned ones were left with two sons in Christ, the first the son of God without a mother, and the second the son of Mary without a father. Actually, Jesus as the son of Mary would have been the third son of God, created by God and adopted as his son. This would imply that we were saved not through God's firstborn and only begotten son, but through Mary's son, created of Adam's impure and sinful flesh. In this case, we should give thanks to the Father not only for his Word, but also for Adam's flesh, which delivered us from death. In the eyes of the prophets this would be idolatry.[54]

Against this view, which Menno understood as heresy, he defended his doctrine of the pure and spotless son of God. Born of the seed of the Father, planted in Mary by the Holy Spirit, nourished and fed in her virgin body, he became in due time a genuine man, undivided and whole as a new creation and incarnation of the Word of God.[55] Although Mary made no substantial (bodily) contribution to Christ, he still was her son as well because she conceived him, nourished him and gave him birth.[56] The mystery of the incarnation cannot be explained in a natural and carnal sense,[57] but only according to the true explanation and sense of the Holy Spirit, since it is the work of the Holy Spirit.[58] Menno knew that there were few who could understand this intricate matter even after it was explained to them, and feared that on this account he and his brothers would be judged to be sectarians and heretics.[59]

In his debate with Mikron in 1554, Menno tried to avoid any kind of philosophical speculation about the incarnation. The statement in John 1:14 that "the Word became flesh" was clear enough.[60] For Menno, this meant that Christ was the true son of God and not born of the sinful flesh of Adam.[61] Mikron accused Menno of inconsistency: ten years earlier Menno had written that he did not teach this article to his followers, but now the doctrine seemed to be crucial for salvation. Menno conceded that in 1544 the preaching of repentance and forgiveness of sins seemed to be enough,[62] but since that time his understanding of the incarnation had changed and deepened.[63]

Menno now compared Mary to a field into which seed is being sown; she nourished and gave birth to Jesus, but made no substantial contribution to the son of God. If she had, Christ would have participated in her sinful flesh.[64] For Menno this was clear and easy to understand, but to make it even simpler for his opponents Menno used the illustration of his own son. He is called Menno's and Ghertruyd's son: Menno's son because he is of his substance, and Ghertruyd's son because she carried him in her body, nourished him and gave birth to him. In the same way Christ is the son of God because he is of his substance, and the son of Mary because she gave birth to him.[65] When he was pressed by Mikron Menno made contradictory statements, but he always returned to the basic principle of John 1:14.[66] If he had continued to confine himself to this basic statement, Menno would have saved himself and his followers considerable trouble.

In his *Reply to Martin Mikron* of 1556 Menno accused Mikron of partiality, of omitting the most important questions and of twisting Menno's words[67] while dressing up and decorating his own. Menno was now the one who dominated the disputation and refuted the arguments of his opponent. When Mikron was forced to concede that Christ was pure and without sin because he was not born of marital intimacy nor of the seed of man,[68] and that a woman does not have seed but only the blood of menstruation, he had lost the debate as far as Menno was concerned.[69]

Many of the more systematic questions about the heavenly flesh doctrine were left unanswered by Menno.[70] For him, the crucial point of this doctrine was the sinlessness of Christ. If Mary had made any substantial contribution to Christ's nature, Christ would have had a part in Adam's sinful flesh,[71] and consequently he would have been unable to atone for our sins. But reconciliation or atonement was only one side of the coin; the other side was the incarnation as God's new creation.[72]

In Menno's understanding of the Melchiorite incarnational teaching, the Word of God which became flesh and lives among us, God's kingdom becomes visible reality in believers, but that kingdom is defined by Christ himself. In his life of perfect harmony with God's will, Christ anticipated the new creation of justice and peace, and his life became the ultimate standard for all human life. His way as the suffering servant became the unsurpassed way of life for all. As long as heaven and earth exist, there will be no other. It was here that Menno parted ways with the direction taken by the Münsterites. Jan van Leiden and the Münsterite kingdom were an aberration without any biblical foundation, for only by following Christ's way of suffering love could believers participate in the anticipation of God's kingdom. Since the Word became flesh and lived among us, God's *utopia* had already become *topia* for Menno. There was no need for pretended new revelations, or for a second David; all that was needed was to repent, to be born again and to follow Jesus Christ.

Whereas for Menno the incarnation of the Word of God meant forgiveness, brotherly love, suffering service and a new life, for the Münsterites it became the justification for an apocalyptic crusade. After Münster had become Anabaptist and the bishop had started the siege, a nonresistant suffering Christ seemed of little or no help to them. The apocalyptic vision of Christ as the coming avenger and judge of the unbelievers was much more attractive. Does not the Lamb which was slain turn into the Lion of Judah in Revelation 5:5? And does it not "tread the wine press of the fury of the wrath of God the Almighty" and "rule the nations with a rod of iron" (Rev. 19:15)? Hoffman's revolutionary ideas about the extermination of the wicked before the day of judgment, his vision of an earthly kingdom of the elected 144,000 in cooperation with a militant king David, and his expectation that Christ would not return before a kingdom of peace was established[73] were further developed and applied to the Münsterite situation by Rothmann in his *Restitution* and *Van der Wrake*. Münster was not a return to the New Testament, but the anticipation of the apocalyptic events of the millennium.

In Münster the presence of the incarnate Word of God served to legitimize new revelations of a culminating stage in salvation history in which "the weakness, suffering, and the ethics of the early Church and the corruption of the medieval Christendom would both be left behind."[74] In the community of regenerated brothers and sisters, the coming kingdom of righteousness and peace was already being anticipated in Münster. Had it not been for the immediate siege of the bishop, the Anabaptist kingdom of Münster might have remained peaceful. But given the historical circumstances, the New Jerusalem had to defend itself against the vicious attacks of the wicked, and so the elect became God's instruments for the execution of his wrath.

If in Münster the incarnation was seen as the beginning of radical new revelations, for Menno, on the contrary, the incarnation of Christ meant that his words and his earthly life had a normative revelatory significance. He was not willing to go beyond Christ, either backward to David or Adam, or forward to a new unaccountable "spirit" or kingdom.[75]

Unless a man is born again,
he cannot enter the Kingdom of God

Regeneration and Restitution in Münster

Although regeneration was not a major theological issue in the Münsterite kingdom, Rothmann defined it clearly from the beginning. The Münsterites believed that "Christ died for our sins ... in order that we from now on walk our way of life, pure and spotless as befits our calling."[76] Luther's *sola fide* was definitely not enough for the Anabaptists in Münster. Although believers have free access to the Father through Jesus Christ, they need to do more than simply believe in his sacrificial death:

> Two things are needed, which I must observe in Christ if I want to be saved; first, I have to recognize him as my saviour and entrust to him with firm faith the redemption from my sin; second I must see Christ as an example ... so that from now on I become like him, following in his footsteps, if I want to inherit the heavenly kingdom.[77]

Thus faith, reconciliation and sanctification went hand in hand for Rothmann.[78] Conversion should always be the spontaneous response to the proclamation of the gospel.[79] For Rothmann, the sum of the gospel was simply, repent and believe in the good news, which means repentance, faith in Jesus Christ, dying to sin, baptism in his name and the gift of the Holy Spirit which turns obedience to God's will into joy.[80] Rothmann outlined a procedure for proclaiming the gospel almost like that of a modern evangelist. First, convince people of their sinfulness. If they repent, tell them about the forgiveness of their sins through Christ. Then they should be baptized and received as fellow members into the body of Christ. As brothers and co-heirs with Christ they must now live in obedience, righteousness and holiness in order to be saved.[81]

Regeneration without baptism to integrate the believer into the body of Christ and without a new life of obedience, righteousness and holiness made no sense to Rothmann. Regeneration was equal to restitution. [The born again believer was not only saved from sin and death, but also restored to the prelapsarian state of Adam before the Fall] For Rothmann and the Münsterite kingdom, restitution was not the restoration of the New Testament church but the recreation of fallen humankind into the image of God before the Fall, with its moral and perfectionist implications.[82]

The emphasis on regeneration and moral perfection seemed to increase as the Münsterite kingdom declined. If signs and miracles revealed Münster to be the New Jerusalem during its first stage under the leadership of Jan Matthijs, the achievement of moral perfection in its later stages would prove the incarnation of the Word of God among them. The inscription on the new coins issued in September 1534 was a reflection of this Münsterite claim: "Unless a man is born again, he can not enter the Kingdom of God; one Lord, one faith, one baptism; the Word has become flesh and lives among us."

Because the last day, the day of judgment was very near, the proclamation of the gospel of Jesus Christ had become urgent. It was the last call to repentance and salvation,[83] and whoever accepted it would still be saved. When Jan van Leiden became king, he prophesied that all the nations which rejected the gospel would be punished.[84] One's response to the doctrines of incarnation and regeneration as restitution now had ultimate consequences in Münster: one either accepted them and was saved, or rejected them and was lost forever.[85]

Menno's Doctrine of Regeneration and the "Spiritual Resurrection"

The doctrine of spiritual regeneration was central in Menno's early writings, and echoes Melchiorite emphases. The earliest and most eloquent of Menno's known writings is probably his tract on the *Spiritual Resurrection*.[86] This meditation on Ephesians 5:14, or sermon, as Bornhäuser calls it,[87] concentrates on the sole subject of conversion, and could well have been written already in 1534.

The spiritual regeneration of the sinner begins with the call to wake up from the sleep of death.[88] This confrontation with the gospel of Jesus Christ is followed by mortification, spiritual sickness, pain and anguish. The third step in the process of transformation is repentance, affliction and godly sorrow over the sinfulness and lostness of life. After reaching this stage, the sinner is ready to crucify his sinful body with Christ, to die to sin, and to be raised with Christ to new life. This is then followed by the symbolic act of baptism. The seventh step in this almost mystical experience is sanctification, with the proper fruits of new life in Christ.[89] [Regeneration is entirely the work of the Holy Spirit, because only the

Spirit can give birth to a new spiritual life, whereas flesh can bring forth only flesh.[90]

Through the incarnate Word of God, the carnal human being can be regenerated into a spiritual son or daughter of God and a brother or sister of Jesus Christ. What is born of the flesh is corrupt, carnally minded, earthly and motivated by material things. It is deaf, blind, ignorant, hostile to God, unjust, unclean, disobedient, sinful and unable to do good. Born of the first Adam, this fruit of death is transformed by the Word of God. The godly seed of life, implanted into the heart of the sinner, gives birth to a new spiritual being, which is recreated into the image of God, one that is humble, peaceful, holy, forgiving, able to do good, like-minded with Christ and with God, and able to conquer sin and death.[91] This regeneration, which is like an ontological change of the human nature from earthly into heavenly, from fleshly into spiritual, is irreversible as long as the believer remains in God.[92] Those transformed in this way have received the sign of Thau on their foreheads and have arrived at the city of God, the heavenly Jerusalem. As the spiritual bride of Christ they are his holy congregation, bone of his bone and flesh of his flesh. Menno describes the regenerated believers as a holy nation, the new people of God (1 Peter 2).[93]

In this process of regeneration[94] the church as the bride of the Lord receives seed from the Father and bears new children into his likeness.[95] Clothed with power from above, baptized with the Holy Spirit and so united and mingled with God, the born again believer becomes a partaker of the divine nature and is made conformable to the image of his Son.[96] Menno concluded that "in short, in these people the old things have passed away, behold, all things have become new" (2 Cor. 5:17).[97]

The *Spiritual Resurrection* was a universal evangelistic call to repentance and regeneration:

> Therefore we counsel and admonish all in general, whatever their name, rank, class, or condition, to take good heed to the Word of the Lord which we have briefly presented according to our limited gift and simple talent.[98]

Menno's radical understanding of regeneration was clearly based on the Melchiorite doctrine of incarnation. He saw the church as the bride who receives the heavenly seed for the regeneration of new believers. Baptism symbolized death to sin and resurrection to new life with Christ. Like the sign of Thau received by the servants of God on their foreheads, baptism identified the believers as members of the people of God who had already arrived at the New Jerusalem, the city of the living God, which had descended from heaven.[99]

In the *Spiritual Resurrection*, the effects of regeneration were limited to the individual. Although the writer had obviously experienced regeneration and received the sign of Thau himself, he was careful not to identify himself with or commit himself to any Protestant, Reformed or Melchiorite group. He could be called an evangelical preacher because he knew and used Scripture well, but we can postulate that Menno could still have been a Catholic priest when he wrote this tract[100] because he said and did nothing to confront the church. The emphasis on the sign of Thau and the presence of the heavenly Jerusalem which has already descended from heaven betray the writer as a Melchiorite, but one who avoids any apocalyptic speculations and is very independent and secure in his own scriptural convictions:

> And we add that all doctrines which do not agree with the doctrine of Jesus Christ and His apostles, let them appear ever so holy, are accursed. For His Word is the truth and His command is eternal life.[101]

Menno could have written this tract in 1534.[102] He already had "brothers" among his readers who shared with him the same call and election,[103] but he did not yet call them covenanters as he does later in the *Blasphemy*. His ambivalent position as both an evangelical priest and a regenerated believer soon became a luxury Menno could not afford over a longer period of time. On the one hand, he lost the confidence of his own evangelical parishioners, who joined the Münsterites for lack of any clear alternative;[104] on the other, he had problems convincing the Münsterite delegations that he was not one of them, even if he did share their doctrines of incarnation and regeneration. In addition, he failed to give his much needed leadership to those less aggressive Melchiorites like Obbe and Dirk Philips who, though seriously tempted[105] by the promised New Jerusalem, did not join the Münsterite kingdom.

Even when Menno did finally identify with the non-aggressive covenantors by rejecting the messianic kingship of Jan van Leiden, he was still able to avoid any direct confrontation with his church and to retain the security of his position as a priest. After all, should preaching repentance and spiritual regeneration not be the central message of any evangelical priest? And considering that the primary significance of the Melchiorite baptism with the sign of Thau was apocalyptic rather than ecclesiological, this baptism as a confirmation of his own identification with and commitment to the kingdom of God might not be in contradiction with the basic understanding of faith in the Catholic Church either. Why could he not handle his baptism as a priest in the same way as he handled the eucharist and child baptism, which he had not believed in for years?

It was not until Oldeklooster[106] (March 30-April 7, 1535) that Menno accepted responsibility for his own compromising involvement and culpability with respect to the Münsterite kingdom, because he was "one of those who had disclosed to some of them a part of the abominations of the papal system."[107] After much prayer and spiritual struggle, Menno finally left the Catholic church in January 1536. He spent the following year at a solitary place studying and writing. The *New Birth* (1539-40) and *Meditation on the Twenty-Fifth Psalm* (1539-40) were probably written at least in part during this time.[108]

The *New Birth*, published in 1539-40, was a call to repentance and regeneration addressed to all those who called themselves Christians but continued to live in sin.[109] If they did not repent and change their way of life, Menno warned, they would certainly die, whether they were kings or emperors, rich or poor, men or women. The message of John 3 is unmistakable: unless a man is born again, he can not enter the kingdom of God.[110] There may be one or two among a thousand so called Christians who understand this clear evangelical principle, said Menno, but most are fooled by child baptism, false suppers, masses, confessions and other ceremonies which have replaced the true gospel of Jesus Christ. It is not through ceremonies and false doctrines that we receive salvation, but only through new birth in Christ Jesus.[111] In the process of regeneration we become like Christ, who is the firstborn among many brethren (Rom. 8).[112] Crucifying our sinful flesh with its lusts and desires, burying our sins in baptism and rising with Christ to new life, we are the pure bride of Christ, flesh of his flesh and bone of his bones.

In the *New Birth*, the church as the body of Christ comes more to the forefront than it did in the *Spiritual Resurrection*.[113] Those born again by the power of the Holy Spirit are the true children of God, the spiritual house of Israel, the spiritual Mount Zion, temple and Jerusalem.[114] There are some who claim to be born again, but their life has not changed. Those regenerated by the power of the Spirit must also bear the fruits of the Spirit.[115] Menno challenged the pope with his cardinals and councils to prove that the sinner who claims to be a Christian can enter the kingdom of God. If this is possible, then Moses and the prophets, Christ and the apostles are liars and false witnesses, Menno concluded.[116]

In opposition to the *concilium* of Rome, the true *concilium* which Christ brought down from heaven and sealed with his blood, stands on its own and will not be overcome even by the gates of hell. Whoever rejects this *concilium* of true faith, love, baptism, Lord's Supper, obedience and a blameless life is also rejecting God and Jesus Christ, and is looking for human doctrines.[117]

In the *New Birth* regeneration and new Christian life have become central themes in Menno's theological discourse. He still considers the kingdom of God the spiritual Jerusalem. The church represents the body of Christ, which is the symbol and norm of sanctification,[118] but as the spotless bride of Christ it has no dominating function yet. Going beyond the *Spiritual Resurrection*, Menno now challenges the doctrine as well as the life of the Catholic church, although he is not yet as abusive as he will be in his later writings. There still seems to be a possibility of reformation from within, if Roman Catholics will only repent and be born again.

A significant ecclesiological shift is visible in the revised edition of the *New Birth* of 1556. In this revision, the church as the community of believers has become identical with the kingdom of God. Proper baptism has now become essential, still symbolizing death with Christ and rising to new life, but also implying integration into the spotless bride of Christ as obedient members of his church, according to the true ordinance and Word of the Lord.[119] The kingdom of God is now the spiritual city of Jerusalem where the regenerated believers live together in peace and serve each other with their spiritual and material gifts. They prove their new life by their actions, because if they do not, the "ban of excommunication descends on all the proud scorners—great and small, rich and poor, without any respect of person ... until they repent."[120]

We are fortunate that most of the first editions of Menno's writings have survived the centuries, although they are not easily accessible. They are not to be found in the two *Opera Omnia* of 1646 and 1681, nor in the English translation of 1956, even if the date on the title-page indicates the contrary.[121] Because of the many shifts in Menno's theological concepts, the study of the first editions of his early writings must be considered indispensable for any scholarly research.[122] In the case of the *New Birth* tract, later revisions reveal the growing importance of the church in Menno's understanding of the spiritual life.

Genuine Repentance and New Life in the New Jerusalem

Together with the *Spiritual Resurrection* and the *New Birth*, the *Meditation on the Twenty-Fifth Psalm* is one of Menno's earliest writings, and must have been written after he left the Catholic church, before his ordination as elder.[123] Horst calls the *Meditation* a vindication of Menno's spiritual integrity.[124] Given the ambiguity of Menno's position during and after Münster, both the militant and the more peaceful Melchiorites must have questioned his integrity. These questions apparently did not disappear after Menno's ordination as elder, because he felt the need for an extra introduction to the 1539 publication to defend himself against "all kinds of slander and lies."[125] He was accused of adultery, of being a Jew who teaches the law and circumcision,[126] of being an insurgent and of longing for what he had left behind. Some called him a false seducer, others an accursed heretic.[127] He was accused of libertinism as well as legalism. Some suspected him of being a revolutionary, while others seemed to sense his longing for the safety and comfort of the Catholic priesthood. These accusations reflect perceptions of Menno's indecision and wavering between the extremes of legalism and libertinism, of insurrection and quietism in the period during and after Münster.

In the *Meditation*, which we may also call a personal confession, Menno is transparently honest about his deep inner struggle. He is unsure of himself. In a situation of extreme danger he might deny the name of the Lord, as he has already done many times. Through the guidance of the Holy Spirit, he has finally understood that his previous life was motivated by selfishness, that it was earthly and consequently evil.[128] As an evangelical preacher he had considered himself to be a spiritual and honest Christian,[129] but through the process of repentance and regeneration he learned to see himself as a deeply corrupted sinner.[130] Like many others, he had been using his faith in the grace and compassion of the Lord as a safety net to enable him to continue his selfish and sinful life. Not until he left the Catholic church and started a new life under the cross of Christ did he become a genuine Christian, and he concluded that if repentance and regeneration did not lead to a new Christian life with its proper fruits, they are nothing but empty talk. In fact, Menno's confessional description seems to fit his former life, since his basic motivation seems to have been ambition.[131]

Looking forward to a new life as a committed Christian, Menno envisions the heavenly Jerusalem on earth. Describing life in the church of the living God, Menno became as excited about this communal vision as he had been about individual regeneration in his *Spiritual Resurrection*. Those who know the Lord will live upon Mount Zion, in the heavenly Jerusalem, in the congregation of the righteous whose names are written in heaven. Delivered from hell, sin and death, they serve the Lord in peace and joy of heart all their days. They worry about nothing because the Lord will provide for their needs. They have pleasure in the law and speak of the Word of the Lord day and night. Their thoughts are upright; their words are words of grace: holy, faithful and true. What they seek, they find; what they desire, they obtain. Their souls dwell in the fullness of the wealth of the Lord. And although for a time they must endure much misery, suffering and trouble in the flesh, they know that the way of the cross is the way that leads to life. With Christ they contend valiantly, running with patience the race set before them until they have seized the prize and have received the promised crown. They neither waver nor turn aside and nothing can hinder them, since they have become partakers of the Spirit of the Lord. Their house is firmly built upon the rock and they walk in the ways of the Lord all their lives.[132]

The exuberance of these passages is hardly surpassed in Menno's writings. It reflects the enthusiasm of someone who has recently been regenerated from the sinfulness and lostness of this world and now has become part of God's new creation. All battles have been won, and from now on everything will be joy and happiness. Menno has finally entered the New Jerusalem, which has descended upon this earth.[133]

Menno's understanding of regeneration and the new life is more qualified and realistic in his later writings. As children of God, believers are *being* reborn from the wicked nature of Adam into the godly nature of Jesus Christ.[134] In a discussion of baptism as the symbol of death and resurrection with Christ in his earliest *Fundament-book*, Menno comes to the conclusion that the regenerated sinner no longer sins.[135] The Christian is still tempted by sin, but sin no longer dominates his life and he now has the power to overcome it.[136] Menno quotes 1 John 3:6: "Whoever is born of God does not commit sin; for his seed remains in him; and he cannot sin because he is born of God."[137] What at first glance seems to be a literal quotation is actually a paraphrase with the interesting interpolation, "for his seed remains in him." This addition is certainly not part of the text, nor can it be found in contemporary translations.[138] It simply is a reflection of Menno's doctrine of incarnation and regeneration. The same seed of the Word of God which was planted in Mary and became a new creation in her is planted into the hearts of believers, transforming the unholy nature of Adam into the holy nature of Christ.[139]

It is this unholy or sinful nature of Adam, from which and into which every human being is born, that Menno calls "original sin." This original sin, the lust and desire of the flesh, is the human inclination to sin rather than actual sin, but this inclination inevitably produces actual sins like adultery, hate, jealousy, lies, robbery, murder and idolatry. Although believers die to actual sin through regeneration, baptism and new life in Christ, this original inclination toward sin, or possibility of being tempted by sin, will stay with them as long as they live. Actual sins can be forgiven, but the power of original sin can be broken only by constant faith, prayer and obedience.[140] Obedience is crucial, because if regeneration does not lead to a triumphant resurrection to new life, it is meaningless.[141]

Regeneration as Menno understood it and described it is a long and difficult process with six to seven stages, or steps:

> First, there must be the preaching of the gospel of Christ, Matt. 28:19; then, the hearing of the divine Word, Rom. 10:17; third, faith by hearing the Word, Rom.10:17; fourth, there must be the new birth by faith; fifth, baptism out of the new birth, Titus 3:5, in obedience to God's Word; and then follows lastly the promise.[142]

It took Menno almost ten years to make his final commitment. In his *Renunciation of Rome*,[143] (1554) he describes his own process of conversion, which began when he started to question the doctrine of transubstantiation in 1524 and to study the Bible seriously for the first time. He says that through the power of the Holy Spirit he was illuminated and became knowledgeable in Scripture, but this first illumination led to spiritual pride rather than to repentance and conversion. He misused his new insights to criticize the Catholic church, to impress people in public and private disputations,[144] and to make himself a name as an evangelical preacher. Under the influence of his preaching, some of his parishioners joined the Melchiorites; others became hypocrites like Menno himself, misusing the gospel to fulfill their selfish ambitions. When Menno finally realized his complete failure as an evangelical preacher, after the Oldeklooster disaster, he faced the deepest crisis of his life:

> My heart trembled within me. I prayed to God with sighs and tears that he would give me, a sorrowing sinner, the gift of His grace, create within me a clean heart, and graciously through the merits of the crimson blood of Christ forgive my unclean walk and frivolous easy life and bestow upon me wisdom, Spirit, courage, and a manly spirit so that I might preach His exalted and adorable name and holy Word in purity, and make known His truth to His glory.[145]

Upon this experience of deep repentance, forgiveness and regeneration, Menno should have been baptized as a symbol of dying with Christ to sin and rising with him to new life as a logical next step,[146] but he makes no reference at all to his baptism.[147] He says that he immediately began to proclaim the gospel in his parish without restriction, and nine months later in January 1536 he finally left the Catholic church. A year later, after much hesitation, he accepted the call to become an elder of the scattered and confused Melchiorites.

> And so I, a miserable sinner, was enlightened of the Lord, was converted to a new conviction, fled from Babylon, entered into Jerusalem, and finally, though unworthy, was called to this high and heavy service.[148]

It was this final, unconditional commitment to the service of the Lord which made Menno's conversion complete. Whatever he said, wrote or did before had been done half-heartedly, and Menno would later refuse to take any direct blame or credit for it.[149] The turning point in Menno's life was when he fled Babylon and entered Jerusalem.

Conclusion

A review of Menno's early writings and later editorial emendations, read against the background of contemporary events, allows us to fill in more details of Menno's spiritual and intellectual biography. In Münster the Melchiorites considered the incarnation of Christ to be the crucial act of salvation and transformation. If the utopian God had become flesh and lived among them, and if the covenanters already shared in this new reality through faith, regeneration and the covenant, then Münster was the anticipation of the New Jerusalem. As the visible expression of God's kingdom of righteousness and peace, it was already transforming all areas of life. The introduction of high moral standards and rigorous discipline, the practice of brotherly love, the institution of communism, the provision of housing and work for everyone, the abolition of the use of money and the absence of any kind of exploitation were all reflections of this transformation.

The same doctrine of incarnation led Menno first to the experience and then to the writing of the *Spiritual Resurrection*. As the Word of God was sown in Mary, it was now being planted into the hearts and minds of those who were willing to listen to the gospel and ready to receive it. In Mary it became Christ Jesus, a totally new creation; in the believer it recreated heart and mind to its prelapsarian adamic condition, and produced a new creature. Delivered from the domination of sin, the regenerated believer now had the power to do what was right.

In the early stages of Menno's own process of conversion, he saw regeneration as an individual and spiritual experience, with explicit apocalyptic implications but few ecclesiological commitments. Any good Catholic could and should have had this experience. The Lord's Supper, baptism and membership in the body of believers had only marginal importance for Menno. At this stage in Menno's thought, changing one's life to produce spiritual fruit was seen as an individual effort and not as a result of new life as a member of the body of Christ.

Although the *Spiritual Resurrection* was based upon the same doctrine of incarnation and regeneration as was the Münsterite kingdom, not even Menno's own parishioners ever saw a purely spiritual regeneration as a real alternative to Münster. His second tract, the *New*

Birth, was still very individualistic on the subject of conversion.[150] When Menno revised it in the 1550s, however, ecclesiology had moved to the centre of his theological discourse. Menno's shift from being a spiritualistic fellow-citizen of the heavenly Jerusalem to becoming a rigourous proponent of the church without spot or wrinkle would be gradual. In his *Fundament-book* of 1539, Menno was clearly moving in that direction. In that writing he defined his concept of baptism,[151] the Lord's Supper, separation from the world and excommunication. The church now was seen as God's alternative for the recreation of the entire society. But Menno's ecclesiology was still evolving in 1539. It would not be until the 1550s that Menno came to view the church as a more exclusive minority of truly regenerated believers who lived new lives and focused on their own perfection and holiness.

In his adoption of the Melchiorite incarnational teaching, his understanding of spiritual regeneration, and his expectation of a new life for believers, Menno Simons stood firmly within the Melchiorite line of thought. At the same time, Menno definitely shaped these inherited doctrines in his own manner and way. His own interpretation of the "celestial flesh" doctrine moved him away from the Münsterite expectation of new revelations and Davidic kingdoms on earth. For Menno, the fact that "the Word became flesh" meant that the revelatory Word still ruled on earth, and would rule until Christ came again on the last day; the revelation of God's will in Christ remained in force. For Menno, Melchiorite incarnational doctrine signified a heightened Christocentrism and emphasis on the words and the life of Christ as normative for believers. Menno's acceptance of the Melchiorite doctrine of spiritual regeneration also was central to his spiritual thought, and was as closely linked to the "celestial flesh" doctrine for him as it was for other Melchiorites.

Nevertheless, as time passed Menno's emphasis shifted from individual spiritual renewal, to the ecclesiological implications of spiritual rebirth. By the 1556 edition of the *New Birth*, Menno identified the "reborn" by their membership in the community of believers. The same sure evolution is evident in the area of repentance and a new life which, in Menno's early writings, highlighted individual and personal dimensions, but shifted later to an emphasis on the church as the guardian of repentance and new life. Menno's writings demonstrate not only that he appropriated central Melchiorite spiritualist doctrines, but also how he reshaped them into a unique ecclesiology, over time.

CHAPTER FOUR

The Eschatological Anticipation of the New Jerusalem

Menno Simons' thought evolved steadily towards a clearer ecclesiological conception. Having developed his Melchiorite spiritualist inheritance in the face of Münsterite claims to be establishing the New Jerusalem on earth—in a specific city in Westphalia—he soon faced challenges from the Davidjorists, who were more radically spiritualist than he was. For the Davidjorists, the church was essentially invisible, made up of those who were believers inwardly, but outwardly appeared to be conforming to the external religious requirements of the state. Menno became convinced that the idea of a spiritual and "hidden" New Jerusalem was not in accord with the witness of Scripture. Over against Davidjorist "nicodemism," a concrete and visible faithfulness in this material world, and the subsequent "separateness" of the community of the faithful became increasingly important to Menno. At the same time, however, the increasingly hostile political context of unrelenting persecution meant that the church as the visible foretaste of the New Jerusalem would necessarily exist as a persecuted minority, not a ruling majority as Menno had once thought. By the time of Menno's last writings, his vision of the New Jerusalem had taken final form.

Spiritual and Individualistic Anticipation of the New Jerusalem

Not all Melchiorites joined the exodus to Münster, and not all of them agreed with the developments there. One of the most outspoken opponents of the apocalyptic anticipation of the kingdom of God was Menno Simons. As an "evangelical priest" and "honest spiritual Christian" he developed his early understanding of the New Jerusalem in his first tract, the *Spiritual Resurrection*. Those who have received the seed of the word of God into their hearts, he wrote, who have repented and died to sin, and who have been raised with Christ to new life have already arrived at the heavenly Jerusalem.[1] Because they have been given the Spirit of

Christ, they understand God's will and keep his commandments. As a royal priesthood and a holy nation they have now become God's people, although they were not a people in the past.² As individual believers they anticipate the kingdom of God in everyday life through faith and obedience. The restitution of God's people thus happens in the hearts and minds of the new citizens of God's kingdom, not in special places or towns. In Menno's early understanding, the New Jerusalem does not depend on a geographic location or a political or socio-economic organization, but becomes visible in the lives and actions of individual believers who do not even need to be organized into communities.

The language and the imagery of this tract sound apocalyptic. The sign of Thau, the seal of the living God from Revelation 7, has been associated with the end times throughout church history, changing its symbolic meaning in response to new historical situations.³ For the Melchiorites the sign of Thau was the symbol and confirmation both of their election and of their participation in the final apocalyptic events of history. Menno certainly shared the contemporary expectation of the last day of judgement and salvation. For him as well the sign of Thau represented election, even though its most important function was to represent dying with Christ and rising with him to new triumphant life.

Although apocalyptic, however, Menno's expectation was clearly not millennialistic, unlike that of the Münsterites. He assures his readers that this present time of grace is also the last time, the last invitation to the wedding of the Lamb before the final day of judgment.⁴ In a letter to his sister-in-law in the late 1550s, he writes that as long as she feels the presence of the Holy Spirit in her life she is a child of God and will inherit everlasting life. Even if she and Menno did not see each other again in this life, they would praise God together in his everlasting kingdom.⁵ Now and to the end of time, Christ as the incarnate Word of God is the absolute norm and content of all Christian life.⁶ "For no one should lay any foundation other than the one already laid, which is Jesus Christ" (1 Corinthians 3:11)⁷ already was the motto Menno used in this the earliest of his writings. In other words, unlike the later Münsterite leaders, Menno's expectation for the imminent coming of the Lord did not go beyond the message of the gospels. The fact that Christ and the gospels remain normative for the anticipation of the New Jerusalem makes Menno's expectation eschatological, but not apocalyptic in the Münsterite sense.

Menno's self-identification with the covenanters in his *Blasphemy* does not imply a basic change in this position. Although the term "covenanter" always seems to have apocalyptic overtones when used in connection with Münster, it actually meant many different things at the time. Hoffman, who probably introduced this concept to the Netherlands,[8] applied the term "covenant" to the new relationship between the believer and Christ, a relationship like the marriage bond. Baptism with water is the true sign of this covenant.[9] As the bride gives herself to the bridegroom, believers give themselves to Christ, giving up their own will, life, desire and spirit and submitting unconditionally to the will of God and Jesus Christ.[10]

For Jan Paeuw, an Anabaptist deacon in Amsterdam, this covenant had a different meaning, with clear apocalyptic implications. At his trial which began on December 29, 1534, he confessed that baptism is the sign of the covenant and that everyone who has made this covenant has also been baptized.[11] The content of the covenant is simply the promise to walk in the ways of the Lord and does not include any promise made to others who have also made the covenant. However, the "simple ones" do have to promise not to go to any church or keep any human institution. Those who are stronger in the faith do not need to make this promise because they already understand that everything that has been instituted by the popes and all that is being done in the churches is contrary to Scripture and the teaching of the apostles.[12] Jan Paeuw also knew about Münster and about the expectation that Amsterdam would be given into the hands of the covenanters.[13] For the early Rothmann also, the covenant was related to baptism as the pledge of a good conscience toward God and the promise to live according to his will (1 Peter 3:21).[14]

In the *Blasphemy* Menno interprets the covenant with God to include keeping the pure doctrine of Jesus Christ, a good conscience and an unfeigned faith as well as being baptized upon the cross of Christ.[15] True covenanters recognize that Christ is already Lord and King over the entire earth and over his believing congregation, that no one else can ever claim to be "the joyous king over all and the joy of the disconsolate" as Jan van Leiden does,[16] that the Christian congregation will never confess any other King and Lord than Jesus Christ,[17] that Christ fought only with the spiritual sword of the word of God and won his kingdom through service and suffering, that Christ will return in his own time for the salvation of believers and the judgement of the wicked and will receive his kingdom from no one else but his Father,[18] and that the true covenanters have not been baptized upon the sword of David but upon the cross of Christ, and now are ready and willing to suffer.[19]

Menno's preaching of a spiritual covenant and baptism upon the cross of Christ in 1534-35 did not convince radical Melchiorites.[20] They were not ready to listen to a man preaching an individualistic spiritual anticipation of the kingdom while they were busy conquering the entire world. But for those who wanted to remain in the security of their positions and offices, Menno's message of a spiritual resurrection and a personal covenant with God was attractive. Menno recalled that they were quite eager to learn from him how to dissimulate[21] and lead hypocritical lives.[22]

From spiritual regeneration Menno moved to a personal covenant with God, still without any apparent ecclesiological implications. If Christ is the unchallenged king of heaven and earth, and if born again believers enter into a covenant relationship with the Lord which is confirmed by the sign of baptism, then they are already citizens of the heavenly Jerusalem. This personal covenant with God does not carry with it any special responsibility for fellow citizens of the kingdom. Not until some of his parishoners and his own brother Peter lost their lives at Oldeklooster did Menno become aware of his own culpability with respect to the Münsterite kingdom, because he was "one of those who had disclosed to some of them a part of the abominations of the papal system."[23] Menno then experienced a deep spiritual crisis which led to the final stage of his conversion.[24] At this point he began to warn everyone against the Münsterite heresy and to preach true repentance, right baptism and the right Supper, but for nine more months he managed to stay in the security of his parish without truly facing the cross of Christ.[25] If he did denounce the false doctrines and practices of the Catholic church for nine months from the pulpit of his church, as he claims,[26] his superiors must have considered his criticism harmless enough to be tolerated.[27]

Menno saw the service and sacrificial suffering which characterize the way of Christ as the strategy by which God's kingdom is established. Suffering is seen not as weakness but as the consequence of healing love, forgiveness and reconciliation, the spiritual weapons of Jesus Christ. Because Christ succeeded in submitting to God's will, his followers also must reject the use of the sword.[28] In Menno's view, the Münsterites placed themselves outside the New Jerusalem the moment they decided to conquer the kingdom with the sword.[29]

Menno was consistent in his spiritual anticipation of the kingdom in both the *Spiritual Resurrection* and the *Blasphemy*, but his view was shaped by his Christocentrism: because our attitude towards the wicked must be the same as Christ's, this individual and spiritual anticipation may lead believers to personal suffering as well.

The New Jerusalem after Münster

After the Münsterite debacle there was much confusion among the Melchiorites. Once they had lost their leaders, the former pluralism[30] of the movement resurfaced and everyone read and interpreted Scripture as they saw fit.[31] Menno describes the covenanters as innocent sheep without a shepherd.[32] Impelled by his own conscience because of his compromising involvement with the covenanters[33] he finally decided to leave the priesthood and give leadership to the scattered and confused brothers and sisters.

The picture Menno paints of the contemporary church in his *Meditation on the Twenty-Fifth Psalm* (1539) is rather gloomy. Many of those who only recently escaped the Babylonian captivity and submitted to the cross of Christ have been seduced again by false prophets, and their erring has become a thousand times worse than it was before.[34] The lamentation of 4 Esdras 10:21-23 might very well be a description of the condition of the covenanters after Münster.[35] The Christian church, which should be a beautiful vision of the heavenly Jerusalem of peace, has changed into an inhuman guzzler of innocent blood. The city of the great king has been destroyed. The temple of the Lord has become a place of adultery and fornication. The bride of Christ has become a disgraceful harlot. Christ the blessed King of glory is rated a simpleton and despised as a fool, and his apostles are dismissed as liars. The Word of God is displaced by the preaching of false doctrines and by the use of violence. Antichrist rules in every place. Wherever Menno goes he finds nothing but vain obstinacy, perversity, blindness, avarice, pride, pomp, wantonness, strife, envy and ungodliness. The learned ones seemed to be the only hope of change for Menno, but they speak like the beast and both their teaching and their actions are motivated by ambition, avarice, lust and the desires of men.[36] Those few people who are searching for the truth are forced to carry the cross of Christ.[37] In 1539 Menno did not yet see the church as a suffering minority, but when he read the Old Testament as the history of God's people, he could hardly avoid the conclusion that even in Israel only a few were faithful to the Lord. He saw the same situation in the contemporary church.

Facing the tremendous task of restoring the New Jerusalem, Menno developed a new programme. He prayed for protection in the Word of God so that he might preach nothing but a living faith, a genuine love, true baptism, the right Supper, a blameless life and a justified excommunication of those who cause offence in doctrine and in life. He continued to pray for strength to obey the external magistracy in all earthly things[38] not contrary to God's Word, so that the holy city and temple of the Lord might be rebuilt, the erring sheep gathered and the adulterous bride forgiven. A special concern for Menno was the restoration of the house of the Lord as a light for the nations.[39] He wished to see all nations come to the mountain of the Lord and serve him in peace and freedom of conscience under the protection of a Christian government[40] and the leadership of good teachers, for the praise and honour of the Lord.[41] This New Jerusalem would become an example for the nations, a place where people from around the world would come to worship and learn to walk in the ways of the Lord.[42]

Freedom of conscience for Menno meant freedom of choice, but never pluralism. In the introduction to the 1539 edition of the *Meditation* he rejected any form of coercion in matters of faith. If he himself was in error with respect to the truth about Jesus Christ, he would gladly submit to instruction rather than be persecuted.[43] In a statement of his own confession of faith he says that he is seeking nothing other than the unadulterated Word of the Lord Jesus Christ, but at the same time there is no doubt in his mind that his interpretation, his doctrine and his ordinances are the only correct ones. If he errs, Menno writes, he should be admonished once with brotherly love and then excommunicated like the heretics in the early church. He is willing to suffer the tyranny of Nero, Diocletian, or Maxentius if he is proved wrong in his faith and doctrine and does not repent. One can only wonder what would have happened to an unrepentant sinner and heretic in a "Mennonite" society with the protection of a "Mennonite" government.

In a Latin postscript, probably dating from 1539, Menno claims that all that has been said so far is a true reflection of his doctrine and life: "Here you have my doctrine and my attitude of mind, from this you can see what I teach and what I live."[44]

Up to 1539, Menno had provided no definition of a Christian government, evangelical baptism, the true Supper or right excommunication. All we know is that, unlike the practices of all contemporary churches, these must be in accordance with the norms and doctrines of the Word of God because he prayed, "O Lord, preserve me pure and simple in thy truth that I may neither believe nor teach anything that is not in conformity with thy holy will and Word."[45]

In the *New Birth*, Menno divided humankind into two major groups: those who are born from above and have forgiveness of their sins, correct doctrines, faith, baptism, Supper, prayer, truth, light, promise and eternal life; and those who have not been born from above and consequently have nothing but lies, darkness, false sacraments, human promises, ungodly life, the wrath of God and eternal pain in hell.[46] If the unregenerated read the Scriptures, they will soon discover their own sinfulness and the false doctrines and sacraments of their church. Through the power of the Holy Spirit they are free to make their own choices, and it is Menno's first call and responsibility to call them to repentance and regeneration.[47] The statement that among a thousand there are only one or two who have grasped the true meaning of the heavenly birth[48] agrees with the conclusion of the *Meditation* that there are very few regenerated Christians.

A careful reading of the *Meditation* and the *New Birth* supports the conclusion that both tracts were written after Menno's resignation from the priesthood and around the time of his ordination as an elder of the covenanters, that is sometime in 1536/37. Addressing Roman Catholics in particular in his *New Birth*, Menno writes as one of them: "Tell me, my most beloved, where and when have *we* ever read in the Word of the Lord..."[49] This engaged "we" is replaced in the revised edition by an impersonal "you."[50] Catholics were still considered to be Menno's brothers in the first edition, whereas in the revised edition he simply addresses them as "you," or outsiders.[51] Although he was disassociating himself from the Catholics at this stage, Menno was careful not to identify himself with any of the Protestant or Anabaptist groups.[52] When Menno divided humankind into those who have the right doctrines and those who have the wrong ones in the first edition, he avoided giving names to any of the groups concerned. In the revised edition false doctrines go together with priests and masses, implicating the Catholic church.[53]

In his call to repentance and regeneration, Menno challenged theologians, scholars, councils, popes, cardinals and bishops to prove from Scripture that an unrepentant sinner can enter the kingdom of God.[54] It is certainly not enough to know Christ only after the flesh, without any change of life, because "he who is in Christ is a new creature, because the old things have passed away, it has all become new."[55] Once the spiritual baptism has happened the believer can be baptized with water and incorporated into the holy and blameless body of Jesus Christ, which is the congregation.[56] As the holy church of Christ, believers now bear the right fruits of the Spirit.[57] In 1536-1537 Menno optimistically wrote that whoever read his epistle and compared it with the Scriptures would not only recognize its truthfulness, but also accept it.[58]

Since Menno had come to the insight that there are only believers and unbelievers, that there is only one gospel, one baptism, one Supper and one true church, all that remained was to call unbelievers to repentance, and to baptize the believing with water. His goal was nothing less than the evangelizing of unbelievers and the restoration of the true church of Christ.[59] At this stage, in 1536/37, Menno would probably have refused to identify this church with any existing Protestant church or Anabaptist group. He did not represent any specific name or tradition, but only the "Council of the Lord Jesus Christ" which would stand on its own forever.[60]

The New Jerusalem, built on the Right Foundation

The only complete summary of Anabaptist-Melchiorite ideas before Menno wrote his *Fundament-book* was the *Restitution*, written by Bernhard Rothmann in 1534 to justify developments in Münster.[61] Although it was written with conviction and had a remarkable ability to engage the ordinary reader,[62] the *Restitution*, with its legitimation of Jan van Leiden's kingship, polygamy, and the use of aggressive violence could never serve Menno as a foundation for the true church of Jesus Christ. Menno found his foundation elsewhere: "No other foundation may be laid except the one that has been laid which is Jesus Christ" (1 Cor. 3:11).

After his universal call to repentance in the *New Birth*, Menno continued to struggle with the Münsterite heritage of the covenanters on the one side and the growing spiritualistic emphasis of David Joris and his followers on the other. Menno's convictions were severely tested[63] and strengthened in this process, and his vision of the true church of Jesus Christ began to take a more definite shape. In 1539 Menno began to write the *Fundament-book*, which was published in 1540.

Convinced that he had understood Scripture better than anyone else of his time, Menno now developed his understanding of the true foundation of faith and life in the New Jerusalem. If the magistrates would check his doctrine, he stated, they would soon discover that it is the genuine teaching of Christ, the eternal word of truth which will last forever.[64] This self assurance was already present in Menno's *Meditation* where he stated that with his teaching, which is simply the Word of God, he will judge not only princes but also angels on the last day of judgement.[65] At the conclusion of the *Foundation* he once more asserted the infallibility of his doctrine, the only way to salvation.[66]

Writing with the authority of the Word of God, then, Menno paraphrased 1 Corinthians 3:11 from "For no one can lay any foundation other than the one already laid, which is Jesus Christ" to "No other foundation may be laid except the one that has been laid, which is Jesus Christ."[67] What he wanted to make clear to his readers from the beginning is that no one should ever be allowed to lay another foundation than Jesus Christ. Although Paul stressed the impossibility of doing this, the Münsterites, at least for a short time, proved that this could indeed be done. Menno's point now seems to be that this should never happen again.[68] The fact that he did not revise this paraphrase in his later editions[69] indicates that it did not apply only to the Münsterites. It is always possible to replace the true foundation of the church, not only by new revelations as happened in Münster, but also by human doctrines, institutions and ceremonies.

Menno confronts all magistrates[70] and men of whatever land, class, or rank they might be with the *Fundament-book*,[71] which in his view was not just one foundation among many others, but was the only true foundation of Christian doctrine. He desired for them the illumination and true knowledge of God the Father and of our Lord Jesus Christ which is indispensable for everlasting life. Menno aimed at nothing less than the conversion all of Christianity using a selection of key evangelistic verses from Matthew, John, Mark and Isaiah.[72]

Menno's goal in the *Fundament-book*, as it was already in the *New Birth*, was the restoration of the true church of Jesus Christ, a church which might very well include entire nations, if they would repent and accept baptism upon the name of Christ. The first message for everyone is that we still live in the time of grace,[73] the time to repent, to turn away from the ways of the sinful flesh, to die to sin and to rise with Jesus Christ to new life. The prophecies of the Old Testament have been fulfilled and the one who was promised has come. Anointed with power from above and armed with the sword of the Spirit, he has proclaimed the good news of the kingdom of God and overcome the rule of Satan. By giving his life for our sins he has reconciled us to the Father, and we are again the chosen children of God. But this is also the last time before the coming day of judgement, the last call and invitation to the wedding celebration of the Lamb. Those who do not respond now may be too late tomorrow, and those who are still waiting for a gospel that does not include the cross of Christ should listen very carefully. If Christ conquered his kingdom through suffering, what else can the members of his body expect?[74] Menno understood what he was saying to be not human wisdom but the true Word of God as taught by Christ Jesus,[75] the promised king David and the seed of life through whom everything can be renewed.

In the next chapter of the *Fundament-book* Menno deals with the genuine penance which produces real fruits of repentance and leads to new life,[76] changing the old sinful human being and his works into a new one created after Christ in righteousness and holiness.[77] The key to regeneration and new life is faith in the gospel of Jesus Christ,[78] which transforms and renews one's entire life by recreating the sinful human being into a new one marked by obedience and peacefulness in Christ.[79]

After genuine repentance and a change of life has taken place by the power of the Holy Spirit and through faith, the born again Christian is ready for baptism.[80] Believers' baptism is a commandment. The water of baptism has no power in itself,[81] but it symbolizes the incorporation of the believer into the church of Christ, the inner washing from our sins and the new covenantal relationship of obedience to the Lord.[82] During this entire discourse on baptism, however, Menno still does not connect baptism to mutual responsibility between brothers and sisters. Repentance, regeneration, faith and baptism are experiences and commitments of individuals. Menno's ecclesiology is emerging, but not yet clearly formed.

When Menno begins to argue against the Spiritualists, however, especially when he focusses on the followers of David Joris, participation in church life suddenly becomes important.[83] Like the bread composed of many different grains, individual believers become the body of Christ when they come together to celebrate the Lord's Supper. It is still not the local congregation that Menno is focusing on, but the church of God composed of Jews and Greeks, of men and women, of slaves and free, of all of God's children scattered all over the world.[84] As members of one body they are united not by a mutual covenant, but by the love of God and love for each other. Since they are like-minded as the different members of one body ought to be, they serve each other with all their material and spiritual goods.[85] As they celebrate the Lord's Supper, breaking bread and drinking wine in remembrance of Christ's death, the spiritual gifts of service for the building of God's kingdom become manifest, such as are described in Ephesians 4 and 1 Corinthians 12.[86] The celebration of the Supper as the body of Christ might very well lead to what we today would call a charismatic experience, where the participants are drunk with God's wisdom and play and dance for joy before the Lord.[87]

Just as the incarnation of the living Word of God is the precondition for regeneration, so Christ's life of love, service, suffering and death becomes the foundation for the church. Regeneration, new life, the covenant with God and commitment in baptism can be experienced individually, but the celebration of the Lord's Supper must be a communal experience in which the church, composed of many individual members, becomes the visible body of Jesus Christ. In the same way as Christ committed his life to service and suffering love, the believers now commit themselves and all their spiritual and material gifts to the service of each other.[88]

The Eschatological Anticipation

Menno's ecclesiology is built not upon the baptismal vow[89] or a new covenantal relationship with God and with each other,[90] but upon the cross of Christ. The church as the body of Christ can be built only upon the ultimate love of God which finds its highest expression in the life, teaching and cross of Jesus Christ.

In the *Blasphemy* Menno also had related baptism to the cross of Christ, but there he simply rejected the use of any kind of violence for the conquest of the kingdom. In the *Fundament-book* Menno's deepened understanding of the cross enabled him to work out the positive content of the cross as a new relationship between the members of the body of Christ. In the celebration of the Supper they commit themselves to the way of the cross and become Christ's visible body in this world, ready to be broken in the loving service of their fellows. The real transubstantiation happens not in the bread and wine, but in the many individual believers who are being transformed into the body of Christ, a new incarnation of his healing, forgiving and reconciling love. Menno asserts that the traditional doctrine of transubstantiation prevents this miracle from happening by concentrating attention on a mere piece of bread and a glass of wine which are presented as a sacrifice for the individual believer. When the bread and wine are worshipped as the flesh and blood of Christ, they replace the true body of Christ and become idols so powerful that they have always prevented the true church from being realized and are used by the Antichrist to dominate the entire world.[91]

Admission to this celebration of the Supper is subject to certain preconditions. Those who have not committed their lives to the service of Christ and are not willing to serve their fellow-members with all their material and spiritual gifts should not participate in the celebration of the Supper, because they are not members of the body of Christ and do not belong to his church. Separation from unbelievers and their evil deeds is the ultimate consequence of this ecclesiology, for only in this way can the holy city of Jerusalem, the city of peace and prayer which is the church of God, be kept clean and alive.[92]

From a dogmatic point of view, Menno said very little about any specific Christian doctrine in his writings prior to 1539. He was working on the foundation for such doctrines, a foundation which would consist of repentance, regeneration and new life, baptism and the right celebration of the Supper. Where these are present, the kingdom of God or the New Jerusalem is becoming reality. If the community of believers built upon the cross of Christ is the true foundation for the development of Christian doctrines, Menno should now be ready to develop them—but instead he continues to write about the call and mission of preachers and teachers of Christian doctrines. Menno is not so much a theologian as an evangelist, developing doctrines only as far as is necessary for his preaching the gospel and building the church of Jesus Christ.

Menno believed that, like doctrines, the call and mission of preachers must emerge from the right foundation of Christ and his body. Preachers full of the love of God for their neighbours and moved by the power of the Holy Spirit are called and confirmed by the church of Jesus Christ for no other purpose than to teach, to admonish, to discipline, to baptize, to celebrate the Lord's Supper, to oppose false doctrines and to lead the church by right doctrine and life.[93] An evangelical preacher who does these things may consider himself called and commissioned in the same way as Christ and his apostles[94] or Moses and the prophets. Those who have not been called in this way may be very learned and well-spoken, but they will never produce the spiritual fruits of the kingdom of God.[95] This very responsible role of the preacher is defined by Menno as an *ampte* or office, rather than as service or ministry.[96]

Menno is as concerned about the message of the evangelical preacher as he is about his calling. He must preach "the" Word of God, serving only as the mouth of God and avoiding any kind of diversion.[97] Even Christ did not preach his own wisdom and understanding, but only the Word and doctrine of his Father.[98] Wherever the Word of God is being preached in this way, people will be set free from their captivity to the sinful flesh, as Menno had discovered. It took him years to break free[99] from the Babylonian captivity of his worldly ambitions and his desire for security and comfort[100] to go to Jerusalem, where he now enjoyed the freedom of the spirit of Christ. However, it is a freedom which has its price: it very well might lead to physical suffering.[101]

By presenting the right understanding of grace, regeneration, baptism, the celebration of the Supper, rightly called preachers and the proclamation of the gospel of Jesus Christ, Menno claims to have solved the major problem of the Babylonian captivity of the church. If the ordained governments and all the people of the nations[102] would read carefully what he has to say, they would have to admit that his doctrine, faith and life are the only way of life.[103] In the same way as there was only one house of Israel, one Jerusalem and one temple, so there is now only one Christ and one church, which has one gospel, one faith, one baptism, one Supper and one way to eternal life. Those who have not built their lives on this foundation are not members of the church of Jesus Christ,[104] regardless of name, fame or position.

In a final appeal to the magistrates, Menno challenges them to study the word of God as the pious kings of the Old Testament did.

They should not misuse their power to persecute innocent believers, but use their office (which included the practice of torture and capital punishment) in accordance with God's calling and ordinance.[105] It is the responsibility of pious magistrates to punish evildoers and to remove blind and false teachers from their positions.[106] By the time the revised edition of the *Fundament-book* was published in 1558, Menno's concept of the role of the government had grown to include the establishment of justice, the defence of freedom by delivering citizens from the hands of oppressors, and the prevention of the spreading of heresies. In the first edition Menno simply wanted false teachers and prophets removed;[107] in the revised edition he was concerned that the means to be used for this purpose be reasonable and without violence. A God-fearing government must promote and defend God's Word and doctrine.[108] A non-Christian government should take Cyrus (Ezra 1:2) as its example and allow God's people to rebuild the spiritual Jerusalem on the old foundation of the twelve apostles.[109]

In a final chapter, Menno calls scholars and learned ones, common people and corrupt sects to repentance and to new life. The message is the same: listen to the proclamation of the pure word of God, repent and build your new life upon the right foundation, which is Jesus Christ.

The anticipation of God's kingdom in the *Fundament-book* is universal and holistic. The time of God's grace includes all people and all nations and affects all areas of life. Repentance and regeneration must lead to baptism, the sign of a good conscience and of obedience to God's will and the symbol of dying to sin and rising with Christ to triumphant new life. Although Menno states that those who have died and risen with Christ to new life no longer sin, he immediately modifies his statement to say that desire and temptation are still present in the Christian life, even though they no longer dominate a believer's actions.[110] At the celebration of the Lord's Supper, when individual believers commit themselves unconditionally to the service of the Lord and their brothers and sisters with all material and spiritual gifts, the many different members of Christ become one visible body, his chosen bride and holy church. As they live in disciplined harmony and peace with each other, they already anticipate the heavenly Jerusalem.

Although only true Christians are to be admitted to the celebration of the Supper and the members of the body of Christ need to shun the false doctrines and ceremonies of the Babylonian harlot,[111] Menno never gives up the vision and hope of a Christian people living under the leadership and protection of a Christian government. In 1554-55 he still is calling the magistrates to repentance and new life, and confronting them with the examples of the pious kings of the Old Testament. If the magistrates would listen and repent, they not only would carry the sword for the punishment of the wicked and the protection of the good, but also would establish justice, implement righteousness and prevent the spread of any false doctrine and the teaching of any heresy in their nations. As they carry out their true calling and ordinance from God, they will become establishers and defenders of God's word and protectors of the church of Jesus Christ.

In a community of believers where everyone shares everything and where born again Christians through the power of the Holy Spirit no longer sin, even though they are still susceptible to temptation, the restoration of prelapsarian humanity becomes reality. Menno seldom discusses the concept of restitution in the way that Rothmann and Dirk Philips do.[112] It is the anticipation of the kingdom of God, inspired by the example of Christ and his apostles, that really matters. This anticipation, built on the only right foundation which is Jesus Christ, looks forward to his second coming and lives by his life, teaching, death and resurrection.

In the *Fundament-book* of 1539-40 Menno does not yet conceive of the godly gathering of believers, the body and church of Jesus Christ, as a suffering minority, but he was always aware of this possibility.[113] If Christ conquered his kingdom through suffering, what else can the members of his body expect?[114] There may be times of goodwill and peace for the body of Christ in this world, but the anticipation of the kingdom of God will always stand under the sign of the cross of Christ.[115]

In the *Fundament-book* the framework for the anticipation of the kingdom of God is not complete. Menno has not yet given any definition of the ban. The "cutting off" of sinners had been part of Menno's theological discourse since he left the Catholic church,[116] but he had yet to articulate a clear exposition of its meaning, content and method of implementation. His failure to define this concept is a good example of the way Menno wrote theology, namely in response to the questions and problems arising from everyday church life.

When the Melchiorites became carried away by the excitement of the anticipation of the New Jerusalem in Münster, Menno wrote the *Spiritual Resurrection* to make them aware that regeneration and new life in Christ are indispensable preconditions for the anticipation of the kingdom of God. After the self-proclamation of Jan van Leiden as the messianic King David, Menno used clear scriptural evidence in the *Blasphemy of Jan van Leiden* to demonstrate that Christ is the promised Messiah and Lord of heaven and earth, and that Jan van Leiden's kingship is heresy based upon false prophesies and misinterpretation of Scripture. After Münster, Menno finally provided the Melchiorites with desperately needed leadership and developed the basic points of his new programme for the true church of Jesus Christ. In the *Fundament-book*, the most complete of his theological attempts, he proclaims the need for repentance and regeneration to unbelievers during this time of grace, he leads born again Christians into the fellowship of believers, and develops the theological content and ethical implications of citizenship in the New Jerusalem. The focus of Menno's theological discourse is still not dogmatics, but the anticipation of the kingdom of God which comes as a result of the down-to-earth proclamation of the gospel of Jesus Christ rather than by abstract philosophical speculations or theological deliberations. But as Menno himself soon realized, wherever people repent and join the church of Jesus Christ a minimal foundation of sound biblical doctrines becomes indispensable.

Completing the Foundation

The cutting off and shunning of the unrepentant sinner

The *Kind Admonition on Church Discipline*, Menno's first systematic exposition of the ban, appears to have been written in 1541, first in the form of a personal letter[117] and later published in a revised form[118] addressed to his brothers and sisters in the local congregation.[119] Although from the beginning of his ministry he claimed that the ban was one of the signs of the true church, he did not mention it in his *Fundament-book*. His reason for omitting it cannot be that it was the kind of information to be given only to insiders, like the Melchiorite doctrine of incarnation. The most probable explanation is that in 1539 the ban had not yet become the public issue that it became in the 1550s, when Menno had to defend it against Gellius Faber[120] and wrote expositions on it for the general public in his *Instruction on Excommunication*[121] and *A Kind Admonition on Church Discipline*.[122]

The ban is the logical consequence of Menno's doctrine of incarnation and regeneration, of baptism and the covenant of a good conscience with God, and of the celebration of the Supper and the formation of the body of Christ from many individual believers. In his first writing on the ban, Menno presents a summary of these doctrines before he proceeds to the biblical concept of excommunication and shunning. His concept of regeneration is still based upon the Melchiorite doctrine of incarnation. The decision of believers to become God's children was based upon their own free choice.[123] Born again of the heavenly seed of the Word of

God, they become like Christ in their minds, spirits, hearts and wills,[124] living unblameably and sinning no more.[125] Celebrating the Lord's Supper together, they become members of the same body of Christ and love, admonish and discipline one another with the Word of God.[126]

If, in this process of growing together into the fullness of Christ, a member fails, Menno continues, his brothers and sisters will not allow him to be lost, but will teach and admonish him in love in order to bring him back into the community of believers.[127] This kind of caring and restoring discipline can be practiced only with godly wisdom, modesty, goodness and care.[128] If the apostate brother deliberately remains in sin and does not repent, he has cut himself off from the congregation and should be shunned.[129] He no longer is accountable to the congregation, but only to God. The formal excommunication of the unrepentant sinner is neither more nor less than the public confirmation of what has already happened when the believer removed himself from the body of Christ. The ban practiced in this way is nothing other than the highest expression of love for the erring sinner.[130] How do sinners benefit by continung to participate in the fellowship of the believers, Menno asks, if in their hearts they are no longer living in the community of Christ?[131]

In 1541 Menno was confident that unrepentant sinners would accept the ban as a consequence of their own free choice.[132] In the same way as born again Christians originally committed themselves freely to the covenant with God and with the church, they now freely leave the fellowship of believers once this covenant has been broken. In this process the congregation can only love, admonish, heal, reconcile and save; she should never reject, judge, or condemn the sinner. Even formal excommunication is practiced only to open the way for repentance and for restoration.[133]

In a short addition to this instruction on the ban, Menno once more describes the community of believers as those who no longer sin because they have become partakers of the nature of God. Marked by the sign of Thau on their foreheads, they are already God's holy people, the temple of the Lord, the spiritual Mount Zion and the New Jerusalem.[134] The emphasis in Menno's early writing on the ban is the individual, not the maintenance of a pure corporate body.

True Christian faith as the instrument of transformation

Around 1542 Menno published a tract concerning the *True Christian Faith*. Because he was no longer allowed to teach and to preach in public, Menno was forced to share his God-given, Scripture-based wisdom in writing.[135] Thanks to this godly wisdom, Menno had learned to understand that everything in the Christian life depends on a sincere and active faith.[136] The only instrument powerful enough to make a regenerated life possible is faith based on the promise of Scripture and evidenced by the power and the fruits of the gospel of Jesus Christ and the apostlic teaching.[137] Such life-transforming and fruit-bearing faith is a spiritual gift from God.[138]

True faith first leads the sinner to the recognition of God's holiness and righteousness on the one hand and his own human sinfulness and lostness on the other. The biblical term for this understanding is "the fear of God,"[139] which is also wisdom because it frightens the believer away from what is evil and destructive in life and leads him to genuine repentance.[140] This first step of true faith bears no fruit. It is love, the second consequence, that makes the difference and compels believers to obey all the commandments and teachings of Christ.[141] This love is a response to God's unlimited grace which he has bestowed so richly upon all humanity in his son Jesus Christ, healing, restoring and saving lives.[142] The fruits of righteousness and holiness are born of this love, which is powerful enough to overcome all resistance and able to bear anything, even the cross of Christ if necessary.[143] The fear of God, a response to his justice and holiness based upon the law, and the love of God, fully expressed in his son Jesus Christ, cannot be separated. Together they transform all human life.[144]

Menno's assessment of contemporary forms of faith is quite negative. The papists, although they believe in Christ's sacrifice for the atonement of human sin, have made this life-transforming faith depend on an institution whose ceremonies and sacraments add up to nothing less than idolatry.[145] Luther's *sola fide* led to a comfortable, fleshly life.[146] Mikron and the Zwinglians taught that Christ is not only the Son of God, but also the product of the menstrual blood of an unclean woman,[147] a doctrine of incarnation which for Menno is simply blasphemous. Faith in such an unclean, human Christ can have no transforming or saving power.

Menno presents his readers with biblical examples of the power of faith, of whom his favourite Old Testament examples are Abraham and King Josiah. Abraham's life was changed radically by his trust in the Lord's promise and his obedience to his commands.[148] King Josiah (2 Kings 23ff) is the foremost example of a Christian king and ruler who, once he came to know the law of the Lord, repented and changed his own life and the life of his entire nation. If contemporary kings and rulers would repent in the same way as King Josiah did, they also would become spiritual kings and priests, ruling their nations in the fear of God and with Christian wisdom.[149]

The major causes of injustice and exploitation in his society, from Menno's point of view, were ambition, selfishness, lust and greed. But examples from the New Testament show that true Christian faith has the power to transform even a corrupt tax collector, a greedy businessman, an ambitious prince, a cold-blooded murderer, a fallen woman or a hypocritical clergyman. If everyone in society would experience what Zacchaeus did, everything would change for the better.[150] Born again believers would freely share all their possessions with the needy with joyful hearts and minds. Injustice, exploitation, hunger and suffering would cease. Everything would be used for the benefit of everyone, because wherever there is faith everything is used in a pure and right way.[151] People who believe like Zacchaeus belong to the church of the Lord and are the true citizens of the New Jerusalem.[152] Utopia becomes reality, because it is the nature of the believer not to cheat or to harm, but to help and to do justice to everyone.[153] True Christian faith has the potential to transform society.

A holistic vision of the New Jerusalem

In *Why I do Not Cease Teaching and Writing* (1539) Menno again emphasizes the identity between his teaching and the gospel of Jesus Christ.[154] Although he recognizes that those who proclaim the Word of God have always been persecuted,[155] he has again been seriously tempted to stop teaching and writing,[156] but he cannot because there are too many people who need to hear the clear gospel of Jesus Christ. He has come to the understanding that the entire world has always been misled by ignorant preachers and teachers who, motivated and influenced by their fleshly desires and ambitions, have sought nothing but temporal things. With the help of unfaithful princes and rulers they have invented false doctrines, sacraments and ceremonies and have seduced the common people to idolatry.[157] In countries where the preachers are selected and installed by the magistrates without receiving a call and commission from Jesus Christ, the situation is even worse.[158] When he looked around, Menno could see hardly any God-fearing government, any true evangelical preacher or any irreproachable church.[159]

In this situation Menno and his brothers desired nothing else but to work toward the restoration of God's people.[160] For this restoration to be complete, Menno put forward seven signs of the true church:

> 1. no bishop, pastor or teacher should be admitted in the church of Jesus Christ unless he follows Christ's doctrines and lives unblameably before the Lord, since Christ himself is the norm for the life and teaching of any evangelical preacher;[161]

2. no gospel should be proclaimed other than the true gospel of Jesus Christ;[162]
3. true faith and life in Jesus Christ which proves itself in deeds of love should be practiced;[163]
4. only true Christian baptism, first with Spirit and fire and afterwards with water should be practiced;[164]
5. no other supper than the Supper of Jesus Christ should be celebrated;[165]
6. all strange ceremonies and actions of worship which are contrary to the Word of God should be abolished;[166]
7. all magistrates should be converted so that they rightly administer and execute their office in the fear of the Lord for the protection of the good and the punishment of the evil.[167]

Standing in the way of this complete restoration are princes, preachers and the common people who are still fleshly and earthly minded; they all are drunk with the enchanting wine of the Babylonian harlot; they do not fear the wrath of the Lord against all evil; and they do not acknowledge the marvelous deeds of love and grace of the Lord.

The entire creation of heaven and earth with its abundance of life was been given by God to humankind.[168] In addition, God has given us his Word, first in the form of natural law, then through Moses and the prophets, and finally in his only begotten son Jesus Christ, the incarnation of his wisdom and power. He has delivered us from the bondage of sin, hell and death. Calling us daily to repentance and new life, he has opened heaven for us and given us eternal life.[169] Once people recognize this unlimited love of God, they will have to repent and change their lives.[170] For Menno it is not fear but faith and love[171] which are the most powerful instruments of transformation.[172] The fruits of this evangelical faith are works of healing, forgiveness, reconciliation and peace.[173]

After a seven-page call to repentance, Menno states that he will not cease teaching and admonishing as long as he lives. If princes and rulers and their subjects, all who call upon the name of the Lord, recognize and accept this teaching of Christ, there will be no further need for any fortifications, army or sword. The only instrument of violence that will still be necessary is the sword of justice for the punishment of the wicked and the protection of the good.[174] Then what the prophets Isaiah and Micah foresaw will become reality: swords will be beaten into plowshares and spears into pruning-hooks. There will be no wars anymore and all people will live in joy and in peace,[175] because those who have become members of the body of Jesus Christ seek nothing but love, peace and unity.[176]

Defending his faith and doctrine in a written statement[177] to Jan a Lasco in 1544, Menno distances himself and his followers from Münster and describes the new community: We do not belong to the Münsterite heresy. As Christians, born of the powerful seed of the Word of God in Jesus Christ, partakers of his nature and his Spirit, we can not participate in any kind of insurrection or turmoil. Our prince is the prince of peace. His kingdom is a kingdom of love, unity, peace and betterment of life. Whoever has this peace in his heart will never participate in any kind of violence or injustice. For this reason we reject the use of all violence *Excepto ordinario potestatis gladio, in debitum usum verso*.[178] We fight only with the two-edged sword of the Word of God, and hope, through the power of the Holy Spirit, to free all men from the bondage of evil. Our goal is nothing less than the restoration of the true Church of Jesus Christ.[179] No magistrate needs to fear us, because we are not trying to destroy them but to correct them and to save them.[180]

There is a strong rationalistic element in Menno's approach to ethics. Once people acknowledge the unlimited love of God which he has expressed so marvelously in his creation of heaven and earth with their abundance of life, in natural law, in the law of Moses and the prophets and finally in the gospel of his son Jesus Christ, they will have to repent their sinful way of life and begin a new life of unconditional love for God, for his creation and for their fellow man.[181] Abundance of life, justice and peace for everyone will result from this transformation.[182] Out of love humankind has received the abundance of life of God's creation; out of love they will then freely share this abundance with their fellows. Under the leadership of truly Christian bishops, pastors and teachers, by means of the celebration of the right sacraments of baptism and the Supper, protected and supervised by a Christian government, the restoration of God's original creation—which at the same time anticipates the coming kingdom of Jesus Christ—will become reality.

It is clear that as late as 1544, Menno is still not dreaming of a sectarian minority separated from the world, but of an all-inclusive new society of regenerated Christians, the new people of God, the New Jerusalem which already anticipates the coming kingdom of God.

The Anticipation of the New Jerusalem in Menno's last decade

Menno's theology, based upon the Melchiorite doctrine of incarnation, is mainly a theology of the new creation or the anticipation of the kingdom of God. Suffering and the cross of Christ are not mentioned as an explicit sign of the church by him until his *Reply to Gellius Faber* of

1554.[183] Although Menno had always been aware that the cross is a part of the Christian life, he accepted it only reluctantly and never ceased to complain about it. The *Reply to False Accusations* (1551) is a good example of his attitude.[184] Even though he knows that the truth has always been persecuted,[185] Menno has a hard time accepting this fact. It might have been easier for him, he says, if he and his followers had been persecuted, tortured and burned by unbelievers and heathens, but now they are being slandered by the preachers, theologians and scholars and persecuted by their own Christian magistrates. The preachers and learned ones have been piling up lie upon lie so effectively that Menno and his followers are not even allowed to defend their doctrines and confess their faith publicly.[186] The so-called Christian governments have not fulfilled their responsibility to listen carefully to both parties, to check their expositions of faith against Scripture and then to support what is biblical and condemn what has been identified as false teaching.[187]

The main accusations against Menno and his followers in 1551 were still that they were Münsterites, rebels eager to take over cities and lands, that they practiced sharing their wives as well as their possessions, that they claimed to have reached perfection, and that they taught that salvation can be gained by merit.[188] Community of goods never became a sign of the true church as such, and it was never compulsory among the Anabaptists except among the Hutterites and the Münsterites. In his defence, Menno wrote that since regenerated believers have been baptized into the body of Christ and participated in the same bread, they love each other and care for each other[189] as the entire Scripture teaches that true Christians should do. Using the analogy of the body, Menno stated that it would be against the law of nature if one half of the body were to neglect the other half.[190] In the same way, all those who have been born again, received the Spirit of God and become members of the body of Christ do not neglect each other, but stand ready to serve their fellow members with all their material and spiritual goods:

> They show mercy and love, as much as they can. No one among them is allowed to beg. They take to heart the need of the saints. They entertain those in distress. They take the stranger into their houses. They confort the afflicted; lend to the needy; clothe the naked; feed the hungry; do not turn their face from the poor; do not despise their own flesh.[191]

The Anabaptists do not advocate taking the land and property of others,[192] but teach and practice unconditional love and mercy as did Jesus Christ. Even if they were teaching and practising community of goods, they would only be following the example and practice of the apostles.¹⁹³ For seventeen years Menno and his followers had practiced this kind of mercy, love and community. Many had lost their property and even their lives, but so far "none of those who have joined us nor any of their orphaned children have been forced to beg."¹⁹⁴ For Menno it was intolerable hypocrisy that the rich and powerful lived in their abundance and luxury while many of their poor brothers and sisters, baptized with the same baptism, sharing in the same bread and belonging to the same church had to beg for their daily bread.¹⁹⁵ How could the preachers celebrate the Lord's Supper if they did not practice mercy and love?¹⁹⁶ And how could they accuse Menno and his followers of heresy for simply following the example and teaching of Jesus Christ and his apostles?

Menno claims that because of the shameless lies of these preachers, Charles V issued his so-called Blood Placard in 1550. Since then "in Brabant, Flanders, Friesland, and in Gelderland God-fearing pious hearts are led daily to the slaughter like innocent sheep."¹⁹⁷ In this critical situation, Menno was not pleading with his Christian readers for his own life and the lives of his followers, but calling the magistrates to repentance and confronting them with the duties of their God-given office. As a Christian government they must first follow the instructions of Deuteronomy 17:[14-20]. They should then make themselves a copy of the law so that they would be able to read in it every day and act accordingly.¹⁹⁸ Referring to Romans 13, Menno concludes that because the magistrates have been given their office by God, they should bend their knees before the Lord and rightly and reasonably execute this function.¹⁹⁹ If they would listen carefully to him²⁰⁰ instead of to the shameless lies of the preachers, they would soon discover that Menno and his brothers and sisters were not Münsterites but sincere Christians who seek only the Christian way of life and peace.²⁰¹

The greatest enemies of the covenanters in the 1550s, Menno maintained, are the preachers who use whatever means of slander and defamation²⁰² they can find against the covenanters in order to protect their own positions as religious ministers and counsellors of the magistrates. If he were allowed to defend his doctrine and faith in a public debate, and if the magistrates listened impartially, they soon would discover the truth and the roles would change. A truly Christian government, which would have to listen to and follow the doctrine and teaching of Menno Simons, would use nonviolent means to stop heresies from spreading and would develop a new society of justice and peace under the protection of Christian magistrates, as a result of the proclamation of the true gospel of Jesus Christ. But if the preachers continue their slander and false accusations and the magistrates do not listen to Menno, then the covenanters will have to submit to the will of the Lord and continue to suffer persecution and martyrdom.[203] By 1552, Menno's counterattack had become acrimonious. He no longer considered his opponents to be regenerated Christians or to have the Holy Spirit or the Word of God. All their actions, he says, are motivated by their sinful flesh, and they seduce and encourage the common people to a similar lifestyle.[204]

In the same year some of the covenanters wrote and published an anonymous letter in which they accused and slandered both the preachers and the magistrates and pointed to their corruption as a reason for not attending public worship services or celebrations of the Lord's Supper. Gellius Faber responded to this letter in 1552 with his *Antwert ... up einen bitter hoenischen breff der Wedderdoopers*. Although Menno was not the author of this letter, all the major points[205] to which Faber responds could very well have been made by him, and Menno was eager to defend them in his *Reply to Gellius Faber*. The attack of the covenanters on the preachers was effective enough to cause Faber to complain that the preachers had lost their credibility and lacked the moral authority to enforce the ban properly.[206]

Menno discussed the question of the oath for the first time in 1551. Although he admitted that swearing was lawful in the Old Testament, he argued that it is not allowable in the perfection of Christ in the New Testament. This is the first time in his writings that he characterized the law of the Old Testament as imperfect and the gospel of Jesus Christ as perfect, and it seems curious that he should do so in relation to the God-given office of government, which for him is deeply rooted in the law and kingly tradition of the Old Testament. He may have been influenced at this point by the separatist ideas of the Swiss Brethren, expressed in the *Schleitheim Confession*, which set the "perfection of Christ" over against the imperfection of the sword and the oath. This is the only statement where Menno uses the terms "dat volkomene" and "dat onvolkomene."[207]

Separation from the sinful world had become imperative for Menno and his followers by 1551. In answer to questions from members of his congregations, Menno points to Paul: "whatever Paul says about separation, he says it mostly in the imperative."[208] Thus we have to avoid any fellowship with those who confess that they are Christians but do not live accordingly, even if they are marriage partners or children or parents.[209] But Menno cautions the brothers not to carry shunning to excess[210] because he knows from his own experience the negative effect of compulsory shunning. The ban should always remain a work of godly love, and Menno agreed with Dirk Philips that the intent of the ban is not the ruin of people, but their recovery.[211] How controversial the ban had already become is shown by Menno's closing observation that if all the brothers would follow the teaching of Christ and his apostles in brotherly love and peace, disunity and quarrels would cease at once.[212]

The ban must have been used relentlessly in the early 1550s. Faber maintained that the implementation of the ban by the covenanters had created more disunity than unity, and that out of the hundreds of excommunicated members not more than five had changed their lives, the rest of them having become so bitter that they would rather have been called papist than Christians.[213] Menno does not deny Faber's accusations, but argues that the ban has helped eliminate all kinds of heresies from the ranks, helping to eliminate the suspicion that they were Münsterites, and leading to radical obedience to God's ordinances.[214] There is no question that for Menno the fruits of the ban are unity and a church without spot or wrinkle, even if only a few of the excommunicated do repent and return to the church.[215]

Menno's ecclesiology gets its final definition in his *Reply to Gellius Faber*. Defending the five articles of the anonymous letter of the Anabaptists against the Reformed, Menno discusses the true signs by which the church of Christ may be known:

1. unadulterated doctrine
2. scriptural use of the sacramental signs
3. obedience to the Word
4. unfeigned brotherly love
5. a bold confession of God and Christ, and
6. suffering oppression and tribulation for the sake of the Lord's Word.[216]

If we compare these signs with the seven conditions[217] for the restoration of the church Menno set out in 1542, there are several interesting differences. The election of right bishops, pastors and teachers is no longer a key issue, nor is the conversion of all magistrates a prerequisite for the anticipation of the New Jerusalem. By the 1550s Menno had become resigned to the fact that the cross of Christ is part of the kingdom of God. This major polemical tract contains hardly anything else that is new, but simply repeats Menno's previous arguments. Even suffering as a sign of the church of Jesus Christ receives no further exposition, but remains a tremendous injustice to which Menno and his followers are certainly not looking forward.

Did Menno finally resign his dream of converting the entire world and his vision of a Christian nation under the leadership and protection of a Christian government? Certainly not! His definition of the function of a Christian magistrate remained basically unchanged in the 1554-55 revised edition of the *Fundament-book*.[218] But while he was waiting for the repentance and regeneration of princes and kings, the New Jerusalem was being anticipated even without the protection of a Christian magistrate and the church of Jesus Christ was growing in spite of persecution. It depended on the love and grace of God, the illumination of the Holy Spirit, and the faith and obedience of believers.[219]

After appealing to human reason and common sense and demanding public debates as an instrument for the discovery of the truth for so many years, in 1554-55 Menno came to the conclusion that reason is useless for the recognition of truth because of its corruption by sin.[220] The truth can be discovered only through the illumination of the Holy Spirit. Any tendency to argue and to debate is now seen by Menno as a sign of the Antichrist because the Spirit of God is a spirit of love and peace.[221] The conclusion of the long introduction to his *Instruction on Excommunication* is simply mind boggling. Menno now uses this important biblical insight to warn against any opposition to his authoritarian instruction on the subject of the ban. All those who seek unity and peace will receive his instructions with joy and thankfulness to the Lord, simply because his teaching, based on God's holy Scripture, is the truth[222] and there is no other truth.

Menno accepted the cross of Christ as a true sign of the church in the 1550s, but for him and his followers suffering remained a human injustice and a result of rebellion against God's rule and order. Community of goods was not accepted as a sign of the church of Jesus Christ because it was never commanded by Christ or by his apostles. But the practice of unconditional love and mercy, which does not limit the love for the neighbour to the sharing of material goods only because it is all-inclusive, continues to be the proof of Christian faith and life. Poverty, exploitation and oppression remain intolerable for Menno in a Christian society. If the magistrates, the rich and the powerful as well as the poor would repent, a new society of justice, righteousness and peace would be the result. Menno never surrendered his vision of the anticipation of the New Jerusalem in the context of a Christian society, even though he accepted the fact that the true church would have to suffer because of present sinful conditions in the world.

Menno's attitude to the implementation of the ban hardened in the 1550s. The ban, a commandment from Christ and from Paul, began to be carried out in an almost legalistic way. It proved to be a most effective way for Menno and his followers to disassociate themselves from the Münsterite debacle by causing many well disposed citizens and magistrates to recognize the difference between the emerging "Mennonites" and the Münsterites. It also definitively separated the "Mennonites" from the Davidjorists, who spiritualized regeneration and negated a visible ecclesiology.

In his *Reply to Gellius Faber*, Menno concentrated his attention on the signs of the true church of Jesus Christ and those of the church of the Antichrist. Hardly any new theological contribution can be found in this longest and most polemical of Menno's tracts. The continued confrontation with the preachers apparently absorbed all of Menno's energies and blocked his creative capabilities in the later 1550s. By then Menno had learned from experience that it was possible to anticipate the New Jerusalem in the context of a small, although growing, minority of believers without any interference and protection from the magistrates. And last but not least, Menno had discovered that human reason and public debates were inadequate instruments with which to discover truth. It is the Holy Spirit who illuminates and transforms hearts and minds. What had not changed was Menno's conviction that his doctrine and teaching were the only true foundation for Christian faith and life.

Menno's Understanding of a Christian Magistracy

Menno wrote his theology in response to the immediate needs that arose in the growing fellowship of believers, in the context of shifting political realities. In the process of defending himself and his followers against the suspicion of harbouring Münsterite aspirations, he was forced to develop his own understanding of a Christian government. In view of the way he fiercely denied any intention of taking over cities and lands, it is strange that he never criticized the taking over of Münster by the Anabaptists in February 1534. His rejection of Anabaptist Münster begins only with the proclamation of Jan van Leiden's messianic kingship, the introduction of the sword for the propagation of the gospel and the punishment of the wicked by the covenanters. In this regard he is consistent in his *Blasphemy*, in the *Meditation*, in both editions of the *Fundament-book* and in the rest of his writings.

In the *Meditation*, Münster does not become evil in Menno's eyes until the self-proclaimed kingship of Jan van Leiden and the introduction of scandalous polygamy.[223] The only mistake, and this was a minor one, of his dear Münsterite brothers and sisters was the use of the sword for the defence of their faith. The formation of a genuine Anabaptist society under the protection and rule of an Anabaptist government even seemed praiseworthy, because these dear brothers and sisters in Christ "sought nothing other than Jesus Christ and eternal life, and for this reason left house, farm, land, ... father, mother, wife, children, and even their own lives."[224]

Menno's radical rejection of Münster in the 1550s, although more differentiated, is still based upon the same critique as in his earlier writings. In his *Reply to False Accusations* of 1551 he writes "let us say in our defence, that we considered the Münsterite doctrine, dealings and actions, as for example concerning king, sword, insurrection, self defense, vengeance, many wives, and the external kingdom of Christ upon earth ... to be a seductive heresy ... which is far removed from the spirit and example of Christ."[225] However, Menno never repudiated the early peaceful phase of the magisterial Anabaptist reformation of Münster.

Against the public accusation that "we are rebels who desire to take over cities and countries, if we just had the power,"[226] Menno argues that the kingdom of God is a kingdom of peace and that its citizens are peaceful. If the magistrates could only be conquered with the peaceful weapons of this kingdom, then at last there would be "a Christian, wise, true and God fearing government."[227] Such a government would follow the example of Moses, Joshua, David, Hezechiah and Josiah and make Deuteronomy 17:2 its guideline.[228] Calling the governments of his time to repentance, Menno time and again admonished rulers to "exercise their service, to which they have been called, in a right way ... wielding the sword, which has been given to them by God with justice in the fear of God in true brotherly love ... to the protection of the good and the punishment of the evil, as is said in the word of God, Rom. 13:3, 1 Pet. 2:13."[229] Such a God-ordained magistracy would have the responsibility to stop all false teachers, preachers and prophets from propagating their heresies. Although the example of the Old Testament kings who exterminated the false prophets and priests with their altars[230] seems very close to Menno's heart, he rejects the use of any physical violence to suppress heresy in the revised edition of the *Fundament-book* of 1554/55.[231]

A Christian government is not just a pious wish for Menno, but is one of his seven preconditions for the restoration and rebuilding of God's people.[232] Even if Menno assured contemporary governments that the Anabaptists were not seeking their overthrow,[233] still he envisions the acceptance of his understanding of the gospel as the starting point of a new society of justice and peace for everyone,[234] except for the wicked and the false teachers and prophets, who would still be subject to the sword of the God-ordained government.

In Menno's early writings there are no stated restrictions on the use of the sword for a government exercising its God-given function. This had changed by the time of his debate with Mikron in Wismar in 1554. There Menno stated that although a Christian can serve in the office of government, and it would also be his responsibility to punish the evildoer, this would have to be done without the shedding of any blood. A criminal who deserves the death penalty should not be executed, because this would take away the possibility of repentance, and thus possibly destroy his soul.[235]

In spite of this shift, we can observe in conclusion that for Menno, government is not "an ordering of God outside the perfection of Christ," as it is described in the *Schleitheim Confession*.[236] On the contrary, Menno conceives of a Christian government which would have the tremendous responsibility of realizing the kingdom of God here and now by implementing justice and peace, by promoting the proclamation of the gospel and protecting its purity against any false teachers and prophets, and by protecting the good and punishing the wicked. This might have opened the door to the use of violence to defend the good against aggression by the empires of evil, as happened in Münster—a use of the sword by the "dear Münsterite brothers and sisters" for the defence of their faith that was once described by Menno as a minor mistake.

But in the end, for Menno the actualization of the kingdom of God—the establishment of the New Jerusalem—did not depend on the participation of any given government. The kingdom of God has always been present in this world; it became visible reality among us through the incarnation and life of Jesus Christ. Only through repentance, regeneration and new life can we become part of it. Although Menno time and again called contemporary magistrates to conversion, he did not believe that the restoration of God's people depended on their response.

In Menno's view, any government wishing to be called Christian will have to submit unconditionally to the law of the Old Testament and the gospel of Jesus Christ—as taught and preached by Menno Simons.[237] In this regard he makes no concessions. According to Menno, the greatest mistake of the Reformed "preachers and learned ones" is their willingness to compromise the pure doctrines of Jesus Christ for the sake of power and influence, so that they allow governments to call themselves Christian without the radical experience of true repentance and regeneration. Implicitly Menno blames the preachers for his failure to gain the protection and support of any of his contemporary magistracies.

The New Jerusalem, or Menno's people of God, was never conceived *a priori* as a suffering minority.[238] The theology of incarnation was in the first place a theology of new life,[239] and then possibly of suffering and martyrdom.[240]

We can only guess what life in a "Mennonite nation" under the leadership of a "Mennonite government" might have been like in the sixteenth century, although we do have later examples of "Mennonite states within a state" in the Mennonite colonies of nineteenth-century Russia and currently in Latin American countries such as Paraguay and Mexico. It is possible that a sixteenth-century Mennonite commonwealth would have come quite close to Calvin's Geneva, except that it would have included believers' baptism and the freedom of choice. Freedom of choice becomes meaningless, however, if there is only one right choice to be made within a believers' commonwealth; one can imagine that baptism in such a commonwealth might soon have become a precondition for any public responsibility or office.

In any case, the scenario is hypothetical. Given the historical conditions and realities, a "Mennonite nation" was a practical impossibility for Menno and his followers in the Netherlands, even though it seemed to remain a hoped-for theoretical possibility for Menno, to the end of his life.

CHAPTER FIVE

Conclusion

When we survey the entire range of Menno Simons' extant writings we can clearly distinguish three major phases or shifts in the development and evolution of Menno's theological discourse. Our research has shown basic differences between the fifteen-thirties (from 1534-1537 up to 1539), the fifteen-forties (from 1539-1542 up to 1550) and the fifteen-fifties (1551-1558). The first period corresponds to Menno's spiritualistic anticipation of the kingdom as an established Catholic priest and fellow member of the Melchiorite convenanters. The second period reflects Menno's vision of the transformation of society as a whole, when he was an ambitious and quite successful reformer and hunted heretic in the patrimonial provinces of Charles V during the early forties. The third period corresponds with the anticipation of the New Jerusalem as the separated spotless bride of Jesus Christ, now without any support or protection from the magistrates.

The first period begins with Menno's confession of faith in early 1534 as reflected in the *Spiritual Resurrection* and continues with his opposition to the Münsterite kingdom in private and in public debate and the writing of the *Blasphemy*. The *Meditation* and the *New Birth* still belong to this period in regard to their spiritualistic tenor, but introduce the transition to the next period with the introduction of a basic programme for the anticipation of the kingdom of God.

The *Spiritual Resurrection* is the earliest and most individualistic of Menno's writings. It reflects strong Melchiorite influence in regard to the doctrine of incarnation and the apocalyptic anticipation of the New Jerusalem. Using apocalyptical imagery and key references from John and Revelation, its basic argument is spiritual and eschatological, but not apocalyptic in the Münsterite sense. Although Menno probably had received the apocalyptic sign of Thau already, the major thrust of this tract is anti-Münsterite. Because the heavenly Jerusalem has already descended from heaven and its anticipation is spiritual through repentance and regeneration, there is no need to go to Münster, or even to leave the Roman Catholic Church.

When the *Spiritual Resurrection* had no effect on the development of the Münsterite kingdom and Jan van Leiden proclaimed his messianic kingship, Menno wrote his *Blasphemy*. In Jesus Christ all the promises of the Old Testament have been fulfilled. He was the promised Messiah and now is the all-powerful king of heaven and earth. Until the second coming of the Son of Man the anticipation of his kingdom will have to happen through regeneration and a new life of unconditional love and possible suffering.

After Oldeklooster, Menno was converted in a new and more radical way. Spiritual regeneration and a personal covenant with God without radical commitment and any ecclesiological implications are not enough. Although Menno began to develop a new programme for the church of Jesus Christ in his *Meditation* and *New Birth*, he still was reluctant to identify himself with any of the existing reform movements. Menno's goal for the future was nothing less than the restoration of the true church of Jesus Christ. The means for this purpose would be the Word of God, a living faith, genuine love, right baptism and Supper and the ban. Under the protection of a Christian government the anticipation of the New Jerusalem as a Christian society would become an example and light for the nations.

The second phase in the anticipation of the kingdom of God began with the publication of the *Fundament-book*, Menno's framework for the development of Christian doctrines. Addressing the magistrates, the common people, the erring churches and their preachers and the corrupted sects, his message was clear: listen to the proclamation of the gospel of Jesus Christ while we still live in the time of grace. Dying to sin in true repentance and baptism, the sinner will be raised with Christ to triumphal new life. Celebrating the Lord's Supper, the individual believer is integrated into the body of Jesus Christ, where every member is committed unconditionally to the service of God and his fellow members, ready to share with them all of his material and spiritual gifts. Although bread and wine remain the same in the Supper, the real transubstantiation now happens within individual believers, when they are transformed into fully responsible members of the body of Jesus Christ, or citizens of the New Jerusalem. Under the leadership of truly called evangelical preachers and with the promotion and protection of a Christian government, the kingdom of God is now anticipated as a fellowship of believers, or the new people of God.

The *Fundament-book* does not provide a fully-developed presentation of Christian doctrines, but rather is the foundation or framework for such doctrines. In other words, Christian doctrines can be developed only where true repentance, regeneration, baptism and triumphal new life with the right celebration of the Supper are being proclaimed and practiced. They can only be written in the context of the fellowship of believers and never in the studies of falsely-motivated preachers and teachers, or in the libraries of the scribes and learned ones.

In a personal letter to the leaders of the Church in Franeker, Menno for the first time in 1541 extensively presented and detailed his concept of the ban. It was not yet the powerful tool of authoritarian elders for the punishment of the unfaithful, but rather the ultimate expression of love for the unrepentant fellow member of the body of Christ. Not responding to the exhortations and rebukes of the church, the sinner is finally cut off, not as punishment, but as confirmation of his voluntary disassociation from the body of Christ. Menno first conceived of the ban as a powerful call to repentance.

Responding to the needs of the growing "Mennonite churches," Menno wrote more extensive tracts on faith and baptism in the same period, which became more aggressive in opposing the false doctrines and practices of all other churches.

In 1539 Menno also presented his seven demands for the restoration of the kingdom of God. Under the leadership of truly Christian bishops, pastors and teachers, with the celebration of the right sacraments of baptism and the Supper, protected and supervised by a Christian government, the kingdom of God can be anticipated, and the New Jerusalem can become a visible reality.

With the publication of Menno's doctrine of incarnation by Jan a Lasco in 1544, Menno's association with the Melchiorites and possibly with the Münsterites became undeniable. After leaving his homeland and living as an exile for the rest of his life, Menno's hope for the formation of a "Christian nation" became unrealistic, even though he never gave up its dream and vision.

The third change in Menno's anticipation of God's kingdom coming to earth came about in the 1550s. Menno now was convinced that his proclamation of the gospel did not fail because it was not powerful enough, or because it was not the right one, but rather it failed because corrupted preachers and teachers, motivated by selfish ambitions, had compromised the true gospel of Jesus Christ to the point where any could call themselves Christians without living a Christian life. Maintaining the vision of the kingdom, Menno now limited his attention to the building of the true Church of Jesus Christ as a bride "without spot or wrinkle." Separation from the sinful world now became imperative.

Menno's optimism and hope of the 1540s for the conversion of humankind crumbled rapidly under the impact of the Blood-Placard of Charles V, published in 1550, the growing influence of "Zwinglian" preachers and teachers—which his followers tried to stop with slander and letters of defamation—and increasing disunity among his own followers. If the true people of God are meant to be a minority—as they always were in the Old and New Testament—all that finally matters is to keep this minority alive in the purest form possible. But apparently in the same proportion as the church became an end in itself, it lost its appeal for most people and became more authoritarian and legalistic, especially in the application of the ban.

Menno's major success in the 1550s seems to have been the recognition of his radical disassociation from Münster by many well-disposed German citizens and magistrates. Finally they recognised the peacefulness and harmlessness of the pious followers of Menno Simons, whose growing quietism in the anticipation of the New Jerusalem no longer posed a threat to worldly kingdoms.

APPENDIX

Evidence of Menno's Authorship of the *Blasphemy*

Arguments and scriptural references from the *Blasphemy* regarding the messianic kingship of Christ and the use of the sword compared with those of the *Meditation*, the *Van de Wedergeborte* and the two editions of the *Fundament-book* from 1539/40 and 1554/5 respectively support the authenticity of Menno's authorship of the *Blasphemy*.

We will use the first edition of the *Fundament-book* as a guideline because its list of references is the most complete and it summarizes the argument of the *Blasphemy* in a few paragraphs. A print-out of the corresponding texts will demonstrate textual parallels.

Fundament-book
1939/40 (Meihuizen, 174-175)

This we will tell you in Christ Jesus, that we do not teach, know or acknowledge any King David other than the invisible king Christ Jesus, who has all power in heaven and on earth, who alone is the Lord of Lords and the King of Kings Ps. 2 [:6,7], 46 [:11], Isa. 83 [:22], Jer. 23 [:5], 30 [:9], 33 [:15], Zach. 9 [:9], 2 Macc. 1 [:24], Matt. 21 [:5], Luke 19 [:38], Heb. 7 [:7], 1 Tim. 6 [:15], Rev. 1 [:5], 17 [:14], 19 [:6]. And anyone who declares himself for a King in the Spirit, has to be punished from God with Adonai, because the true Solomon Christ Jesus shall and will remain the only wise king, who will sit on the throne of His Father. 1 Kings 1 [:50-53], 2 [:25], Luke 1 [:32, 33].

We do not teach, know or acknowledge any sword, but only the sword of the Spirit, which is the Word of God, Eph. 6 [:17], which is sharper than any double edged sword, Heb. 4 [:12], which is the sword of the mouth, Rev. 1 [:16], 2 [:12], 19 [:15]. And whoever takes a different sword will be defeated by the same. Gen. 9 [:6], Matt. 26 [:52], Rev. 13 [:10].

Meditation on the Twenty-Fifth Psalm
1539 (Verduin, 83)

Preserve me from the wiles of the devil who would fain teach us of another king after the spirit, besides the true King of Zion, Jesus Christ, who rules over Thy holy mountain with the holy scepter of Thy Word, who is King of kings and Lord of lords, is seated at Thy own right hand in the heavenly places, far above all principality and power, and might and dominion and every name that is named, not only in this world, but also in that which is to come; under whose feet all things are put, who hath all power in heaven and on earth, before whom every knee must bow and every tongue confess that He is Lord to the glory of Thy great name.

The New Birth
1539 (Verduin, 94)

These regenerated people have a spiritual king over them who rules them by the unbroken scepter of His mouth, namely, with His Holy Spirit and Word. He clothes them with the garment of righteousness...

Their sword is the sword of the Spirit, which they wield in a good conscience through the Holy Ghost. ....

Their kingdom is the kingdom of grace, here in hope and after this in eternal life. ....

Their doctrine is the unadulterated Word of God, testified through Moses and the prophets, through Christ and the apostles, upon which they build their faith, which saves our souls. Everything that is contrary thereto, they consider accursed.

Their baptism they administer to the believing according to the commandment of the Lord, in the doctrines and usages of the apostles...

Foundation of Christian Doctrine
1554/5 (Verduin, 199-200)

We write the truth in Christ and lie not, that as to the spirit we acknowledge no king either in heaven above or upon the earth beneath, other than the only, eternal and true king David in the spirit, Christ Jesus, who is Lord of lords and King of kings.

And if anyone declares himself king in the kingdom and dominion of Christ, as John of Leiden did at Münster, he with Adonijah shall not go unpunished, for the true Solomon, Christ Jesus Himself, must possess the kingdom and sit eternally upon the throne of David. ....

We teach and acknowledge no other sword, nor tumult in the kingdom or church of Christ than the sharp sword of the Spirit, God's Word, as has been made quite plain in this and our other writings: a sword which is sharper and more penetrating than any sword, two-edged, and proceeding from the mouth of the Lord. With it we set the father against the son and the son against the father, the mother against the daughter and the daughter against the mother; the daughter-in-law against the mother-in-law. But the civil sword we leave to those to whom it is committed. Let everyone be careful lest he transgress in the matter of the sword, lest he perish with the sword. Matt. 26:52.

In the chart below we shall give the *Fundament-book*, the *Blasphemy*, the *Meditation*, the *The New Birth* and the revised edition of the *Fundament-book* the numbers and columns I, II, III, IV, and V respectively. Using the quotations from 1539/40 as the baseline, the following picture emerges.

1. References regarding the lordship of Christ

Text	I	II (*Opera Omnia*)	III	IV	V
1. Ps. 2:6	x	x 624b; 626a	x		x
2. Ps. 46; 47:2-3	x	x 622a			x^1
3. Isa. 33:22	x	x 622b; 624b			x
4. Jer. 23:5	x	x			
5. Jer. 30:9	x				
6. Jer. 33:15	x				
7. Zach. 9:9	x	x		x	
8. 2 Macc. 1:24	x	x 623a			
9. Matt. 21:5	x	x			x^2
10. Luke 19:38	x	x 624a			
11. Heb. 7:7	x	x 623a	x^3		
12. 1 Tim. 6:15	x	x 623a		x^4	
13. Rev. 1:5	x				
14. Rev. 17:14	x			x	
15. Rev. 19:6	x				x
16. 3 Kings 1:50-3	x^5				
17. 3 Kings 2:25	x				
18. Luke 1:32-33	x	x			x
19. Isa. 9:5		x 622b		x^6	
20. Jer. 51:14		x 629a		x^7	
21. Ps. 89:19		x 625b; 626a-b			x^8

2. References regarding the use of the sword

Text	I	II (*Opera Omnia*)	III	IV	V
1. Eph. 6:17	x	x 627a		x	
2. Heb. 4:12	x	x 627a			
3. Rev. 1:16	x	x 627a		x	x
4. Rev. 2:12	x	x 627a	x	x[9]	
5. Rev. 19:15	x			x	x
6. Gen. 9:6	x		x		
7. Matt. 26:52	x	x 628a		x[10]	
8. Rev. 13:10	x				

Because we have been using the first edition of the *Fundament-book* as the guideline, some of the key references of the earlier publications, the *Blasphemy* and the *Meditation*, do not appear. Eph. 1: 20-21 and Matt. 28: 18,[11] which support the universal rule and kingship of Christ are quoted literally by Menno in the *Blasphemy*[12] in support of the same argument. From out of six references in the *Meditation* in this regard, four fulfill a key function in the *Blasphemy*. 1 Pet. 2 and Phil. 2 are quoted as well in the *Blasphemy*, and are prominent in the *Meditation* as well. Thus all six of these references in the *Meditation* were used before in the *Blasphemy*, in support of the same arguments.

The same happens when comparing the references in *The New Birth* with those in the *Blasphemy*. Luke 17: 24 and 1 Tim. 6: 13-15 are quoted literally in the *Blasphemy*.[13] The John 18: 11 citation in the *Blasphemy*,[14] which refers to the rejection of the sword used by Peter in defense of the Lord, however, only indirectly supports the argument of the *The New Birth*.

NOTES

Introduction

1. Menno Symons, *Opera Omnia Theologica* (Amsterdam, 1681), 258b. From now on we will refer to this edition as *Opera Omnia*. See also *The Complete Writings of Menno Simons, c.1496-1561*, translated by Leonard Verduin and edited by J. C. Wenger (Scottdale, 1956), 672. From now on we will refer to this translation as: Wenger: *CW*.
2. Gerald R. Brunk, ed. *Menno Simons. A Reappraisal* (Harrisonburg, VA: Eastern Mennonite College, 1992), 20.
3. Karel Vos, *Menno Simons 1496-1561* (Leiden: E. J. Brill, 1914), 217.
4. W. J. Kuehler, *Geschiedenis der Nederlandsche Doopsgezinden in de zestiende eeuw* (Haarlem: H. D. Tjeenk Willink & Zoon, 1932), 215-216.
5. See Jakob P. Bekker, *Origin of The Mennonite Brethren Church*, trans. by D. E. Pauls and A. E. Janzen (n.p.: The Mennonite Brethren Historical Society of the Midwest, 1973), chapter 8.
6. Cornelius Krahn, *Menno Simons* (Karlsruhe: Heinrich Schneider, 1936), 179.
7. Walter Klaassen, in Gerald R. Brunk, ed., *Menno Simons. A Reappraisal*, 21.
8. Sjouke Voolstra, *Menno Simons. His Image and Message* (North Newton, Kansas: Bethel College, 1997).

Chapter One
The Social and Religious Context

1. Steven E. Ozment, *The Reformation in the Cities* (Yale, 1975), 8-9.
2. Decavele, *Dageraad van de Reformatie* (Brussels, 1975), 635.
3. A. J. van Houtte, and others, *Algemene Geschiedenis der Nederlanden* (12 vols., Utrecht, 1949-1958) IV, 267-268. C. Augustijn, *Erasmus en de Reformatie* (Amsterdam, 1962), 289. In Rothmann's view the Anabaptist Reformation of Münster began with Erasmus, Luther and Zwingli and then continued with Melchior Hoffman, Jan Matthijsz and Jan van Leiden. R. Stupperich, *Die Schriften Bernhard Rothmanns* (Münster in Westfalen, 1970), 219.
4. Most of these humanists remained within the Catholic church because they still believed in the possibility of a reformation from within. Decavele, *Dageraad*, 636.
5. Ibid., 115.
6. How powerful this medium of communication had become already is reflected in the fact that in Gent from 1521 to 1535 the battle against heresy consisted mainly in the suppression of heretical literature. Decavele, *Dageraad*, 235.
7. This literacy was probably more common in Flanders, Brabant and Holland, where most of the people, including the rural population, were literate by 1567. Alistair Duke, "The Face of Popular Dissent in the Low Countries, 1520-1530," *Journal of Ecclesiastical History* 16 (Jan. 1975): 45.
8. A. J. Van Houtte, *Algemene Geschiedenis*, VI, 226.
9. Someone whose property was valued at less than a hundred pounds was considered to be a pauper. Ibid., 237-238.
10. Export duties on wool at the warehouse in Calais, where the Dutch bought the English wool, averaged 15,000 pounds between 1510 and 1520, 10,000 between 1520 and 1530, and 5700 pounds between 1530 and 1538. The embargo on the export of wool from England forced the Dutch to buy lower quality wool from Spain. The cloth produced from this

wool was of inferior quality and led to the loss of traditional markets, resulting in further deterioration of the industry. For more details, see N. W. Posthumus, *Geschiedenis van de Leidsche Lakenindustrie. I. De Middeleeuwen* (Den Haag, 1908), 208-209, also 405-406.

[11] Ibid., 407.

[12] L. Knappert, *De Opkomst van het Protestantisme in een Noord-Hollandsche Stad* (Leiden, 1908), 135.

[13] *Correctie Boek*, October 22, 1521. Gemeentearchief Leiden.

[14] The unemployed workers received some support from the city. For example Leiden decided in 1522 to double the weekly allowance of the poor (*Vroedschapsresolutie*, 1522, fol. 2. Gemeentearchief Leiden). In 1529 the number of poor or unemployed was 1832 (Ibid., 1529, fol. 30v). This number had increased to five or six thousand by 1545. In order to keep them from starvation, they were given a weekly ration of bread (Ibid., 1545, fol. 35v). The crisis in the textile industry affected the rural as well as the urban population, because much of the spinning and dyeing of the wool was assigned as piecework to rural areas. In Holland about half of the population of 37 villages was working for Leiden (Posthumus, *Geschiedenis van de Leidsche Lakenindustrie. I. De Middeleeuwen* [Den Haag, 1908], 294).

[15] J.en A. Romein, *De lage Landen bij de Zee* (Utrecht, 1936), 179.

[16] *Vroedschapsresolutie*. December 1, 1530. Gemeentearchief, Leiden. See also Posthumus, *Geschiedenis van de Leidsche Lakenindustrie. I. De Middeleeuwen*. (Den Haag, 1908), 362.

[17] J. A. van Houtte, *Algemene Geschiedenis*, IV, 237-238.

[18] J. Wagenaar, *Vaderlandsche Historie* (Amsterdam, 1751) V, p33-42. R. Häpke, *Niederländische Akten und Urkunden zur Geschichte der Hanse* (München, 1913) I, 189.

[19] J. A. van Houtte, *Algemene Geschiedenis*, IV, 241.

[20] Ibid.

[21] R. Haepke, *Niederländische Akten und Urkunden*, I (München, 1913), 189

[22] A. F. Mellink, *De wederdoopers in de noordelijke nederlanden, 1531-1544* (Leeuwarden, 1981), 11; 13.

[23] A. Duke, "Face of Popular Dissent," 42.

[24] A. J. van Houtte, *Algemene Geschiedenis*, IV, 252.

[25] *Vroedschapsresolutie*, April 28, 1517, Gemeentearchief Leiden.

[26] J. Blok, *Geschiedenis ener hollandschen Stad* (Leiden, 1912).

[27] Because of their privileges, religious institutions became unbeatable competitors in the textile markets. The same thing happened when they decided to dump their overproduction of food and spirits. Ibid., 131.

[28] Posthumus, *Geschiedenis van de Leidsche Lakenindustrie I. De Middeleeuwen*. (,s-Gravenhage, 1908), 151.

[29] Ibid., 152. See also *Bijlage III.*, 415. As early as 1455 a summons from the weavers' organization was issued against the beguinages in all of the major cities of Holland, instructing them to stop any production of linen and woolen cloth for marketing purposes. At that time the Court of Holland ruled in favour of the Beguines. In 1504 the weavers were successful.

[30] Knappert, *Opkomst van het Protestantisme*, (Leiden, 1908), 35, estimates that there were 550 monks in the monasteries of Leiden in 1514. Posthumus, *Geschiedenis van de Leidsche Lakenindustrie. I. De Middeleeuwen*. (,s-Gravenhage, 1908) 161, gives the following numbers: in 1524, there were 450; in 1542, 280; in 1556, 150.

[31] Duke, "Face of Popular Dissent," 44.

[32] *Vroedschapsresolutie*, Jan. 23, 1524. Gemeentearchief Leiden.

[33] *Vroedschapsboek A*. Fol.37. Gemeentearchief Leiden.

[34] *Derde Memoriaelboek van Sandelin*. Fol.152, Rijksarchief Den Haag. Fredericq, *Corpus documentorum inquisitionis haereticae pravitatis Neerlandicae. Versameling van stukken betreffende de pauselijke en bisschoppelijke inquisitie in de Nederlanden* (Ghent-The Hague, 1889-1902), 353. Hereafter: Fredericq, *C. D.*

[35] J. G. de Hoop Scheffer, *Geschiedenis der Kerkhervorming*, 82

[36] Ibid. See also J. J. van Toorenbergen, ed., *Het oudste Nederlansche verboden boek, 1523*.

Oeconomica christiana. Summa der godliker scrifturen, (Leiden, 1882), Monumenta Reformationis Belgicae I.
[37] A. J. van Houtte, *Algemene Geschiedenis*, IV, 254 observes that the government was tolerant or "Erasmus-minded." Criticism of the Catholic church was generally not viewed with disfavour.
[38] Fredericq, *C. D.* IV, 245-246.
[39] Duke, "Face of Popular Dissent," 45.
[40] Fredericq, *C. D.* IV, 368-373.
[41] Ibid., 396-397.
[42] S. Voolstra, *Het Woord is Vlees geworden* (Kampen, 1982), 33. Voolstra laments that the origins of this doctrine are still unknown, but the minutes of the interrogation of Willem de Cuiper show that this doctrine was already public knowledge before Hoffmann, Münster and Menno Simons.
[43] Fredericq, *C. D.* IV, 452-495. This report was printed by Nicolaas van Oldenborch between Sept.15, 1525 and Dec.1, 1529.
[44] Ibid., 475, 478.
[45] Ibid., 481.
[46] Ibid., 461.
[47] Pistorius was sentenced to go on pilgrimage to Rome for three years, but instead went to Wittenberg where he stayed for only three months.
[48] Ibid., 469, 473.
[49] Ibid., 458.
[50] Ibid., 477.
[51] Ibid., 468.
[52] Ibid., 477.
[53] Ibid., 464.
[54] Ibid., 465.
[55] Ibid., 469.
[56] Ibid. 488. If there were "thousands" of Sacramentarians in the Netherlands at that time, this suggests strong grass roots organization. This should modify C. Augustijn's statement crediting Dutch Anabaptists for being the first to organize such groups: "This tendency of the Dutch Anabaptists, their need for organisation and group-forming, is important and deserves emphasis, especially since there was no other organisation-forming movement during the time between 1520 and 1550." C. Augustijn, "Anabaptism in the Netherlands: Another Look," *Mennonite Quarterly Review* 62 (1988): 205.
[57] There are great similarities between Jan de Bakker's statements and the Schleitheim Confession of 1527. See H. Fast, *Der Linke Flügel der Reformation* (Bremen, 1962), 60-71; in English, John H. Yoder, *The Legacy of Michael Sattler* (Scottdale: Herald Press, 1973), 34-43.
[58] See R. R. Post, *Kerkelijke Verhoudingen in Nederland voor de Reformatie van 1500 tot 1580* (Utrecht, 1954), 522. Post argues that the report from Gnapheus lacks objectivity, since Gnapheus is himself a Sacramentarian. Ibid., 524.
[59] See H. Isaak, "The struggle for an evangelical town," in *The Dutch Dissenters*, editor I. B. Horst, Kerkhistorische Bijdragen XIII (Leiden, 1986), 68.
[60] A. J. van Houtte, *Algemene Geschiedenis*, IV, 165.
[61] J. J. van Toorenbergen, *Summa der godliker scrifturen*, 118. J. Trapman comes to the conclusion that the *Summa* must have been published in 1523 by J. Seversz in Leiden. On March 23, 1524 it appeared already on the index of forbidden books. J. Trapman, *Summa der godliker scrifturen* (1523) (Leiden, 1978), 5; 17; 18.
[62] J. J. Toorenbergen, Ibid, 146.
[63] Ibid., 142.
[64] Ibid., 125-126.
[65] Ibid., 188
[66] Ibid., 191.

[67] Ibid., 184.
[68] Ibid., 215.
[69] W. Gnapheus was a fellow student of Pistorius at the Hieronymus school in Utrecht. Imprisoned in 1523 with C. Hoen in Den Haag he was eventually freed. In a personal letter he then attacked the monastic way of life and was shut up in a monastery to repent of his views. Here he wrote his tract: *A comfort and mirror for the sick*, which was soon printed and reprinted without his permission, as he explains in the introduction to the revised edition of 1557, fol. A4b. The only known copy of this edition remains in the Universiteitsbibliotheek in Leiden. For our purpose we will follow the 1525 version in a print of 1531, reprinted in *Bibliotheca Reformatoria Neerlandica*, editors S. Cramer and F. Pijper, (The Hague, 1903), I. Hereafter: *BRN* I.
[70] Gnapheus may be referring to the "many thousands of like minded brothers" Pistorius was talking about at his trial. Fredericq, C. D. IV, 488.
[71] *BRN* I. fol. Aijr.
[72] Ibid., fol. Aiijr.
[73] Ibid., fol. Aiijv.
[74] Ibid., fol. Avr.
[75] Ibid., fol. Avjv.
[76] Ibid., fol. Avijr.
[77] "... he who knows the will of the Lord and doesn't do it, will be punished..." Ibid., fol. Avijr.
[78] "... that we ourselves follow the Lord, when he calls us ..." Ibid.
[79] Ibid., fol. Aviijv.
[80] Ibid., fol. Aviijv.
[81] Ibid., fol. Biv-Bijr.
[82] Revised edition of 1557. Ibid., fol. A2b, B3b.
[83] Ibid., fol. G4a.
[84] A. F. Mellink, *De wederdopers*, 334; 339.
[85] Ibid., 339; 345.
[86] C. A. Cornelius, *Geschichte des Münsterischen Aufruhrs*. II (Leipzig, 1855-1860), 11.
[87] The earliest reports of public manifestations of irreverence during processions in Leiden date back to 1512. *Aflesingsboek A*. fol. 35. Similar incidents happened in 1517, when the abbot of Egmont donated a piece of the holy cross to the Pieterskerk. Ibid. Sept. 28, 1517. Offensive leaflets were spread in 1522. Ibid. Sept. 28, 1522, and other incidents are reported in the years following as well. See Ibid. Jan. 20. 1526, *Correctieboek*, Jul. 31, 1528, *Tresorriersrekenboek*, Aug. 30, 1530 fol. 54r. Gemeentearchief Leiden.
[88] *Correctieboek*, March 27, 1526. Gemeentearchief Leiden.
[89] J. G. de Hoop Scheffer, *Geschiedenis der Kerkhervorming*, 513.
[90] *Aflesingsboek*, Apr. 30, 1530. Gemeentearchief Leiden.
[91] When Erasmus in a letter dated August 28, 1525 observed that the major part of the population in Holland, Zeeland and Vlaanderen knew the doctrine of Luther, it certainly was more than an empty phrase. J. Decavele, *De Dageraad der Reformatie* (Brussel, 1975), 597.
[92] Duke, "Face of Popular Dissent," 61.
[93] J. G. de Hoop Scheffer, *Geschiedenis der Kerkhervorming*, 618.
[94] Kuehler, *Geschiedenis der nederlandsche Doopsgezinden*, (Haarlem, 1932), 46.
[95] Mellink, *De Wederdopers*, 345.
[96] Duke, *Face of Popular Dissent, Journal of Ecclesiastical History*, 1975), 66; 67.
[97] Ibid., 66.
[98] K. Deppermann: *Melchior Hoffman*, (Göttingen, 1979), 280. It was these people who were most open to radical, social revolutionary ideas.

Chapter Two
Menno and Münster

1. This essay was written by Menno as a personal letter in response to a Lasco's petition, after the debate with the preachers of Emden; it was then published by the former without Menno's permission. He never permitted a reprint and refused to endorse its contents fully in his debate with Martin Micron. See Horst, *Bibliography*, 94. Thus Menno never willingly gave any public information about the time and circumstances of his baptism.
2. *Opera Omnia*, 525a.
3. In his *Een weemoedige ende Christelycke Ontschuldinge*, from 1551, Menno claims to have opposed the Münsterites for more than seventeen years. *Opera Omnia*, 497a, which brings us to 1534. Since the Melchiorite doctrine of incarnation was one of the cornerstones of the Münsterite kingdom, Menno must have known about it no later than early 1534.
4. *Opera Omnia*, 497a.
5. *Dat Fundament Des Christelycken Leers, 1539-1540*, edited by H. W. Meihuizen (Den Haag, 1967), 202-203. Subsequent references to this first edition will be: *Fundament-book*.
6. *DAN*. III, 100.
7. *Opera Omnia*, 179ff.
8. Horst, *Bibliography*, 96.
9. Menno states that he has been fighting the Münsterites for more than seventeen years, *Opera Omnia*, 497a. Later he repeats that he has been consistent in his faith, *Ibid.* 504a.
10. *Opera Omnia*, 258b. Cf. the modern rendition of this text reads in *Doperse Stemmen* 6, 42.
11. *Opera Omnia*, 636a.
12. K. Vos, *Menno Simons*, 42.
13. *Opera Omnia*, 54b-55b. This statement is missing in the edition from 1939-40. See *Fundament-book*, 170-173.
14. *DAN.*, 113.
15. C. Sepp, *Geschiedkundige Nasporingen* I (1872), 128-136.
16. Ibid., 120. "...truly no confession or justification could be considered stronger proof and witness more powerfully about Menno's aversion to the Münsterites, than this tract against Jan van Leiden, if it had been known to be from Menno's hand before 1600." See also Ibid., 132 and 134. Sepp's basic argument remained the same in 1889. "Where Menno in his own defense could and should have mentioned it, he is silent, namely in the biography published by him in 1554." C. Sepp, *Verboden Lectuur. Een Drietal Indices Librorum Prohibitorum* (Leiden, 1889), 128.
17. De Hoop Scheffer, *Doopsgezinde Bijdragen* (1889): 64-83, and (1892): 1-28. *Doopsgezinde Bijdragen* henceforth *D.B.*
18. Ibid., (1892), 14-15.
19. *Opera Omnia*, 257b. In the margin: "My faithful warning about the Münsterite abominations, even during my time in the papacy."
20. Ibid., 497a.
21. *D.B.* (1905): 89.
22. Vos, *Menno Simons*, 42-51.
23. Kuehler, *Geschiedenis*, 165ff.
24. Horst, *Bibliography*, 117-118.
25. Krahn, *Menno Simons*, 31-32.
26. Christoph Bornhäuser, *Leben und Lehre Menno Simons* (Neukirchen-Vluyn, 1973), 25.
27. *Fundament-book*, 174-175; *Opera Omnia*, 55b-56a.
28. These three references are Matt. 10:35, Rom.13:1 and I Pet. 2:13. *Opera Omnia*, 56a.
29. Karl-Heinz Kirchhoff, in his landmark article "Was there a peaceful Anabaptist

congregation in Münster in 1534?" in the *Mennonite Quartely Review*, (henceforth *MQR*), 44 (1970): 357-370, was able to gather enough evidence for his conclusion that "contemporary sources show that there was a peaceful Anabaptist congregation in Münster until the arrival of Jan Matthys." Ibid., 369. A key source for his thesis is the letter of Bishop Franz to the Landgrave of Hesse dated January 21, 1534, in which he characterizes the Anabaptists as rather innocent people, practising community of goods, wanting to belong to Christ alone and eager to live a life of perfection. The Bishop of Münster had not yet noticed any inclination to militancy. Ibid., 362-363.

A second source is the testimony of Jakob von Ossenburg, captured as emissary to the convenanters outside Münster on February 16, 1534. He confessed that Münster was the New Jerusalem, that peace and safety would be found only in Münster on the day of God's judgment which would take place before Easter, that the Anabaptists had no intention of ruling over the heathen or taking over government offices, and that they were eager to obey the magistracy as long as it was not against God's will. Kirchhoff concludes that Ossenburg's testimony reveals the pious and disciplined lifestyle of the early Anabaptists in Münster. Ibid., 367.

In his latest publication on Anabaptist Münster, J. Stayer states that "The Anabaptist regime in Münster arose from a peaceful Anabaptist movement established in the town since the summer of 1533..." J. Stayer, *The German Peasants' War and Anabaptist Community of Goods* (Kingston, 1991), 123.

Finally there is Rothmann's testimony in his *Restitution*, that he and fellow leaders of the Münsterite Reformation were baptized on January 5, 1534 upon the cross of Christ, and not upon the armour of David. R. Stupperich, *Die Schriften Bernhard Rothmanns* (Münster in Westfalen, 1970), 280. Hereafter cited as Stupperich, *Schriften*.

[30] The law of the Holy Roman Empire permitted a lesser magistracy to defend itself by force of arms against an illegal attack by a higher government. The Anabaptists of Münster claimed that their legally constituted government was defending itself against the illegal siege of the bishop. J. Stayer concludes that "the Münsterites were forced out of a peaceful position by the need to defend themselves, and ... the idea of an apocalyptic crusade developed only after the beginning of the siege ..." J. Stayer, *Anabaptists and the Sword* (Lawrence, 1972), 235.

After the Anabaptists gained control of Münster, rumours spread that the Bishop was approaching the city with 3000 soldiers to exterminate them. "Far from passively submitting to persecution, the spontaneous reaction of the Anabaptists in the face of clear and present danger was to defend themselves." W. de Bakker, *Civic Reformer in Anabaptist Münster: Bernhard Rothmann* (Chicago, 1987), 253.

Kuehler always maintained the thesis of a coexistence of peaceful and revolutionary Anabaptist in the Netherlands. The peaceful did not go to Münster and rejected aggressive violence at the meeting of elders in Spaarndam in January 1535. What Kuehler had to admit was that most of these "peaceful" Anabaptists did permit the use of the sword for the purpose of self defence. Kuehler, *Geschiedenis*, 151-152. Although the question is never discussed, this justification of violence for the sake of personal defence would also imply that the use of the sword by the government, even by a Christian one, for the protection and defence of its citizens would be justified.

[31] Wenger, *CW*, 48; *Opera Omnia*, 629-630.

[32] A paraphrase of this summons reads as follows: All believing members of the covenant should be aware that the time of deliverance is at hand, as God has made known to us. Everyone should get ready for the exodus to the New Jerusalem, a city of refuge for the saints. Everyone should come, because the prophet Jan van Leiden of Münster has written to us that no one outside Münster will survive God's coming judgment of the unbelievers. So leave behind everything that might bind you, such as unbelieving wives, husbands or children. There are enough goods for the saints in Münster, so bring along only your money, linen and something to eat for the journey. If you have a knife, a pike or a musket, bring it along. Whoever does not have weapons should buy them, because the Lord wants to deliver his chosen ones through the

mighty hands of his servants Moses and Aaron. Be very careful and wait for us half a mile outside of Bergklooster at Hasselt on March 24 at noon, not earlier and not later. Signed by Emanuel. (Archief der Doopsgezinde Gemeente te Amsterdam, *Inventaris der Archiefacten No. 462.*) In response to the call, several thousand Melchiorites, about seven to eight hundred men and about fifteen hundred women came to Münster during the next few weeks. See Kirchhoff, *Die Täufer in Münster*, 24.

[33] In a letter dated March 25 1534 to the central government of Holland, the city of Kampen reported that on the previous day, 27 boats carrying about three thousand men, women and children were intercepted and fifteen hundred pikes as well as many muskets, swords, halberds and other weapons were confiscated. Because many of these people were said to be poor and ignorant, the local authorities did not know what to do with them and asked for instructions from the government. J. Hullu, *Bescheiden betreffende de Hervorming in Overijssel I. Deventer 1522-1546* (Deventer, 1899), 158-159.

K. Vos, "Revolutionnaire Hervorming," in *De Gids* 84 (1920): 440 reports that in addition to the 27 boats of Kampen, another 7 were captured in Haarlem, 6 in Amsterdam and 12 escaped.

[34] C. A. Cornelius, *Die Niederländischen Wiedertäufer während der Belagerung Münsters 1534 bis 1535* (München, 1869), 29. The seriousness of this massive exodus from the Netherlands is reflected in the report of the secretary of the Company of Merchant Adventurers, John Coke of Antwerp, who wrote in spring 1534. Citation in I. B. Horst, "Sociale en religieuze aspecten van het vroege Nederlandse Anabaptisme. Een tekst met commentaar," in *Historisch Bewogen. Bundel opstellen voor Prof. Dr. A. F. Mellink* (Groningen, 1984), 31.

[35] After the reinstitution of baptism by Jan Matthijsz in late 1533, hundreds of Melchiorites were baptized in Amsterdam and its surroundings. An attempt to take over the city was planned for "Sinte Gregoriusdach" on March 18, 1534: "during the general procession they would create a riot in the city, then they would first kill all the monks and priests, then they would trample on the holy sacraments, and then they would drive all people out of the city and move into their properties." *DAN*, 5, *Amsterdam* (1531-1536), edited by A. F. Mellink (Leiden, 1985) 23. In a letter circulated among the covenanters, miraculous events similar to those that had happened in Münster were anticipated. Ibid., 30-31. The authors of this letter, Jan and Gherrit, later confessed that they had expected most citizens of Amsterdam to join them. Then God would have created fear and confusion among the unbelievers. Most of them would have left the city on their own, and the rest would have been peacefully conducted out of the city by the Anabaptists. Then the covenanters would have had everything in common. Ibid., 34. Jan Paeuw still insisted during his trial of Dec. 29 1534 that Amsterdam would be given by God to those who are "int verbont" (part of the covenant). Ibid., 85-86.

[36] This proclamation happened after the unsuccessful assault on the city of Münster of August 31. See R. van Dülmen, *Das Täuferreich zu Münster 1534-1535* (München, 1974), 147-150.

[37] Ibid. 619, 622b, 623a, 623b.

[38] Gresbeck reports that Jan van Leiden himself claimed that he had received the revelation that he was to become the king of the righteous, called to punish all injustice and becoming second only to God. C. A. Cornelius, *Berichte der Augenzeugen über das Münstersche Wiedertäuferreich* (Münster, 1853), 82. Knipperdoling reported: "Dear brothers and sisters, God has revealed to me that I should announce to you great joy, on behalf of God." Ibid., 102. The prophet Henricus had an experience like Samuel's in the Old Testament. While he was asleep a voice spoke to him three times, "Prepare, prepare, prepare." When this happened on three consecutive nights, he prayed: "Dear Father, what should I prepare?" and received the answer: "You shall proclaim great joy to my people." Ibid., 94-95. The theme of joy is still present in Rothmann's *Van der Wrake* of December 1534. Paraphrasing Ps. 149:1f, he applied the Psalm to Jan van

Leiden as the new King of Zion. Stupperich, *Schriften*, 285. Inviting the brothers to join them joyfully in Münster, Rothmann continues in the spirit of Psalm 149: "all hesitation is over, we now are allowed to see the kingdom, which David will have on earth. This will make us happy forever. The time of the godless is over. O, what a joy." Ibid., 294.

The same theme of joy appears in the letter of Jan and Gherrit to the covenanters in and around Amsterdam. As soon as Amsterdam was given into the hands of the covenanters, a new alliance of righteousness and justice would be established. "Then we will sing, shout and dance for joy." *DAN 5, Amsterdam,* 30-31.

[39] Because written messages became too dangerous to carry, the slogan was probably transmitted verbally.

[40] As long as miracles were happening every day and victories were achieved, the covenanters came to Münster by the hundreds. But after the failure of Jan Matthijsz on Easter morning and the fading away of power under the kingship of Jan van Leiden, attracting new covenanters to the city became crucial for the survival of the New Jerusalem, and also much more difficult.

[41] Not once does Menno refer to any written statement or published document; his refutation is based entirely on what Jan van Leiden claimed and on what people were saying. If Christ is the king over all the earth and his believing congregation, "how can Jan van Leiden call himself a joyous king of all, the joy of the disconsolate?" *Opera Omnia*, 622b. This blasphemous claim was said to have come from Jan van Leiden himself. Again, the greatest blasphemy a man could speak was what Jan van Leiden asserted, that he had become "the joy of the disconsolate." Ibid., 623a.

[42] The 1627 edition reads: "Wy hadden des schrijvens wol ontslagen gewest/ dan die noot dringet ons tho schrijven/ eens deels/ want wy der schandelijcke verleydinge/ vnde de groote lasteringhe Gods/ nicht moghen verdraghen/ dat een Mensche in Christi stede ghestelt wort/ eens deels/ want men ons nicht wil tho woorden staen/ noch sulcke verleydinge ja veel meer grouwelijcke ketterije/ vanden beloofde David/ vnde meer anderen mit Bibelschen schriften verdegenen.

Dan sulcken aerdt hebben alle verleyders/ alle dwalende geesten/ dat sy vlien van Godts woort/ als Christus secht alle de quaet doet/ haet dat licht/ vnde comt nicht by dat licht/ op dat zyn wercken nicht ghestraft en worden." Menno Symons, *Een Gantz duidelijck ende klaer bewijs/ uyt de H. Schriftuere/ dat Jesus Christus/ is de rechte belovede David inden geest/ ...*, Fol. A4r-A4v. The text in the *Opera Omnia*. p621b-622a has some differences in spelling, but otherwise is the same.

Verduin's translation of: "want men ons niet wil te woorde staen" by "because we are not allowed to speak" is a distortion of the original meaning of the text. Menno's reason for writing was that "they are not willing to argue with [me] any more" or "they refuse to be accountable to [me]." Menno was upset because the Münsterites, including his own former parishoners, are not willing to listen to him anymore. Menno's former biblical authority as evangelical priest had been replaced by the visions and teachings of the Münsterite prophets and theologians. Menno had no other choice now but to write against the blasphemy of Jan van Leiden. The third of Menno's reasons for writing was "noch sulcke verleydinge, ja veel meer grouelijcke ketterije van den beloofden David, ende meer anderen met Bybelschen schriften verdedigen." Verduin's translation, "and such deceit and abominable heresy concerning the promised David and other articles are defended with passages from the Bible" is not correct. See Wenger, *CW*, 34. The conjunction "noch" can be translated by "neither" or "nor" as well as by "and." Menno uses this "noch" in the same way in *Opera Omnia*, 625a: "dat Gode de Vader geenen anderen Koninck ingeset heeft, over Sion, noch oock insetten will..." The point Menno is making in the passage above is that the followers of Jan van Leiden have failed to support their claims with scriptural evidence. This reading is confirmed by the next paragraph, even in Verduin's translation, as well as by the entire construction of the argument in Menno's *Blasphemy*. Like all false teachers and prophets, the Münsterites shy away from the clear word of God, by replacing it with

false visions and prophecies.
[43] This heresy consists of nothing less than the replacement of Christ by Jan van Leiden ("dat een mensche in Christi stede gestelt wort..."), *Opera Omnia*, 621b. In the title of the *Blasphemy*, Menno states the heresy even more strongly: Jan van Leiden claims not only to replace Christ, but he is "hem settende in de stede Godts," usurping the place of God. Ibid., 619.
[44] It would take Rothmann a few more months to develop a proper scriptural foundation for the kingship of Jan van Leiden in his *Restitution*.
[45] Ibid., 621a. In his *Meditation on the twenty-fifth Psalm*, Menno makes the same point. Among those who escaped the bondage of Egypt and Babylon and submitted to the cross of Christ are many who are now being seduced by false prophets. The Münsterites knew the Word of God before they where seduced, but now they even defend their heresy "believing that this is the blessed will of God, but this was never what [God] meant." *Doperse Stemmen* 2: 22-23.
[46] Menno was not the only one in the Netherlands who opposed the aggressive use of the sword. When thirty two of the Melchiorite elders met in Spaarndam in December 1534 or early January 1535, the majority voted against the aggressive use of violence. Kuehler, *Geschiedenis*, 141.
[47] *Opera Omnia*, 622a.
[48] Ibid., 622b.
[49] Ibid., 623a.
[50] In a summary of the Münsterite heresies dated October 1534, based upon the confessions of 27 captured apostles from Münster, a similar statement was made: "They also confess that they believe that all of Holy Scripture speaking about Christ our Savior and his spiritual kingdom, point to their king, whom they call David, in which the Scripture now will be fulfilled as promised in Jeremiah 30 (23:5) and Ezechiel 31 (37:24)." R. Stupperich, *Schriften von Katholischer Seite gegen die Täufer* (Münster, 1980), 232. To refute this claim is the chief purpose of Menno's *Blasphemy*. "And so every righteous one will understand, in what horrible heresy those are entangled, who do not want to understand that Christ is the promised king David, but a different man." Jeremiah 30 has been fulfilled in Jesus Christ: "The Christian church does not confess any other King and Lord, than the Christ." Isaiah 33, 1 Cor. 8." *Opera Omnia*, 624b.
[51] Ibid., 624a.
[52] Ibid., 624a.
[53] Ibid., 625a-b.
[54] Ibid., 626a-b. "...he boasts that he is the promised David, of whom all the prophets testify, and will not admit that Christ is our promised one." Ibid., 624a.
[55] *Opera Omnia*, 627a.
[56] Ibid., 628a. From the safety of his position as a Catholic priest it was easy for Menno to speak about suffering as normative for the Christian life. This is probably one of the major reasons that the Münsterites, and even his own parishoners, did not take him seriously. When he later became one of the most hunted heretics of the time, Menno never stopped complaining about the injustice of persecution.
[57] The concept of the punishment and destruction of the unbeliever before the second coming of Christ was already expressed by Hoffman during his trial in Strasbourg on May 29, 1533: "The true Jerusalem can not be built or rise, unless Babylon with all its crowd and following is overthrown and destroyed." Manfred Krebs und Hans Georg Rott: *Quellen zur Geschichte der Täufer. VIII. Band. Elsass II. Teil.* (Gütersloh, 1960), 18; *Opera Omnia*, 629a-b. The summons of March 1534 did not foresee the personal involvement of the covenanters. The punishment of the unbelievers would be carried out by God, but God's chosen people needed to be inside Münster to be safe from God's wrath. *Inventaris der Archiefsacten*, Nr. 462. Archief der Doopsgezinde Gemeente te Amsterdam.
[58] *Opera Omnia*. 630a-b.
[59] Ibid. 631a-b.

[60] Rothmann's *Van der Wrake* was printed in December 1534. The occupation of Oldeklooster took place from March 30 - April 7, 1535.

[61] Vos, *Menno Simons*, 44. Stayer comes to the same conclusion in his article on Oldeklooster and Menno: "The short essay is written in conscious opposition to Rothmann's *On Vengeance*." J. Stayer, "Oldeklooster and Menno," *The Sixteenth Century Journal*, 9 (1978): 51-69.

[62] *Opera Omnia*. 629a. "Now some are saying that the Lord will punish Babylon, and this through his Christians; they will have to be his instruments." In Menno's understanding, the Münsterite claim for vengeance is based upon Jeremiah 51:11. After paraphrasing this pericope in the paragraph above, Menno continues that it is clear from the text that God will use the gentiles for this task, and not the believers. Ibid. But Rothmann's basic argument about God's relentless vengeance on the wicked through his chosen people is not based upon Jeremiah 51:11, but Jeremiah 30:18-24. See Stupperich, *Schriften*, 293, 294, 296.

[63] Stupperich, *Schriften*, 286, 287, 290, 297.

[64] The events of February 9-11, 1534 "were for the Münster Anabaptists an experience of God's intervention in history ... like that of the Israelites crossing the Red Sea." Stayer, *German Peasants' War*, 127.

[65] These new revelations were so unprecedented that Rothmann did not even dare to set them down on paper. Because even he and his fellow leaders had difficulties understanding them, they might cause brothers outside Münster, who had not outgrown the knowledge of the suffering Christ, to stumble. Stupperich, *Schriften*, 286.

[66] The fellowship of true believers or the true church of Jesus Christ has now been restored in Münster after 1400 years of decay, with new revelations and institutions. Ibid., 281.

[67] Ibid. 290-292.

[68] "... that a man is put in the place of Christ ..." *Opera Omnia*, 621b; 623b; 624b.

[69] Stupperich, *Schriften*, 294.

[70] *Opera Omnia*, 630a.

[71] "Some do believe and expect that God himself with his angels will come from heaven and take revenge on the godless." Stupperich, *Schriften*, 292. This is the interpretation Menno defends in his *Blasphemy*. *Opera Omnia*, 629a-b. It is clearly not Menno, but Rothmann in both the *Restitution* and *Van der Wrake* who is on the defensive. Whereas Menno relies only on Scripture, Rothmann is forced to refer to all kinds of new revelations and to a new timetable to explain, justify and legitimize the new developments in Münster. We have no evidence that Rothmann was writing against Menno in particular, but the fact that he feels the need to write such a compromising pamphlet points to a growing opposition in the Netherlands. That Menno was one of the most outspoken and critical covenanters outside Münster is evident.

[72] Menno addresses Jan van Leiden by name in his *Blasphemy* six times. *Opera Omnia*, 619, 622, 623, 630. He further makes nine direct allusions to him by using one or another of his pretended titles, such as king, David, Christus, prince. Ibid., 622, 623, 624, 625, 626, 630.

[73] Kirchhoff quotes Jan van Leiden's assertion that it was Jan Matthijs who "initially introduced the use of the sword and violence against the authorities." Jan Matthijs arrived in Münster just before the elections of the city council on February 24, 1534. *MQR* (1970): 369.

We should remember that Jan van Leiden was present at all the key events related to the rise and development of the Münsterite kingdom between summer 1533 and June 1535. Klopris later confessed: "King Jan van Leiden is not older than thirty years. He has great knowledge of Scripture and is so well spoken that he can win the people to follow him." J. Niesert, *Münsterische Urkundensammlung* (Coesfeld, 1826), 134.

During the interrogation of the 27 captured Münsterite apostles, the leadership of Jan van Leiden as ruler, prophet and teacher was repeatedly emphasized in the testimonies. Johan Klopris stated in his confession that all the errors were introduced by Jan van Leiden, who also started rebaptism in Münster. Stupperich, *Schriften von Katholischer Seite*, 231: "They further confess that Jan van Leiden, a servant and a tailor of trade, posed first as an apostle, then became a prophet and finally made himself a king after the lost attack." Dusentschuer later announced that "God wanted to clean this city and drive out the godless. For this purpose He chose this king to rule over the entire world and to kill and exterminate with the sword all those who would not believe in him." This was confirmed by Rothmann and the preachers as well, "but God wants to renew all things and has given all the earth to the king." Ibid., 232.

74 Menno's frequent repetition of Jan van Leiden's claim supports our argument. If he had been familiar with Rothmann's *Van der Wrake*, he would have had dozens of statements to quote and to argue against.

75 Members of Menno's own parish became evangelical under the influence of his preaching and teaching. When they left for Münster he tried to oppose them, but without much success. *Opera Omnia*, 257a. He knew about the baptism upon the cross of Christ of the Münsterite leaders in January 1534 and recognized that the reformation of Münster was peaceful up to January 1534. "This I want to know from you, if you have been baptized upon the sword or upon the cross? How can you be so foolish, since you started in the Spirit and now you want to continue in the flesh?" Ibid., 630b. From his public and private debates with leaders of the New Jerusalem he must have known about later developments as well.

76 Stupperich, *Schriften*, 285.

77 Ibid., 293.

78 Ibid., 294.

79 Ibid., 295.

80 While Rothmann in his *Van der Wrake* quotes Scripture directly only 11 times and indirectly 14 times, Menno has 213 Scripture references in his *Blasphemy*. In the Old Testament Menno relies heavily on the Psalms (28 references) and Isaiah (22 references). His New Testament references are more balanced: Matthew (24 references); Luke (16 references); Romans (9 references); Hebrews (14 references); I Peter (7 references); and Revelation (14 references). He makes some further reference to most of the other books of the Old and New Testaments.

81 *Opera Omnia*, 624b.

82 Stupperich, *Schriften*, 294.

83 There is evidence that Jan van Leiden's dreams and visions did not always agree with Rothmann's theological and ideological conceptions of the Münsterite kingdom. K-H. Kirchhoff, "Die Endzeiterwartung der Täufergemeinde zu Münster 1534/35," in *Jahrbuch für Westfälische Kirchengeschichte* 78 (1985): 41, points at a difference concerning the millennium: "King Bockelson must have developed his own opinion about the thousand years in opposition to Rothmann." It is quite possible that Jan van Leiden encouraged this popular understanding of his role as messianic king David.

84 Verduin translates "aen allen waren Broeders ende Bontgenooten" (*Opera Omnia*, 619) by "to all the true brethren of the covenant," Wenger, *CW*, 32, which is not quite right. Literally it should read: "to all the brothers and members of the covenant."

85 *Opera Omnia*, 621.

86 Vos asserts that Menno's baptism took place before 1536. Vos, *Menno Simons*, 29. Evidence from contemporary sources (see *B.R.N. VII*, 362) and tradition point to Obbe Philips as the baptizer.

87 The introduction of polygamy encountered strong opposition from the leaders as well as from the covenanters in Münster. After riots and some executions, the resistance of the population slowly broke down. Cornelius, *Berichte der Augenzeugen* (Münster, 1853), 67, 68, 72. Although Gresbeck reports that polygamy finally was generally accepted, we have no statistics for the percentage of those who actually became involved.

88 In his *Bekenntnis des Glaubens und Lebens der Gemeinde Christi*, written in early 1534,

Rothmann complains about the "made up slander ... that they have their women in common ... . But these are ... all stinking lies." Rothmann quotes Matt. 5:27ff. and maintains that if anyone were to commit adultery in Münster "we would in no way tolerate him but he would be put in the ban and handed over to the devil for the rotting of his flesh." Stupperich, *Schriften*, 205.

[89] The theological foundation for polygamy was developed by Rothmann in his *Restitution*. The entire argument in favour of this new institution sounds rather strained. When he finally comes to the statement "Well then, now, the freedom of man in marriage is that he can have more than one wife at the same time in wedlock" it sounds as if he is admitting something his readers might know about already, but not be in agreement with. Stupperich, *Schriften*, 264.

[90] Ibid., 286. A paraphrase of Rothmann's statement would read as follows: We wish that we could present it to you, as it is in truth, but we know that you would respond with surprise and not be able to understand the light, which by the grace of the Father has been rising for us... All we can do is just draw a few lines for you from some of our revelations, but to disclose the true foundations of everything cannot be put in writing or on paper.

[91] *Fundament-book*, 202-203.

[92] The Anabaptists considered Münster's battle of resistance an act of permissible self-defence. "This was believed to such a degree that preachers raised theological objections to the recruitment of mercenaries, for it was right to defend oneself, but not to avenge oneself." Kirchhoff, *MQR* (1970): 369.

[93] In 1539 Menno did not admit this, but in the revised edition of the *Fundament-book* he stated: "We do confess, my dear Lords, that some from the false prophets were baptized with the same baptism as we." *Opera Omnia*, 55a.

[94] Against Stayer's statement in "Oldeklooster and Menno," 59, "Menno certainly became acquainted with Rothmann's writings in the course of warning his flock against 'king, polygamy, kingdom, sword,' all of which, with the exception of polygamy, come to the fore in the *Blasphemy* of Jan van Leyden." A careful reading of Rothmann's *Restitution* and *Van der Wrake* over against Menno's *Blasphemy* and later writings argues against Stayer's conclusion.

[95] *Fundament-book*, 174.

[96] *Opera Omnia*, 55b-56a.

[97] Wenger, *CW*, 64; on the various editions, see Horst, *Bibliography*, 77-81.

[98] *Doperse Stemmen 2. Menno Simons Meditatie op de 25e Psalm*, vertaald en ingeleid door H. W. Meihuizen, (Amsterdam, 1976): 43. Hereafter: *Doperse Stemmen 2*.

[99] Ibid., 41.

[100] Even if he would never deny the name of the Lord directly, Menno knew about the temptation to hide the word of God "under hypocrisy, lies and questionable words," as he himself did for many years. Ibid., 47.

[101] Ibid., 41.

[102] Ibid., 23.

[103] Ibid., 46.

[104] In the *Blasphemy*, Menno describes the conduct of the false teachers in a similar way. After forgetting the pure doctrine of Christ and ceasing to follow him as their master, they introduced the use of the sword. *Opera Omnia*, 621a-b.

[105] "Moreover he has dressed up open adultery under the cover of the custom of Jewish fathers; also a literal king and kingdom, together with many other abuses at which a sincere Christian is astonished and confounded." *Doperse Stemmen 2*: 46. Thus Menno knew about the marriage problems in Münster, but here, as in the first edition of the *Fundament-book*, he refuses to call it polygamy.

[106] *Doperse Stemmen 2*: 46.

[107] Rothmann uses this argument in *Van der Wracke*, basing it on Acts 3:21-23. Stupperich, *Schriften*, 288. Although there is no direct reference to Rothman's assertion, Menno probably encountered this argument in his disputations with the Münsterite delegations,

or in his discussions with his own parishoners who joined the Münsterites.
108 *Doperse Stemmen* 2: 48-49.
109 Ibid., 33-34; 42.
110 Valkema Blouw, in a specialized article on "Drukkers voor Menno Simons en Dirk Philips," in *Doopsgezinde Bijdragen* (Nieuwe Reeks 17, 1991): 31-74, provides evidence that the revised edition of Menno's *Fundament-book* was printed in Fresenburg in 1554-55. This edition has usually been dated 1558. See Horst, *Bibliography*, 54; Meihuizen, *Dat Fundament des Christelijken Leers*, XVII.
111 The first edition was printed in 1539-1540. Horst, *Bibliography*, 51.
112 S. Zijlstra, *Nicolaas Meyndertsz. van Blesdijk. Een bijdrage tot de geschiedenis van het Davidjorisme* (Groningen, 1983), 19. Zijlstra defends the thesis that between 1537 and 1540 David Joris was the most important leader of the Anabaptist movement in the Netherlands. An attempt by Joris to gain the Anabaptist leadership in Strassburg failed because he was unable to prove his calling as the third David with convincing evidence from Scripture. Gary R. Waite thinks that Joris remained a significant leader into the early 1540s: "Evidence suggests that Joris, by his attempts to unite the fragmented Anabaptist movement and by his success at gaining a large and devout following became the most important Anabaptist leader in the Netherlands for the decade following the defeat of the Münsterite kingdom in 1535." G. R. Waite, *Spiritualising the Crusade: David Joris in the context of the early Reform and Anabaptist movement in the Netherlands 1524-1543* (Scottdale: Herald Press, 1986), v.
113 Horst, *Bibliography*, 51-76. See also J. Decavele: "in the reviving Anabaptist movement in Flanders after 1550 there was only one central personality: Menno Simons." *De Dageraad der Reformatie* (Brussel, 1975), 514. And further: "The final shape of the Anabaptist movement in Flanders after 1550 was the work of the followers of this Menno Simons. His writings, first of all *The Foundation of Christian Doctrine*, are the guidelines par excellence for faith and life of the Anabaptists in this land." Ibid., 607.
114 The year 1539 under the title *Foundation of Christian Doctrine*, in Wenger, *CW*, 105 is misleading. In its salutation and preface as well as in the rest of the book this translation follows the revised edition of 1554-55.
115 *Opera Omnia*, 2. The obvious changes in the new edition did not escape contemporary readers. At their Synod in Bolsward in 1588 the Reformed church even considered reprinting the original edition of 1539 because they believed this edition proved the common origin of Mennonites and Münsterites. The same matter came up again at the Synod of Wouden in 1606 and at the Synod of Harlingen in 1610, but unfortunately the reprinting was never done. Finally the Mennonite Jan Theunisz from Amsterdam republished the first edition of 1539 in 1616. In his opinion, Mennonites did not need to disassociate themselves from any of Menno's earlier remarks. Horst, *Bibliography*, 65.
116 *Fundament-book*, XVIII.
117 Karel Vos, *Menno Simons. 1496-1561. Zijn Leven en Werken en zijne Reformatorische Denkbeelden* (Leiden 1914), 40.
118 *Fundament-book*, 8. If there is no other acknowledgement, it may be assumed that the translation is ours.
119 *Opera Omnia*, 4. Wenger, *CW*, 107 simply uses polygamy to translate the Dutch "veelheyt der wijven." The translation is literally correct. But it is interesting to observe, that Menno is very reluctant to use this term in regard to Münster.
120 "What we ask for from all the pious magistrates and all the people by the grace of God is, that you would read our writings seriously at least once; pay attention and understand, so that you finally know what we teach and who we are." *Fundament-book*, 5ff.; 160.
121 Ibid., 57.
122 "...not that we want to have many wives, or expect a kingdom here on earth. No, no, praise be to God forever, we know well what the word of the Lord teaches us concerning that and what it means." *Opera Omnia*, 17a.
123 *Fundament-book*, 170-171.

[124] Ibid., 171.
[125] *Opera Omnia*, 54b-55a.
[126] *Fundament-book*, 172.
[127] Ibid., 172-173.
[128] Ibid., 173.
[129] Ibid., 174.
[130] Menno already used the same argument in the *Blasphemy*: "And it has to happen in this way, that sects arise among us, so that the approved ones will be revealed." *Opera Omnia*, 621a. In his *Meditation* he follows a similar line of reasoning: "Where Christ comes, there the devil soon will be found as well, as I have experienced recently, among many other things." *Doperse Stemmen* 2: 46.
[131] *Opera Omnia*, 55a.
[132] "We confess, dear Lords, that some of the false prophets have been baptized externally and in appearance, with the same baptism as we, ... but they did not belong to us ..." Ibid., 55a. This statement is missing from the first edition of the *Fundament-book*. See 170-171.
[133] *Opera Omnia*, 55b.
[134] "And this without any question did not happen through baptism, because water cannot teach right or wrong, but it happened through the false prophets, about whom we have been warned so faithfully." *Fundament-book*, 173. See *Opera Omnia*, 55b.
[135] *Fundament-book*, 199.
[136] Ibid., 199.
[137] Vos, *Menno Simons*, 28, thinks one of them was Obbe Philips. Kuehler gives the name of Jan van Geel. Kuehler, *Geschiedenis*, 164. S. Voolstra, *Doperse Stemmen* 6: 28, suggests Peter Simons and Albert Beneventura as well as Jan van Geel.
[138] *Fundament-book*, 202-203.
[139] Traditional research on the Münsterite kingdom has focused on communism, polygamy and the reign of terror. Karl-Heinz Kirchhoff, known for his thorough research of the social and economic background of the Münsterite Anabaptists, tries to interpret this religious phenomenon from the perspective of its apocalyptic expectations. The events of January and February 1534, so hard to explain from a rational point of view, then fall into place. Kirchhoff's thesis is that the apocalyptic expectation of 1533-34 substantially influenced the rise and development of the Anabaptist congregation in Münster. K. H. Kirchhoff, *Die Täufer in Münster 1534-1535* (Münster, 1973). See also his article "Die Endzeiterwartung der Täufergemeinde zu Münster 1534/35," in *Jahrbuch für Westfälische Kirchengeschichte*, 78 (1985), 20. Willem de Bakker, *Civic Reformer in Anabaptist Münster: Bernhard Rothmann, 1495-1535*, (Chicago, 1986), 19, states that the religious aspects of the Reformation in Münster were not anomalous. Münster was not a fringe phenomenon on the edge of the Reformation, but was firmly embedded in the theological, ecclesiological and political developments of its time. See also J. Stayer, "Polygamy as Inner-Worldly Asceticism," in DAN Bulletin, nos. 12 & 13 (1980-1981): 59-67.
[140] Probably the most fascinating personality among the Münsterite leaders was Bernhard Rothmann. Starting as a Lutheran reformer in 1530, he joined Zwingli in 1532 and was obviously an Anabaptist by the time he wrote his *Bekenntnis von beiden Sakramenten* in August 1533. Baptized on January 5, 1534 by the apostles of Jan Matthijsz, he soon became the leading theologian of the Münsterite kingdom. In his five major tracts written between January 1534 and June 1535, Rothmann developed the theological foundation for the Anabaptist kingdom of Münster. Starting from Hoffman's theological understanding of the use of violence, Hoffman's Christology, interpretation of Scripture, restitution, justification of polygamy and a negative view of government, Rothman modified these concepts to bring them in line with the thinking of Jan Matthijsz and Jan van Leiden. He began as the theorist of the kingdom, but he slowly lost control and ended up as the spokesman for the ill-conceived inspirations of Jan

van Leiden and his prophets. See Martin Brecht, "Die Theologie Bernhard Rothmans," in *Bibliotheca Dissedentium, no.3,* ed. by J. G. Rott and S. L. Verheus (1987), 149-155. See also Brecht's more extensive article in *Jahrbuch für Westfaelische Kirchengeschichte,* 78 (1985): 49-82 and also J. Stayer, "Polygymy as Inner-Wouldly Ascetism": 59-67.

[141] *Opera Omnia,* 449a.
[142] Ibid, 449b.
[143] Ibid., 437a.
[144] Ibid. 448b.
[145] Ibid., 441a.
[146] Ibid., 497a.
[147] Ibid., 498b.
[148] Ibid., 502a.
[149] Ibid., 504a.
[150] Ibid., 506a.
[151] Ibid., 507b.
[152] Ibid., 509b.
[153] Ibid., 514a.
[154] Ibid., 497a. This is one of the very few places where Menno uses the term *wraeck,* or vengeance. But even when he does refer to vengeance in the context of Münster, he never quotes Rothmann directly or tries to refute the main points of Rothmann's arguments. Verduin's translation of "dat uytwendige Rijck Christi op Aerden" with "the visible Kingdom of Christ" (Wenger, *CW,* 547) is not correct. The difference between "external" and "visible" is very basic for the understanding of Menno's concept of the Kingdom of God. Münster was only external, because it was motivated by selfish ambition, greed and lust. The truly spiritual Kingdom of Christ becomes visible reality through repentance, regeneration and new life.
[155] *Opera Omnia,* 497a.
[156] Ibid., 498a.
[157] Ibid.
[158] *Opera Omnia,* 497a.
[159] Horst, *Bibliography,* 96. Wenger argues that the *Blasphemy* was written in 1535. Considering this to be Menno's first written work, he comes to the conclusion that the *Reply* must have been published in 1552, Wenger, *CW,* 547, note 3.
[160] *Opera Omnia,* 503a. In the margin he writes "I confess my noble Lords ... to the honor of God, that we do not seek insurrection or mutiny." Wenger, *CW,* 556.
[161] *Opera Omnia,* 503a.
[162] J. Decavele, *De dageraad van de Reformatie* (Brussel,1975), 33f.
[163] Decavele, *De dageraad,* 56-57.
[164] Statistics for Friesland show 7 executions in 1549, one in 1550, one in 1551, none in 1552 and 9 in 1553. J. J. Woltjer, *Friesland in de Hervormingstijd* (Leiden, 1962), 109.
[165] *Opera Omnia,* 497a.
[166] Ibid., 504a; Wenger, *CW,* 557.
[167] *Opera Omnia,* 327a.
[168] Ibid., 327b.
[169] Wenger, *CW,* 535; *Opera Omnia,* 333a.
[170] Ibid, 333a-b; Wenger, *CW,* 536.
[171] "Then the sect of Münster appeared, which deceived many pious hearts in our quarters as well." *Opera Omnia,* 257a.
[172] Ibid., 257a.
[173] Wenger, *CW,* 672; *Opera Omnia,* 258a-b.
[174] Ibid., 148f.
[175] Wenger, *CW,* 962; *Opera Omnia,* 188.

Chapter Three
The Heavenly Jerusalem has Descended

1. Hoffman asserts that all men are cursed on account of Adam's sin, and all of Adam's seed belongs to Satan. Adam has brought universal death into the world. Peter Kawerau, *Melchior Hoffman als Religiöser Denker* (Haarlem, 1954), 46.
2. Melchior Hoffman, *Ausslegung der heimlichen Offenbarung Joannis* (Straatsburg, 1530), fol. Z4v; Sjouke Voolstra, *Het Woord is Vlees Geworden* (Kampen, 1982), 11-12.
3. "Medieval natural history supposed that pearls were formed by dew descending from heaven and crystallizing in the oyster, a solid form of celestial water." G. H. Williams, *Radical Reformation* (Philadelphia, 1962), 330.
4. Ibid. We follow the translation of Williams from M. Hoffman, *Die sendebrief to den Roemeren*. BRN V, 311. Williams, *Radical Reformation*, 330.
5. Although Hoffman's view of the incarnation seems to be Valentinian, we have no indication that he ever read any Gnostic or anti-Gnostic text on his own. Like Valentinus, he held that Christ brought his body with him from heaven, taking on nothing of the substance of Mary. Williams, *Radical Reformation*, 329. J. A. Oosterbaan, "Een doperse christologie," in *Nederlands Theologisch Tijdschrift* XXXV (1981): 32-47, argues that Hoffman's Christology is not Valentinian, but is based on Scripture.

    S. Voolstra comes to the conclusion that "qualifications such as 'spiritualistic' and 'docetic' are too general and too polemical in character to adequately describe the intent of the Melchiorite-Mennonite incarnation doctrine.... Hoffman ... makes the incarnation of and the reconciliation through the completely sinless, pre-existent Word of God the basis of his theology. It is not the philosophical distinction between *spiritus* and *materia* but the biblical-theological contradiction of spirit and flesh, especially directed toward the ethical, which constitutes Hoffman's religious thought." Voolstra, *Het Woord is Vlees Geworden* (Kampen, 1982), 211.
6. Williams, *Radical Reformation*, 327. Williams maintains that Hoffman could have seen iconographic representations of what he himself was prepared to make doctrinally explicit. Contemporary woodcuts show the crowned head and upper half of God the Father, while what would be the lower half is taken up by a cloud-enclosed space containing a naked infant bearing a cross and preceded by a Dove, effecting the descent of the body of the Son of God into the womb of Mary. Ibid., 329.
7. As early as 1525 Willem de Cuiper compared Mary to an empty flour-bag. Fredericq, *C.D.* IV., 372. Pieter Florisz of Gouda compared Mary to "a sack that had once held cinnamon, but now only retains the sweet savour." A. Duke, *The Face of Popular Dissent*, 52. In note 7 Duke adds, "This imagery was employed also by English Protestants." Jan Goessen put it more bluntly when he asked rhetorically, "Is our Dear Lady so holy; how holy could the donkey then have been, who carried the entire hodgepodge as well?" Fredericq, C.D. IV., 385. Although Williams expands his documentation on this subject in the revised Spanish edition, he makes no reference to this popular concept among the Dutch Sacramentarians. G. Williams, *La Reforma Radical* (Mexico, 1983), 362-368.
8. M. Hoffman, *Roemerbrief*, 14.
9. Williams, *Radical Reformation*, 331.
10. Kawerau, *Melchior Hoffman*, 49; K. Depperman, *Melchior Hoffman* (Goettingen, 1979), 189f. See Rom. 5.
11. Kawerau, *Melchior Hoffman*, 49-50.
12. "Sinlessness is in this dispensation not yet a question of being, but of becoming." Voolstra, *Het Woord*, 127. Kawerau describes this process as the four-days' journey. On the first day the believer prepares himself for a "truly converted life" (*wahrhaftigen bekehrlichen Leben*). If he continues his journey, he will reach the second stage of holiness, which is the city and the church of the living God. Only the apostolic teachers and prophetic spirits will reach the Holy of Holies, where they learn to recognize God's entire will. This is the third heaven Paul mentions in II Cor.12:12ff. From here

they are allowed to have a look into the fourth heaven which is the throne of God and Jesus Christ, but no human being will ever reach the fourth heaven during his lifetime. Kawerau, *Melchior Hoffman*, 51-56.

13 It was Jan de Bakker of Woerden who as early as 1525 located the presence of Christ in the sacraments within the context of the community of believers. This, together with his secret marriage as a Catholic priest, cost him his life. Fredericq, *C.D. IV.*, 482.

14 Voolstra, *Het Woord*, 44.

15 Ghele Hame confessed during his trial at Kampen, February 1535 that he did not believe "that Christ received anything human from his blessed mother Mary, but was conceived by the Holy Spirit only and born by Mary." *DAN, I.*, 23.

16 For Rothmann's incarnation doctrine, see Stupperich, *Schriften Bernhard Rothmanns* (Münster, 1970), 199.

17 Cornelius, *Berichte der Augenzeugen* (Münster, 1893), 27. The only existing examples of this are two coins minted in 1534. Here the words are: Dat wort is fleisch geworden vn wanet in vns. *Die Wiedertäufer in Münster* (Stadtmuseum Münster, 1983), 69-70.

18 All who were baptized during the three days following February 27 had their names entered into a ledger and were handed a medallion the size of a large coin with the text "The Word was made flesh." W. de Bakker, *Civic Reformer in Anabaptist Münster: Bernhard Rothmann* (Chicago, 1987), 274. See Cornelius, *Berichte der Augenzeugen* (Münster,1893), 28. The DWWF was a reference to the incarnation of Christ in the past and a statement about the present incarnation of the Word of God in the community of the covenanters in Münster. In the same way as the Word of God became flesh in Jesus Christ, God's new creation, or the New Jerusalem, was now becoming visible reality in Münster. Johan Klopris' translation of the DWWF is ". . . das Wort wart fleisch . . . ." (the Word became flesh). J. Niesert, *Münsterische Urkundensammlung I.* (Coesfeld, 1826), 111; 124. This interpretation, confirmed by the inscription of the new Münsterite coins of September 1534, also stresses the presence of the Word of God, which has now come to "live among and in them."

19 Ibid., 111ff.

20 Ibid., 124.

21 Ibid., 116.

22 Voolstra, *Het Woord*, 43.

23 Stupperich, *Schriften Bernhard Rothmanns*, 70; 197.

24 Ibid., 201.

25 Ibid., 202.

26 Ibid., 203.

27 Ibid., 204.

28 Ibid., 203-204.

29 God in his transcendental reality is and will always remain utopian in this world. But in the incarnation of his Son Jesus Christ he became topia, that is, visible reality in this world.

30 The Melchiorite doctrine of incarnation was very much a part of the wild events of February 8, 1534. While Knipperdolling and Jan van Leiden went through the streets of Münster calling for repentance, Georg tom Berge went into ecstasy and combined calls for repentance with warnings of divine wrath against those who still believed that Christ had received his flesh from Mary. Willem de Bakker, *Civic Reformer*, 268-269.

x31 Stupperich, *Schriften Bernhard Rothmanns*, 256.

32 Ibid., 283.

33 Ibid., 207-208.

34 Ibid., 206. Rothmann's and the Münsterites' "peacefulness" lasted only from the day of their baptism on January 5, 1534 until the beginning of the siege of the city by the Bishop on February 28, 1534. All we know about this peacefulness is contained in Rothman's own words in his *Restitution*. At the time of their baptism they "did put down all our defence and weapons and prepared our selves to become sacrificial lambs, because we believed it was not suitable for us to offer resistance to the godless,

but to suffer, even to die with forbearance." Ibid., 280. Was the change from being ready to carry the cross of suffering to organizing an armed defence of the city based upon new revelations? Or were the Münsterite Anabaptists only nonviolent as long as they were a powerless minority? Or had the Melchiorites never denied the government the legitimate use of the sword? In this latter case, it would have been the duty of the Anabaptists to defend the city after the elections of February 15, which gave them a majority on the city council. Obviously Rothmann had not yet developed a theological legitimation of the use of the sword to defend the New Jerusalem, so he simply avoided discussion of the matter. It is clear that violence was not yet being used in the apocalyptic crusade against unbelievers. The judgment of the unbelievers still lay in the hands of God.

[35] Ibid., 206. From later developments it seems to be clear that Rothmann is alluding to the expected coming of Christ on Easter, April 5, 1534. The fact that he is not yet giving explicit information points to the first days of March as the date of publication of this tract.

[36] W. J. Kuehler, *Geschiedenis der Nederlandsche Doopsgezinden* (Haarlem, 1932), 97.

[37] Ibid., 95.

[38] A. F. Mellink, "Beginperiode van het Nederlands Anabaptisme," in D.B. (1986-1987): 34.

[39] Kuehler, *Geschiedenis*, 97.

[40] Gresbeck seems to have captured some of the inner struggle of Matthijsz on the day before his death. At a wedding celebration, Matthijsz was suddenly overcome by the "Baptist spirit... Sitting there he slapped his hands together and banged his head up and down and was sighing and moaning as if he was going to die... Finally he awakened again with a deep groan and said 'O dear Father, not my will but yours be done,' went up, gave everyone his hand and kissed everyone and said 'the peace of God be with you all...'" At this point he left the wedding with his wife. He died the next day. Cornelius, *Berichte der Augenzeugen*, 39.

[41] Melchior Hoffman again provided the basic elements of this new ideology. From him came the idea that the "godless" would be purged before the final judgment, that the Kingdom of the Saints would see cooperation between prophets and worldly rulers, and the expectation that Christ would come following a second Solomon, who would prepare the earth for Christ's arrival. See Deppermann, *Melchior Hoffman*, 229.

[42] "Dat Christus de zoon Godes van onzen vleesche gheen mensch zijn kan, began ick noch in t'Pausdom wel te merken." *DAN III, Marten Micron*, edited by W. F. Dankbaar (Leiden, 1981), 100. See also K. Vos, *Menno Simons* (Leiden, 1914), 34.

[43] *Opera Omnia*, 525a.

[44] *Opera Omnia*, 525a.

[45] Menno describes Christ's birth as follows: "By the kindness of the heavenly Father, I came into this world, and by the power of the Holy Spirit, I became a visible, tangible, and mortal man; in all points like unto you, sin excepted. I was born out of Mary, the unpolluted und pure virgin; I descended from heaven, sprang from the mouth of the Most High, the first-born of all creatures ... ." *Fundament-book*, 25-26. The "wt Maria" (out of Mary) confirms that the Melchiorite doctrine of incarnation was an essential part of Menno's Christology and doctrine of justification by faith. See Voolstra, *Het Woord*, 47-48.

[46] *Opera Omnia*, 527a.

[47] *DAN III*, 89.

[48] Wenger, *CW*, 428; *Opera Omnia*, 525.

[49] Ibid., 526a.

[50] J. A. Oosterbaan's defence of Menno's theology against the charge of being kenotic is convincing. "Precisely because Menno is, above all, concerned with the unity of Christ's person, does he reject the thought that he would ever teach that the Son of God had changed himself into a man and thus laid aside his God-being. The incarnation is, to be sure, a change but not in the essence of His God-being. In spite of the change,

Christ at the same time remained himself." *MQR* (1961), 193. Ooosterbaan then quotes from *Opera Omnia*, 79b-80a: "We teach and believe, ... that the whole Christ is from head to foot, both inside and outside, visible and invisible, God's first-born and only begotten Son; the incomprehensible, eternal Word, by whom all things were created, the first-born of every creature. We teach and believe that He became a true man in Mary, the pure virgin, through the power of the Almighty, eternal Father, beyond the comprehension and knowledge of man. He was sent and given unto us by the Father of mere grace and mercy; the express image of the invisible God and the brightness of His glory." See Menno's *Reply to Gellius Faber, Opera Omnia*, 313.

51 Ibid., 313a.
52 Ibid., 313b.
53 Ibid., 314a.
54 Ibid., 314a-b.
55 Ibid., 315a.
56 Ibid., 319a. M. F. Dankbaar makes an interesting observation in his introduction to *Marten Mikron*: "It is remarkable that the Roman-Catholic doctrine of the immaculate conception of Mary, through which she has been freed from original sin, although opposite to Menno's doctrine of incarnation—for him Mary represented sinful flesh— has the same purport, namely, to preclude any inference that Christ was polluted with sin through Mary." *DAN III.*, XXIII, note 2.
57 In the same way as the work of the Holy Spirit can be understood only through the Spirit, and only the Holy Spirit can give birth to spiritual beings, flesh can give birth only to flesh. The natural law that "like begets like" (*gelyck will van gelyck geboren worden*), becomes for Menno a theological principle and a hermeneutical tool which he applies relentlessly against his opponents and the preachers. If their works are still worldly, then their spirit and motivation must also be worldly. *Fundament-book*, 116.
58 *Opera Omnia*, 527a-b.
59 Ibid. 528a. Oosterbaan's view of Menno's doctrine of incarnation is that for Menno the Word did not take on flesh but himself became flesh. Jesus did not receive his body from Mary; he himself became a body which was received by Mary in faith and through the Holy Spirit, that she might nourish Him and bring Him into the world according to the way of nature. Menno refused to accept the view that Mary made any positive contribution of her own to the incarnation. *MQR* (1961), 192-193. Ooosterbaan then points to the similarity of Menno's and K. Barth's doctrine of incarnation. For Barth, Mary's relationship to the incarnation is much the same as that of the empty grave to the resurrection. K. Barth, *Die Kirchliche Dogmatik*. I/2, 187ff.
60 *DAN III.*, 53; 49.
61 Ibid., 53.
62 Ibid., 54; *Opera Omnia*, 527b; Wenger, *CW*, 431.
63 *DAN III*, 78.
64 Ibid., 57.
65 Ibid., 58.
66 Ibid., 119.
67 *Opera Omnia*, 554b.
68 Ibid., 557a.
69 Ibid., 558b.
70 For a detailed discussion of this subject see Voolstra, *Het Woord*, 149ff.
71 In his *Reply* to Mikron's *Waerachtich Verhaal*, Menno quotes Mikron as saying that "Christ was pure and without sin, because he was not conceived by the process of reproduction by the seed of man." Menno disagreed, saying that sin cannot come from marital intimacy, because sexuality is a gift from God. *Opera Omnia*, 557a.
72 In Menno's theology, the consequence of the Melchiorite doctrine of incarnation is not the deification of the believer, but his sanctification.
73 See Deppermann, *Melchior Hoffman*, 229ff.
74 J. H. Yoder, *The Priestly Kingdom* (Notre Dame, 1984), 125.

NOTES FOR PAGES 65-67

[75] Ibid.
[76] Stupperich, *Schriften Bernhard Rothmanns*, 197.
[77] Ibid., 201.
[78] Ibid.
[79] Ibid., 235.
[80] Ibid., 236. See also *Fundament-book*, 39-40.
[81] Ibid., 236.
[82] "Restitution, then, is in the first place the restoration of the lost, original, creational relationship between God and man through Christ." Voolstra, *Het Woord*, 201.
[83] Niesert, *Urkunden*, 111.
[84] ". . . whoever would not accept this, should be punished." Jan van Leiden, the instrument of God's wrath in his role as King David, would carry out this punishment. Ibid., 111-112.
[85] Stupperich, *Schriften Bernhard Rothmanns*, 233.
[86] Kuehler writes, "Menno's first was a booklet 'On Spiritual Resurrection'" (*Menno's eersteling was een tractaat "Van die gheestelijcke Verrijsenisse"*), Kuehler, *Geschiedenis*, 216. In terms of scriptural references, the *Spiritual Resurrection* is less balanced than any of his later writings. Menno relies heavily on John (16 ref.), Romans (19 ref.), Galatians (10 ref.), Ephesians (14 ref.), Colossians (14 ref.), Hebrews (12 ref.) and Revelation (10 ref.). The remaining New Testament books cited are I Corinthians and I Peter (8 ref. each), Matthew, Luke, II Corinthians and James (5-7 ref. each), and seven books with fewer than five references each. Of the eight books of the Old Testament referred to, the Psalms are quoted ten times and the remaining seven books appear one to three times. The balance changes in the *Blasphemy*, where the Old Testament becomes more prominent and John and Revelation are replaced by the Synoptics. The language and imagery used in the *Spiritual Resurrection* is thoroughly apocalyptic.
[87] Bornhäeuser, *Leben und Lehre Menno Simons* (Neukirchen-Vliuyn, 1973), 176.
[88] Menno opens his sermon with Eph. 5:14: "Wake up, O sleeper, rise from the dead, and Christ will shine on you." *Opera Omnia*, 179a.
[89] Ibid., 180a-b.
[90] Ibid., 180a. The principle that "like begets like" is used by Menno throughout his entire *Opera*, and is related to the Melchiorite doctrine of incarnation. See also *Fundament-book*, 116: "...but where the Spirit of God powerfully moves, nothing but the Spirit will be thought, equal will be born by equal..."
[91] *Opera Omnia*, 180-181.
[92] Ibid., 181a.
[93] Ibid., 183a.
[94] In this early period the role of the congregation was important for Menno only for the "procreation" of new believers. He was more concerned about "the spiritual resurrection of believers than in their gathering together." Kuehler, *Geschiedenis*, 217.
[95] *Opera Omnia*. 182a.
[96] Ibid., 182a.
[97] Ibid., 183a-b.
[98] "In this, as in a clear mirror, man may look at himself and find out in his own judgment of what birth ... essence and nature, life and conduct he is." And then let him pray with Jeremiah: "let us find our ways ... and return to the Lord." Ibid., 183b.
[99] It is obvious in the *Spiritual Resurrection* that baptism and the sign of Thau are identical for Menno. When the regenerated servants of God are being marked with this sign, it confirms them as citizens of the New Jerusalem. Baptism as the covenant with God and the means for reception of believers into the membership of the church does not yet have any importance for him. It is striking that there is as yet no cross in the *Spiritual Resurrection*. Although that which is born of flesh is in its own nature hostile to God and to those born of the Spirit, a confrontation between the two kingdoms does not yet seem to be inevitable. Ibid., 180a.

[100] Vos, *Menno Simons*, 56, note 1, points to the fact that Menno still calls John a "Saint" ("gelijk Sint Johannes seyt," *Opera Omnia*, 182b) as evidence that he is still close to the Catholic church.
[101] *Opera Omnia*, 184b.
[102] Bornhäuser, *Leben und Lehre*, 176, suggests that he wrote it earlier. The *Spiritual Resurrection* is the only tract in which Menno does not allude to Münster, even when he discusses such references as Hebrews 7 (*Opera Omnia*, 108b) or Ephesians 6 (Ibid., 181b), which will become key references in the later *Blasphemy*. All his later writings make some reference to Münster, either directly or indirectly.
[103] Ibid., 184a.
[104] Ibid., 257a.
[105] Obbe Philipps states in his "Confession" (*Bekenntnisse*) that they where impressed and comforted by the dreams and visions of the new teachers and prophets and believed that everything was true and would be fulfilled. "Because we all where untried, simple, innocent, without any malice or deceit. We did not know of any false visions, prophecies and revelations. In our simplicity we believed that when we would stay free of Papists, Lutherans and Zwinglians, then everything would be fine and we would not need to worry." H. Fast, *Der linke Flügel der Reformation* (Bremen, 1962), 327ff.
[106] On this point we agree with Stayer: Oldeklooster was not the breaking point between Menno and the Münsterites, but Oldeklooster forced Menno to identify himself fully with the non-aggressive Melchiorites and finally to leave the Catholic church. Stayer, "Oldeklooster en Menno," *DB*. 5 (1979): 56-76.
[107] *Opera Omnia*, 257a.
[108] We have no evidence that either was published before 1539. Horst, *Bibliography* (Nieuwkoop, 1962), 77-81. However, parts may have been written before that date and even circulated in manuscript form. Vos, *Menno Simons*, 293, dates the *New Birth* ca. 1538. Kuehler, *Geschiedenis*, 218, comes to a similar conclusion.
[109] Kuehler suggests that Menno was primarily addressing Roman Catholics. Ibid, 218. He calls it "an epistle to the Roman Catholics to admonish them and to call them to penance and to regeneration..."
[110] Menno Simons, *Een corte vermaninghe vth Godes woort van die Wedergeboorte, Vnd wie die ghene syn, die belofte hebben 1539-40*. (ME-273), Aiij r.
[111] Ibid., Av r.
[112] Ibid., Av v.
[113] Ibid.
[114] Ibid., Avi v.
[115] Ibid., Bij r.
[116] Ibid., Avij v - Aviij r.
[117] Ibid., Biij v.
[118] Ibid., Bij r.
[119] Wenger, *CW*, 93.
[120] Ibid., 94-95.
[121] The fact that Menno in his later years became stricter and more narrow-minded in his views is reflected in the revisions of his earliest writings. See Kuehler, *Geschiedenis*, 215-216.
[122] This is our major objection to C. Krahn's, *Menno Simons* (Karlsruhe, 1936), 118; 123; 178-179. Because Krahn did not have sufficient access to the early writings of Menno, he was not aware of the many shifts in Menno's theological thinking and easily came to the conclusion that ecclesiology stood always at the centre of Menno's thought: "It has become evident, that a certain concept of the church stands in the centre of his concern. ... For this reason we can say that his theology is eeclesiocentric." Ibid., 178-179. Our study demonstrates that ecclesiology as a narrow concentration on the congregation as the blameless and spotless bride of Jesus Christ did not become a dominant theme in Menno's theological discourse until the 1550s.

[123] According to Meihuizen this "confession" reflects Menno's struggle after he left the Catholic church and before he accepted the office of Melchiorite elder. When he had it printed in 1539, he added the introduction as well as the Latin epilogue. Meihuizen, *Doperse Stemmen* 2: 11. "The recently ordained pastor reveals very little over the time from January 1536 until January 1537. He used this quiet time to read the word of the Lord and to write. This very personal biblically well documented 'Meditation on the twenty fifth Psalm' is the first fruit of this work." Voolstra, *Doperse Stemmen* 6: 32.

[124] Horst, *Bibliography* (Nieuwkoop, 1962), 77. According to the introduction of 1539, this vindication is directed as much to the different factions of the covenanters as to the rest of the Christian church. That Menno is being slandered "... not so much in my presence as in my absence ... " (*Doperse Stemmen* 2: 15), reveals that his position among the covenanters was controversial as late as 1539. In contrast, the revised edition, *Opera Omnia*, 163, has Menno being slandered behind his back by those who wish him ill.

[125] Ibid., 163.

[126] C. Augustijn, "Anabaptisme in de Nederlanden," *DB*. 12-13 (1986-1987): 27 makes a helpful observation on this rather strange accusation: "We find a certain tenacity already in Menno, which is due to the fact that he uses Scripture as a book of law..."

[127] See *Doperse Stemmen* 2: 41-42. In the revised edition of the *Opera Omnia*, 174a, Menno mentions only two of the accusations: "now they accuse me as a false seducer or a cursed heretic..." The former accusations are probably omitted because they were related so closely to Münster and because Menno's integrity was no longer being questioned.

[128] Menno's prayer, "O Lord of heaven and earth, I call you Lord, although I am not worthy to be called your servant, because until now I did not serve you, but your enemy" implies that he wrote this part of the confession before he became a Melchiorite elder. *Doperse Stemmen* 2: 19. In the revised edition this sentence is changed to "...since my youth I did not serve you, but your enemy, the devil..." *Opera Omnia*, 165a.

[129] Before he left the Catholic Church, Menno was considered an evangelical preacher and a good Christian with an established reputation. "Everyone sought me and desired me. ... When I spoke they were silent. ... My word was final in all matters. The desire of my heart was granted." Wenger, *CW*, 71; *Opera Omnia*, 168b. But at that time he confessed that his deepest motivation was selfish ambition. *Doperse Stemmen* 2: 24.

[130] Ibid., 24; *Opera Omnia*, 167b; Wenger, *CW*, 70.

[131] Menno never jeopardized his career by committing any gross sins. His sin was much more subtle: he used his office as a priest to satisfy his selfish ambitions for power and money. Instead of mediating God's love and forgiveness, Menno served the desires of his corrupted flesh. *Doperse Stemmen* 2: 36.

[132] Ibid., 32; *Opera Omnia*, 170b; Wenger, *CW*, 74-75.

[133] Verduin's translation into English of "dat is de eyndelijcke vrucht van die die u bekennen, dat sijn ziele sal woonen in't goede . . . ." *Opera Omnia*, 170b, by "this is the final reward for those who know Thee. Their souls shall inherit that which is good," (Wenger, *CW*, 74), suggests that Menno is describing life after death. But "fruit," "day and night," "misery and suffering," "contending valiantly and running with patience" all point to historical categories. Verduin's translation tends to spiritualize Menno's understanding of the anticipation of the kingdom of God, whereas the original emphasizes life in this world.

[134] *Opera Omnia*, 419a.

[135] *Fundament-book*, 41.

[136] Ibid.

[137] Ibid., 41-42.

[138] In the *Testament (Dat nieuwe) ons liefs Heeren Jesu Christi*, Gher. onde verl. na de copye van Matthens Jacobszoon 1558, I John 3:6 reads "He who remains in him does not sin. And he who sins, has not seen or known him."

[139] *Opera Omnia*, 532b.

[140] *Opera Omnia*, 507b-508a.

[141] *Fundament-book*, 42. This paragraph describing the triumph of the new Christian life is missing in the revised edition of 1554-55. See *Opera Omnia*, 13a-b.

[142] Wenger, *CW*, 265; *Opera Omnia*, 419b.

[143] Ibid., 256a-258b. The *Uitgang uit het Pausdom* is the autobiographical part of Menno's *Reply to Gellius Faber* of 1554.

[144] *Doperse Stemmen* 2: 24. This might very well be the first confession of faith that Menno refers to in his *Reply to False Accusations*; see *Opera Omnia*, 497a. In retrospect (1551) Menno is less harsh with himself and recognizes the value of this first spiritual experience.

[145] Ibid., 257b. Wenger, *CW*, 671.

[146] This is the order in his *Instruction on Christian Baptism*. See *Opera Omnia*, 419b. In the *Fundament-book*, 37, he writes: "But he who hears the word of God and believes, shall be baptized..."

[147] Considering the importance Menno's writings give to baptism and its place in the process of becoming a Christian, this is an inconsistency which has led to much speculation.

[148] *Opera Omnia*, 258b.; *Doperse Stemmen* 6: 42; Wenger, *CW*, 672.

[149] This is probably one of the reasons why in his later writings he makes no reference to either the *Spiritual Resurrection* or to the *Blasphemy*.

[150] Menno is accused of denying the authenticity of this tract. "Yes, you did not want to recognize this booklet from the New Creature as yours." *DAN III*, 199.

[151] In his discussion of the biblical doctrine of baptism, church membership is not even mentioned. *Fundament-book*, 57. It is in the celebration of the Lord's Supper that the body of Christ becomes a visible reality in the congregation. Like the bread of the Supper, the congregation is formed from many individual believers who have become one and are willing to share everything. Ibid., 82-83. He describes this community of believers as the lovely gathering where brotherly admonition, encouragement and thanksgiving are practiced, where everyone is ready to serve, and where moral perfection is pursued. Ibid., 84-89.

Chapter Four
The Eschatological Anticipation

[1] Menno Simons, *Een corte vermaninghe vth Godes Woort van die wedergeboorte/ Vnde wie die ghene syn, die belofte hebben*. The radical Reformation Microfiche Project. Section I. Mennonite and related sources up to 1600. BME-273/1. fol. Biiij r.

[2] *Opera Omnia*, 183a.

[3] Werner Packull writes, "The changing conception of the Thau from a symbol of crusading vengeance against the godless (Rothmann) to one of internal withdrawal (Joris), to the mark of a persecuted remnant (Menno), emphasizes what historians have known all along—namely, that concepts and symbols change their meaning under changing historical circumstances." Werner O. Packull, "The sign of Thau: The changing conception of the seal of God's elect in early Anabaptist thought," *MQR* 4 (1987): 363-374.

[4] *Fundament-book*, 12.

[5] *Opera Omnia*, 434.

[6] *Opera Omnia*, 180b-181a. "On the other hand, all who are born and regenerated from above, through the living word, are of God and are also of the mind and disposition, and have the same aptitude for good that he has of whom they are born and begotten." Christ as the incarnate Word of God is our example in works and deeds, and we must follow him in order to become partakers of his nature in the spirit. Applying the principle of "like begets like," this means "that which is born of the flesh is flesh, and cannot see eternal life; and that which is born of the Spirit is spirit, life and peace, which is eternal life," Menno concludes that born-again Christians will put on meekness, mercy, kindness, humbleness, long-suffering, forbearing and forgiving one

another. Wenger, *CW*, pp. 55-56. All these virtues of individual piety can and should be practiced by any good Christian.
7. In his writings Menno repeatedly changes "can" to "may." The obvious point he is trying to make against the Münsterites is that no one should ever try to lay any other foundation than Christ. For this reason the translation in Wenger, *CW* is not correct on 51, 87, 103, 289, 321, etc.
8. K. Vos, *DB*. 54 (1917): 83.
9. M. Hoffman, *De Ordonantie Gods*, in *Doperse Stemmen* 4, (1980): 23.
10. Ibid., 24.
11. This would imply that when Menno identified himself with the covenanters, he must have been baptized as well.
12. G. Grosheide, *Verhooren en Vonissen der Wederdoopers, Betrokken bij den aanslagen op Amsterdam in 1534 en 1535* (Utrecht, 1920), 50.
13. Ibid., 45.
14. Stupperich, *Schriften*, 202.
15. *Opera Omnia*, 621a-b.
16. Ibid., 622a-623a.
17. Ibid., 624b.
18. Ibid., 629b, 630a.
19. Ibid., 630b-631a.
20. "With my humble gifts I have opposed them, preaching and admonishing, as much as I could. Two times I dealt with one of their leaders... But my admonishment was not effective, because I continued to do what I confessed to be not right." Ibid., p. 257a.
21. Ibid., 257a.
22. Ibid.
23. Ibid.
24. Ibid.
25. Ibid.
26. Ibid., 257b.
27. Menno's prayer in the *Meditation* reflects his lack of courage to face critical situations. "O dear Lord, keep me in simplicity, under your cross, that I may not deny thee and your holy Word in the time of temptation, not conceal your divine truth and will under the mask of hypocrisy, lies and equivocal expressions..." *Doperse Stemmen* 2: 47; Wenger, *CW*, 83. The fact that Menno did not delete this confession of weakness in his later revisions, reveals how serious he considered the problem to be; it also reveals his honesty.
28. *Opera Omnia*, 627b-628a.; 628b.
29. Ibid., 630b.
30. Even among the leaders there was much disagreement. "Some brought the meaning of marriage into question, others taught only in parables. A third group would not receive anybody in grace, or recognize and accept someone as a brother if he sinned even once after baptism, which they interpreted as being malicious and knowing sin to death (Heb. 6:4-6; 10:26). The fourth preferred the baptism of John to the one of Christ. Others insisted on frequent visions, dreams and prophecies. Still others believed that if all brothers and teachers would be killed, they soon would rise with Christ and rule the world for a thousand years and receive back a hundred times more than they left. And so we had almost as many opinions as teachers, and they comforted themselves with lies, promises, visions, dreams and revelations. Some had spoken with God and others with angels..." H. Fast, *Der linke Flügel der Reformation* (Bremen, 1962), 333.
31. This is the contemporary description of the period by Nicolaas van Blesdijk. See S. Zijlstra, *Nicolaas Myndertsz. van Blesdijk* (Groningen, 1983), 4.
32. *Opera Omnia*, 258a.
33. Sooner or later his responsibility for the death of those who joined the Münsterites might be discovered. And besides, if he had already been baptized, he would be

considered one of the covenanters in any case. His own statement that he was accused of being someone who was longing for what he had left, seems to support this interpretation. See *Doperse Stemmen* 2: 41. Evidence from his own writings indicates that Menno never really accepted his status as a legal outlaw and a Christian sojourner but continued to complain about it for the rest of his life. *Opera Omnia*, 327a ff; 493 ff.

On the subject of suffering and the willingness of Menno to carry the cross of Christ, we disagree with Timothy George's statement that "Menno espoused suffering and martyrdom, and was committed to a profoundly otherworldly spirituality." T. George, "John Calvin and Menno Simons: Reformation Perspectives on the Kingdom of God," in *Sixteenth Century Essays & Studies*,10 (1988), 195-214.

34 *Doperse Stemmen* 2: 22-23.
35 "In sorrow I may well lament with Esdras and say: Our sanctuary is laid waste, our altar broken down, our temple destroyed. Our psaltery is laid to the ground, our song is put to silence, our rejoicing is at an end. The light of our candlestick is put out, the ark of our covenant is spoiled, our holy things are defiled." Ibid., 49.
36 Ibid., 47-49. Menno's disappointment with the learned ones, that is the scholars and theologians, lasted for the rest of his life. Although reading Luther freed Menno from the authority of human institutions, and he consulted the writings of Bucer and Bullinger, all of them compromised on the question of child baptism and proved to be of no help in the establishment of the New Jerusalem. *Opera Omnia*, 256a-b.
37 *Doperse Stemmen* 2: 49; Wenger, CW, 84. Menno himself had not yet suffered much. "Although I have drunk a little of the cup of your affliction, yet I have not tasted the dregs (Matt. 20:22-23). *Doperse Stemmen* 2, p. 45. In the revised edition he later adds, "I have not yet resisted unto blood." Wenger, CW, 82.
38 *Doperse Stemmen* 2: 46. The characterization of government as "external" and "earthly" are reflections of Menno's early spiritualism. In the revised editions these words were deleted. *Opera Omnia*, 175b; Wenger, CW, 83.
39 *Doperse Stemmen* 2: 15-17.
40 Menno's vision of the kingdom of God under the protection of a Christian government changed little in his later years. In the revised edition of 1558, "christelijke overheid" has been replaced by "Godvresende overigheden," but the meaning is the same. *Opera Omnia*, 176b.
41 *Doperse Stemmen* 2: 49-50; Wenger, CW, 84-85; *Opera Omnia*, 176a-b.
42 *Doperse Stemmen* 2: 49-50.
43 *Doperse Stemmen* 2: 15-17.
44 Ibid., 50.
45 Wenger, CW, 83. *Doperse Stemmen* 2: 46.
46 *Van die Wedergeboorte*, Aviij v.
47 The conclusion of the *Meditation* that there are very few regenerated Christians is now confirmed with the statement, that among a thousand there are only one or two: "... die des nieuwen hemelschen geboorte rechte sin, verstant, vnd begrip hebben." Ibid., Aiij v.
48 *Van die Wedergeboorte*, Aiij v.
49 Ibid., Aij v.
50 *Opera Omnia*, 123b.
51 "I say indeed dear brothers..." *Van die Wedergeboorte*, Aij v. The *Opera Omnia*, 123b has: "I tell you the truth..."
52 The sentence in the *Opera Omnia*, 124a, that one who tries to be a Christian and admonish them with Christian love "has to be a cursed Anabaptist and a heretic" (*die moet haer vermaledijde Wederdooper en Ketter zijn*) is missing in the first edition.
53 *Van die Wedergeboorte*, Aviij v; *Opera Omnia*, 126b.
54 "...however it is impossible that they could prove and contend with the word of God ... that a disobedient, rebellious and carnal man, even if he appeals to his faith and to the cross of Christ, has entered or may enter the kingdom of heaven." Ibid., Aviij r. He challenges "sola fide" Christians as well as Catholics.

[55] Ibid., B r.
[56] Ibid., Bij r.
[57] Ibid., Biij r.
[58] Ibid., Biiij r. In the revised edition Menno doesn't expect that much any more: "so they will confess that the solid foundation and the truth has been declared." *Opera Omnia*, 130b.
[59] Vos, *Menno Simons*, 55; 58, describes Menno's self confidence as arrogance and spiritual pride. As regenerated Christians, Menno and his followers considered themselves to be God's new creation who alone possessed the truth, unlike Catholics, Lutherans or Zwinglians. As God's messengers they felt they had the same powers as the apostles on Pentecost.

In his writings Menno certainly assumed authority. Building upon the true foundation of Jesus Christ, he never doubted his calling, his ordination, his doctrines or his teachings. Although he invited his opponents to correct him, he never admitted defeat in any of his disputations.
[60] *Van die Wedergeboorte*, Biij v. In the revised edition this statement is again modified. *Opera Omnia*, 130a.
[61] Meihuizen, Introduction to the *Fundament-book*, XII.
[62] Kuehler, *Geschiedenis*, 126.
[63] *Doperse Stemmen* 2: 41.
[64] *Fundament-book*, 31. The same statement in the 1554-55 edition reads: "you will find through the grace of God, that this is the pure and unaltered doctrine of Christ." *Opera Omnia*, 10b.
[65] *Doperse Stemmen* 2: 43. There is no basic change in the revised edition. *Opera Omnia*, 174b.
[66] *Fundament-book*, 157-158. Although the wording in 1554-1555 edition is different, the content of the statement remains the same. *Opera Omnia*, 50a.
[67] Meihuizen, *Fundament-book*, XIII, is convinced that Menno changed this verse deliberately because it is not a literal quotation from either the Vulgate or any of the vernacular translations he used.
[68] Verduin, in Wenger, *CW*, 51, 63, 87, 103, does not even try to translate Menno's paraphrase, but simply quotes the original text from 1 Cor. 3:11. Menno's emphasis is not on "can" or "cannot" but on "may" or "may not." This change is not just from active to passive, but a change of meaning.
[69] See *Opera Omnia*, 1; 71; 121; 133; etc.
[70] By calling the magistrates "ordained authorities," Menno assures them that he recognizes all government as ordained by God, disclaiming any possible Münsterite ambitions. *Fundament-book*, 33. In the revised edition of 1558 Menno mentions only the calling of the magistrates, not their ordination. *Opera Omnia*, 11a. But even an unbelieving government has the responsibility to punish the wicked and to protect the good.
[71] *Fundament-book*, 1. "The foundation of Christian Doctrine" (*Dat Fundament des Christelycken leers*). In the revision of 1554-55, Menno changed not only the content, but also the title. Now it is "A Foundation and clear instruction on the saving Doctrine of Jesus Christ" (*Een Fundament en klare Aenwysinge van de salighmakende Leere Jesu Christi*) *Opera Omnia*, 1. But his claim for the infallibility of his doctrine remains the same.
[72] *Fundament-book*, 4.
[73] *Fundament-book*, 9ff. After Münster, Menno wanted to assure his readers that the time of salvation was still present. It is not too late for repentance and change of life.
[74] Ibid., 13.
[75] Ibid., 9.
[76] Ibid., 17.
[77] Ibid., 20.
[78] Ibid., 25.
[79] Ibid., 27-28. If you believe in the gospel of Jesus Christ, repent and submit unconditionally to God's will, "you will become partners, citizens, children and co-

heirs of the new heavenly Jerusalem. Those who believe on the Son of God inherit eternal life." *Opera Omnia*, 10a.

80 *Fundament-book*, 36ff. Until now Menno has only made the statement that right baptism is indispensable for the true church of Jesus Christ. He now presents his understanding of the meaning of baptism in opposition to the child-baptizers and the spiritualists. There is no foundation in Scripture for child baptism. Ibid., 58, 64, 66. Against the spiritualists he argues that baptism with water is a clear commandment from the Lord. Ibid., 72, 75.

81 Ibid., 47.
82 Ibid., 46, 49.
83 Ibid., 72, 75.
84 Ibid., 77-78.
85 Ibid., 83.
86 Ibid.
87 Ibid., 87. In the *Opera Omnia*, 28a, dancing is too extreme, so the excited believers are allowed only to play and jump before the Lord. For the "plain-clothed" Wenger, *CW*, 148, this is still too much. According to the translation, all that believers are allowed to do is to play and sing before the Lord.
88 This understanding of the meaning of the Lord's Supper had not changed by the early 1550s. In his *Reply to False Accusations*, Menno defends himself and his followers against the false accusations of the "Predicanten." The *Significatum* of the Supper remains unconditional commitment to the service of Christ and to the fellow members of his body, with all the material and spiritual gifts of the believers. See *Opera Omnia*, 504b-505b.
89 For Hubmaier, the baptismal vow is essential to all congregational life and discipline. Before candidates are baptized they must promise to submit to the discipline of the church. As soon as they are baptized the power to bind and to loose is also given to them. *Quellen zur Geschichte der Täufer 9, Balthasar Hubmaier, Schriften*, ed. by G. Westin and T. Bergsten (Gütersloh, 1962), 350. According to the Schleitheim articles, only those can be admitted to the celebration of the Lord's Supper who have been "united to the one Body of Christ, that is to the congregation of Christ, of which Christ is the head, and that through baptism." H. Fast, *Der linke Flügel der Reformation*, 63.
90 The term "covenanter" does not imply mutual responsibility. The covenant is a personal relationship with God, and the covenanters submit only to God and his apocalyptic messengers. The Münsterite Articles have no provision for mutual responsibility either. See Stupperich, *Schriften von katholischer Seite gegen die Täufer* (Münster, 1980), 88-95. Also de Bakker, *Civic Reformer*, 270.
91 *Fundament-book*, 92.
92 Ibid., 105.
93 Ibid., 109.
94 Ibid., 110.
95 Menno could certainly speak from his own experience as a Catholic priest and an evangelical preacher. As long as he put off making his final commitment, the fruits of his preaching were hypocrisy, spiritual pride and insurrection. Ibid., 116.
96 Ibid., 111-112.
97 Ibid., 116.
98 Ibid., 119.
99 Menno first tried to combine inner spiritual freedom with outer life in Babylon. Because he knew all about it, he now warned the Davidites about the same temptation. Ibid., 157.
100 Ibid., 158.
101 Ibid., 156.
102 Ibid. 3.
103 Ibid., 157-158.
104 Ibid., 161.

[105] Ibid., 176.
[106] Ibid., 164-165. In the revised edition the responsibility of the magistrates is increased. Now they have been called by God to punish the wicked, to do justice between arguing parties, to deliver the oppressed from the hands of the oppressor, and last but not least, they should stop the public seducers of the simple people with reasonable means, be they papists, monks, preachers, baptized or not baptized. *Opera Omnia*, 52a-b.
[107] Although the examples of Moses, Joshua, David and Hezekiah, who exterminated the false prophets and priests with their idolatries from their lands, might be very close to Menno's heart, he does not directly recommend their method. The "uthgeroyt" (exterminate) from the *Fundament-book*, p. 165, is replaced in the *Opera Omnia*, 52b, with "afgedaen" (finished), which still was drastic language.
[108] After calling the magistrates to repentance, Menno prays that at last there might be found "a Christian, wise, honest and God-fearing government..." *Fundament-book*, 5-6. In 1554-55 Menno had little hope left that even a Christian government might ever become might ever become "founders and upholders of the Word and doctrine of God." But he still calls the magistrates to repentance and prays that they might become planters of justice and followers of Jesus Christ. *Opera Omnia*, 3.
[109] *Fundament-book*, 162.
[110] Ibid., 41. The wording is different in the later edition (*Opera Omnia*, 13a), although there is no change of meaning.
[111] *Fundament-book*, 104-107; *Opera Omnia*, 33b-34a.
[112] Dirk Philips, *Enchiridion, or Hand Book* (Indiana, 1910), 323-363.
[113] *Doperse Stemmen* 2: 30.
[114] *Fundament-book*, 13.
[115] Ibid., 14.
[116] *Doperse Stemmen* 2: 46.
[117] See Vos, *Menno Simons*, 291. "As the title indicates, this book appeared in 1541. This is rather the date of writing than that of publication." Horst, *Bibliography*, 107-108. The first known edition did not appear before 1556. Horst then continues, "If the 1541 date is the date of writing, this is the earliest writing by Menno Simons on Church discipline." Ibid., 108. From the closing paragraph of *Opera Omnia*, 637b, we may conclude that Menno wrote this tract as a personal letter of instruction to the leading brothers of the congregation in Franeker, Friesland. Vos, *Menno Simons*, 291.
[118] Because two letters to Amsterdam written in 1555 and 1556 respectively are included in this book, we know that it could not have been published before 1556. Horst, *Bibliography*, 107. The letter of 1541 must have been revised by Menno before publication because some of the references and statements are more applicable to the situation existing in 1556 than to that of 1541. In fact, the opening sentence, *Opera Omnia*, 631a-b, doesn't make much sense in 1541, but would very well reflect the situation of 1556. The same applies for Menno's self-vindication in regard to his alleged desire for money. Ibid., 632a.
[119] Ibid., 631a.
[120] *Opera Omnia*, 288b-298b.
[121] Ibid., 185 ff.
[122] Ibid., 337 ff.
[123] Ibid., 632b.
[124] Ibid., 632a.
[125] Ibid., 636a.
[126] Ibid., 633a-b.
[127] Ibid., 633b.
[128] Ibid., 634b.
[129] Ibid., 634a.
[130] Ibid., 634a-b. "In this way the ban is a major work of love, although for those who do not understand, it as a work of hatred..." Ibid., 634b.

[131] Ibid., 634a.
[132] Ibid., 635b.
[133] Ibid., 635a-b.
[134] Ibid., 636a. "We now are the chosen children of God, Jn. 1, Eph. 1, we now are true sisters and brothers of Christ, Luke 8, Heb. 2. We are now similar to Christ, Rom. 8. We are created in the image of God, Col. 3, Eph. 4. We have been marked on our foreheads with the sign of Thau, Ezechiel 9. The kingdom of God is in us, Luke 18. We are the bride of Christ, Jn. 3, the church of Christ, Eph. 5, the body of Christ, 1 Cor. 12, Eph. 1, Col. 1. Christ lives in our hearts, Eph. 3; we are guided by the Holy Spirit, Rom. 8, we are the chosen generation, the royal priesthood, the holy people, the people who belong to God, 1 Pet. 2, the temple of the Lord, 1. Cor. 3 and 6. 2 Cor. 6, the spiritual Mount Zion and the new heavenly Jerusalem, Heb.12, the spiritual Israel of God, Gal. 6, 2 Pet. 1." In his 1555 letter to Amsterdam, which was added to this publication, Menno continues to use the metaphor of the New Jerusalem for the Church of Christ. Ibid., 638a-b, 640b.
[135] Ibid., 73b. There is no doubt in Menno's mind that this wisdom supersedes the knowledge of doctors, theologians and philosophers. On the margin Menno writes "He who is not trained by God remains foolish, James 1:5." Ibid., 74a. Bibiographical observations on this writing in Horst, *Bibliography*, 86-91.
[136] Ibid., 75b.
[137] Ibid., 75b.
[138] This true Christian faith "changes, renews, cleanses, sanctifies and justifies more and more." Ibid., 115a.
[139] Ibid., 76a.
[140] Ibid, 80b.
[141] Ibid., 76a.
[142] Quoting 1 John 4:7, Menno writes: "He who loves is born from God, because God is love." Ibid., 81a.
[143] "Real love overcomes and bears all." Ibid., 81b.
[144] Ibid., 80a.
[145] Ibid., 78a-b.
[146] Ibid., 78b.
[147] The reference to Mikron is part of the second edition. In 1542 Menno had not yet met a Lasco and Mikron. Mikron always denied Menno's claim that he made the statement "This I have to confess, that a woman does not have any seed, but only the blood of menstruation" (*Dat moet ick well bekennen dat een vrouwe geen zaet, maer een menstruael bloedt heft*). Ibid., 79a-b. See also Vos, *Menno Simons*, 119-120.
[148] *Opera Omnia*, 86a.
[149] Ibid., 95b.
[150] Ibid., 99b.
[151] Ibid., 99b.
[152] Ibid., 100a.
[153] Ibid., 99b-100a.
[154] Menno maintains that the reason for his being slandered, hated and persecuted is actually not his own doctrine, but "it is the eternal, heavenly, unchangeable doctrine of our dear Lord Jesus Christ." Ibid., 437a. Nothing can stand up against this teaching, sacraments and life: no imperial placard, no decrees from the pope, no council of the learned ones, no human philosophy, neither Origen, Augustine, Luther or Bucer, because it is the eternal Word of God. Ibid., 445b. This quasi-infallibility of Menno's doctrine, although based upon the Scripture, has almost superseded the written word of God. Ibid., 437a. Menno is no second Enoch, Elijah, third David, visionary or prophet, but what he has to say is in accordance with the letter and spirit of the gospel of Jesus Christ. Ibid., 448b-449a.
[155] Ibid., 439a.
[156] Ibid., 441a.

[157] Ibid., 440b-441a.
[158] Ibid., 441a.
[159] For the first time Menno describes the true evangelical church as one "without spot or wrinkle." Ibid., 441b.
[160] Ibid., 444a.
[161] Ibid., 444a-444b.; Ibid., 534a.
[162] Ibid., 444b.
[163] Ibid.
[164] Ibid.
[165] Ibid., 444b-445a. As in the *Fundament-book* the celebration of the Supper is the initiation into the body of Christ and into mutual responsibility, or brotherly love. *Fundament-book*, 82-83.
[166] *Opera Omnia*, 445a.
[167] Ibid., 445a. Deut. 17:2 is clearly a misquotation. Menno must be referring to Deut. 17:14-20.
[168] Ibid., 445b.
[169] Ibid., 446a.
[170] Ibid., 446a.
[171] Ibid., 446b.
[172] Ibid., 446a.
[173] Ibid., 447a.
[174] Ibid., 455a-b.
[175] Ibid., 455b.
[176] Ibid., 455b.
[177] Not being written for publication, Menno apparently never revised this tract. The first edition was printed without his consent by his opponents in Emden in 1544. No copy of this print is recorded. The second edition came out in 1570. See Horst, *Bibliography*, 94-95.
[178] *Opera Omnia*, 520.
[179] Ibid., 522.
[180] Ibid., 521.
[181] Ibid., 445b-446b.
[182] Ibid., 455a-b.
[183] Hatred and persecution for the sake of Christ have become unavoidable. Christ and the apostles are the proof for this assertion. *Opera Omnia*, 299a-301a.
[184] Ibid., 493.
[185] Ibid., 494.
[186] Ibid., 495. There is no change from the statement in his *Meditation* of 1539. *Doperse Stemmen* 2: 17.
[187] *Opera Omnia*, 495. In the margin: "The worldly authorities should not interfere in the kingdom of God and his justice." Ibid., 499a.
[188] Ibid., 497a, 498b, 502a, 504a, 506a, 509b.
[189] Ibid., 504a-b.
[190] Ibid., 504b.
[191] Ibid., 504b; Wenger, *CW*, 558.
[192] *Opera Omnia*, 504b.
[193] Ibid., 505b.
[194] Ibid., 505a; Wenger, *CW*, 559.
[195] How is it possible that the wealthy and rich live in their luxury and abundance and allow the poor members of their body to suffer? Ibid., 505a-b. The sharing of the same bread refers to the celebration of the Lord's Supper. Wenger, *CW*, 559.
[196] *Opera Omnia*, 505b; Wenger, *CW*, 559.
[197] *Opera Omnia*, 503a.
[198] Ibid., 498b-499a.
[199] Ibid., p. 499a.

[200] Ibid., 516a. If the magistrates were to look impartially at the faith and life of Menno and his followers, they would soon discover "that we are not rebels, murderers and thieves, as we are blamed by the learned ones, but a God-fearing, pious, peaceful people." Ibid., 503a; 501b.
[201] Ibid., 503a.
[202] In his *Brief Defence to all Theologians,* Menno confronts them with the possible consequences of slander and defamation. They should not forget that they would be unable to prove any of their false accusations. *Opera Omnia,* 333b.
[203] Ibid., 335b.
[204] Ibid., 464b.
[205] According to G. Faber in his *Antwert ... up einen bitter hoenischen breef der Wedderdoopers,* these points are: the preachers have not been called properly, either by God or by the people (fol. bi r-v); they baptize children (fol. di r); public sinners are being tolerated at the Lord's Supper (fol. gij v); they do not practice the ban (fol. giiij v); they are not a blameless church of believers (fol. hiij r).
[206] Ibid., fol. hj v.
[207] *Opera Omnia,* 471a. For the *Schleitheim Confession* see H. Fast, *Der Linke Flügel der Reformation* (Bremen, 1962), 66; John H. Yoder, *The Legacy of Michael Sattler* (Scottdale, PA: Herald Press, 1973).
[208] *Opera Omnia,* 473b. This time Menno doesn't need a long introduction to the use of the ban, as he did in his first exposition on excommunication. The fact that Paul makes its use imperative is enough reason for its rigorous implementation.
[209] Ibid., 474b.
[210] Ibid., 474b.
[211] Ibid., 475b.
[212] *Opera Omnia,* 478.
[213] G. Faber, *Antwert,* fol. hi v, fol. hj v.
[214] *Opera Omnia,* 292b-293a.
[215] Ibid., 293a.
[216] Ibid., 300b-301a.
[217] *Opera Omnia,* 444a-445a.
[218] *Opera Omnia,* 52a-b.
[219] *Opera Omnia,* 130b. This statement is part of a pastoral letter from 1556.
[220] Ibid., 187.
[221] Ibid., 189-190.
[222] Ibid., 191.
[223] *Doperse Stemmen* 2: 46.
[224] *Fundament-book,* 202-203. This entire paragraph is missing in the revised edition of 1554-55.
[225] *Opera Omnia,* 497a.
[226] Ibid, 502a.
[227] *Fundament-book,* 5-6.
[228] *Opera Omnia,* 445a. "Read also Deut. 17.2, and there you will find with great clarity, what God commanded all government."
[229] Ibid, 445a. The role of such a government would by no means be passive as T. George states in "CALVINIANA, Ideas and Influence of Jean Calvin," *Sixteenth Century Essays & Studies,* Volume X (1988), 212. It is the non-Christian government which should take no initiative in religious matters.
[230] *Fundament-book,* 165.
[231] *Opera Omnia,* 52a-b.
[232] Ibid., 445a.
[233] Ibid, 521.
[234] In such a society of believers there would be no need for defensive or aggressive weapons. Ibid, 455b.
[235] *DAN* III, 30.

[236] H. Fast, *Der linke Flügel*, 66.

[237] Law and gospel are not contradictory but complementary for Menno. There is continuity between the Old and the New Testaments because there have always been a people of God. *Opera Omnia*, 296a-b. Discussing the similarities between Calvin and Menno, and pointing to Calvin's emphasis on the continuity between the two Testaments which enabled him to find in the Old Testament the pattern for church-state relationships, T. George, CALVINIANA, 205, states: "Menno denied the legitimacy of this appeal to the Old Testament by pointing to the *normative* status of the New Covenant. The radical newness of Christ's Kingdom has displaced the mandate of the Old Covenant." Our findings support the opposite conclusion. Whenever Menno speaks about the legitimate functions of a God-ordained government, he uses the law-abiding kings of the Old Testament as his models.

[238] This is another basic difference from Swiss Anabaptism in the tradition of the Grebel letter to Müntzer. H. Fast, *Der linke Flügel*, 20.

[239] *Fundament-book*, 42.

[240] For this reason we disagree with George's statement that "Menno espoused suffering and martyrdom, and was committed to a profoundly otherworldly spirituality." CALVINIANA, 195.

Appendix

[1] Ps. 46: 11 must be a misreading or misquotation for Ps. 47: 2-3. The former does not support Menno's argument, whereas the latter does. In the revised edition from 1554/5 this error was corrected. Menno's scriptural citations are not always accurate

[2] The *Blasphemy* quotes only chapter 21, without a reference to a specific verse, but it paraphrases verse 5.

[3] Mennos' quotation of Heb. 7: 1 in the *Blasphemy* must be seen as representative for verses 1-10, which speak about the lordship of Jesus Christ, compared with that of Melchizedek, the king of Salem and the king of peace. Since the original version of the *Fundament-book* quotes only the chapters without any reference to specific verses, we may safely consider these two as a match a well.

[4] The reference in the *Blasphemy* is 1 Tim. 6: 13, but Menno paraphrases verses 13-15.

[5] Although the argument in both editions of the *Fundament-book* is the same, the references seem to be mixed up.

[6] Menno's paraphrase in the *Blasphemy* is taken from Isa. 9: 6 of our modern Bible versions.

[7] The *Blasphemy* quotes Jer. 51: 11, but the argument is based upon the entire chapter.

[8] Ps. 89 is one of the most impressive royal or messianic Psalms. Menno quotes this Psalm five times in the *Blasphemy*. Verse 19 in the revised edition should read verse 20, because this verse is paraphrased in the *Blasphemy* and supports the argument in the revised edition.

[9] Again the reference in the *Blasphemy* should read Rev. 2: 12 and not 2: 19. Verse 12 supports the argument. This mistake was corrected in both editions of the *Fundament-book*.

[10] Although the *Blasphemy* quotes Matt. 26: 51, the argument is based on verses 51-53.

[11] Matt. 29: 19 in the *Meditation* (*Doperse Stemmen* 2, 47), must be a mistake, because Menno paraphrases verse 18.

[12] *Opera Omnia*, 622a-b.

[13] *Ibid*, 629b, 623a.

[14] *Ibid*, 628a.

Select Bibliography

I. Bibliographies

Hillerbrand, Hans Joachim. *Bibliography des Täufertums, 1520-1630.* Quellen und Forschungen zur Reformationsgeschichte, 30. Quellen zur Geschichte der Täufer, 10. Gütersloh: G. Mohn, 1962.

Horst, Irvin Buckwalter. *A Bibliography of Menno Simons, ca. 1496-1561, Dutch reformer: with a census of known copies.* Nieuwkoop: B. de Graaf, 1962.

II. Contemporary Sources

A. Manuscript Sources

Gemeentearchief Amsterdam, *Confessieboek, Justitieboek.*

Gemeentearchief Leiden, *Correctie Boek* H. 1528-1548, Vroedschapsresoluties, *Aflesingsboek B.* Beginnende den 9. Mey 1528. Eyndigende den 22. April 1570, Tresorriersrekenboek, *Archief der Secretarie 1253-1575.* No. 1185. Stukken betreffende de anabaptisten, 1535, 25 stuks.

Archief der Verenigde Doopsgezinde Gemeente. Handschriften Kamer U.B. Amsterdam, Catalogus de Hoop Scheffer. Gellius Faber: *Eine antwert ... vp einen bitter hoenischen breeff der Wedderdoeper ... .*

B. Published Sources

Bomelius, Henricus. *Het oudste nederlandsche verboden boek 1523: Oeconomica christiana. Summa der Godliker Scrifturen.* Edited by J. J. van Toorenenbergen. Monumenta reformationis Belgicae, 1. Leiden: E. J. Brill, 1882.

Braght, Thieleman J. van. *Het bloedig tooneel of Martelaers spiegel der Doops-gezinde of weereloose Christenen, die om't getuygenis van Jesus haren Salighmaker, geleden hebben, ende gedood zijn, van Christi tijd af, tot desen tijd toe.* 2nd ed. Amsterdam: Hieronymus Sweerts, 1685.

Cornelius, Carl Adolf, ed. *Berichte der Augenzeugen über das Münsterische Wiedertäufferreich*, Die Geschichtsquellen des Bisthums Münster, 2. Münster: Druck und Verlag der Theissing'schen Buchhandlung, 1853.

Cramer, Samuel, and Pijper, Fredrik, eds. *Bibliotheca Reformatoria Neerlandica.* 10 vols. 's-Gravenhage: Aschendorff, 1903-1914.

Dülmen, Richard van, comp. *Das Täuferreich zu Münster, 1534-1535: Berichte und Dokumente.* DTV wissenschaftliche Reihe. München: Deutscher Taschenbuch Verlag, 1974.

Fast, Heinold, ed. *Der linke Flügel der Reformation: Glaubenszeugnisse der Täufer. Spiritualisten, Schwärmer und Antitrinitarier.* Klassiker des Protestantismus, 4. Bremen: C. Schuneman, 1962.

Fredericq, Paul, ed. *Corpus documentorum inquisitionis haereticae pravitatis Neerlandicae: verzameling van stukken betreffende de pauselijke en bisschoppelijke inquisitie in de Nederlanden.* Vol. 4, *Tijdvak der hervorming in de zestiende eeuw (1514 - 23 September 1524).* Vol. 5, *Tijdvak der hervorming in de zestiende eeuw, eerste vervolg (24 September 1524 - 31 December 1528).* Werken van den practischen leergang van vaderlandsche geschiedenis, 1, 5, 8-10. 's Gravenhage: M. Nijhoff, 1896.

Grosheide, Greta. *Verhooren en vonnissen der wederdoopers, betrokken bij de aanslagen op Amsterdam in 1534 en 1535.* Bijdragen en mededeelingen van het Historisch Genootschap, 41. Amsterdam: Johannes Muller, 1920.

Hoffman, Melchior. *De ordonnantie God's.* 1611. Reprint. Edited by Johannes Arnoldus Osterbaan. Doperse Stemmen, 4. Amsterdam: Doopsgezinde Historische Kring, 1980.

Häpke, R. *Niederländische Akten und Urkunden zur Geschichte der Hanse. I.* München, 1913.

Hubmaier, Balthasar. *Schriften.* Edited by Gunnar Westin and Torsten Bergsten. Quellen und Geschichte der Täufer, 9. Quellen und Forschungen zur Reformationsgeschichte, 29. Gütersloh: Mohn, 1962.

Hullu, J. de. *Bescheiden betreffende de Hervorming in Overijssel: Deventer (1522-1546).* Deventer: Deventer Boek- en Steendrukkerij, 1899.

Mellink, Albert Fredrik, ed. *Amsterdam 1536-1578.* Documenta anabaptistica Neerlandica, 2. Kerkhistorische bijdragen, 6. Leiden: E.J. Brill, 1980.

Mellink, Albert Fredrik, ed. *Amsterdam 1531-1536.* Documenta anabaptistica Neerlandica, 5. Kerkhistorische bijdragen, 12. Leiden: E.J. Brill, 1985.

Mellink, Albert Fredrik, ed. *Friesland en Groningen 1530-1550*. Documenta anabaptistica Neerlandica, 1. Kerkhistorische bijdragen, 6. Leiden: E.J. Brill, 1975.

Micronius, Marten. *Een waerachtich verhaal der t'zamensprekinghen tusschen Menno Simons ende Martinus Mikron van der menschwerdinghe Jesu Christi (1556)*. Edited by W. F. Dankbaar. Documenta anabaptistica Neerlandica, 3. Kerkhistorische bijdragen, 10. Leiden: E.J. Brill, 1981.

Niesert, Joseph, ed. *Urkunden zur Geschichte der Münsterischen Wiedertäufer*. Münsterische Urkundensammlung, 1. Coesfeld: Bernard Wittneven, 1826.

Pekelharing, Klass Rutger, ed. *Bijdragen voor de geschiedenis der hervorming in Zeeland 1524-1572*. Middelburg: J. C. & W. Altorffer, 1866.

Philips, Dirk. *Enchiridion or Hand Book*. LaGrange, Indiana: Pathway Publishing, 1966.

Rothman, Bernhard. *Die Schriften Bernhard Rothmanns*. Edited by Robert Stupperich. Veröffentlichungen der Historischen Kommission Westfalens, 32. Die Schriften der münsterischen Taüfer und ihrer Gegner, 1. Münster: Aschendorffer Verlagsbuchhandlung, 1970.

Simons, Menno. *The Complete Writings of Menno Simons: c. 1496-1561*. Translated by Leonard Verduin. Edited by John S. Wenger. Scottdale, Pa.: Herald Press, 1956.

Simons, Menno. *Dat Fundament des Christelycken leers*. Edited by H.W. Meihuizen. Den Haag: Martinus Nijhoff, 1967.

Simons, Menno. *Een gantz duidelijck ende klaer bewijs, uyt die H. Schriftuere, dat Jesus Christus, is de rechte belovede David inden geest. . . . Tegens de grouwelijcke ende grootste blasphemie van Jan van Leyden*. n.p., 1627.

Simons, Menno. *Meditatie op de 25e Psalm*. Edited by Hendrik Wiebes Meihuizen and J. P. Jacobszoon. Doperse Stemmen, 2. Amsterdam: Doopsgezinde Historische Kring, 1976.

Simons, Menno. *Opera omnia theologica, of, Alle de godtgeleerde wercken*. 1681. Reprint, edited by Hendrik James Herrison. Amsterdam: De Betaafsche Leeuw, 1989.

Simons, Menno. *Uyt Babel ghevloden, in Jeruzalem ghetogen*. 1600. Reprint. Doperse Stemmen, 6. Amsterdam: Doopsgezinde Historische Kring, 1986.

Mellink, Albert Fredrik, ed. *Friesland en Groningen 1530-1550*. Documenta anabaptistica Neerlandica, 1. Kerkhistorische bijdragen, 6. Leiden: E.J. Brill, 1975.

Simons, Menno. *Vele goede en christelijke lessen getrokken uit de vijfentwintigste psalm bij wijze van gebed*. Edited by Hendrik Wiebes Meihuizen. Doperse Stemmen, 2. Amsterdam: Doopsgezinde Historische Kring, 1976.

Stupperich, Robert, ed. *Schriften von katholischer Seite gegen die Täufer*. Münster: Aschendorffer Verlagsbuchhandlung, 1980.

Stupperich, Robert, ed. *Schriften von evangelischer Seite gegen die Täufer*. Münster: Aschendorff, 1983.

Williams, George Huntston and Mergal, Angel M., ed. *Spiritual and Anabaptist Writers*. The Library of Christian Classics, 25. Philadelphia: SCM Press, 1957.

Yoder, John Howard, trans. and ed. *The Legacy of Michael Sattler*. Scottdale, PA: Herald Press, 1973.

III. Secondary Works

Augustijn, Cornelius. *Erasmus en de reformatie: een onderzoek naar de houding die Erasmus ten opzichte van de Reformatie heeft aangenomen*. Amsterdam: H. J. Paris, 1962.

Augustijn, Cornelius, "Anabaptisme in de Nederlanden." *Doopsgezinde Bijdragen* Nieuw Reeks 12-13 (1986-1987): 13-28.

Bornhäuser, Christoph. *Leben und Lehre Menno Simons.: ein Kampf um das Fundament des Glaubens (etwa 1496-1561)*. Neukirchen-Vluyn: Neukirchener Verlag, 1973.

Bloch, Ernst. *Thomas Münzer als Theologe der Revolution*. Frankfurt-am-Main: Suhrkamp Verlag, 1967.

Brunk, Gerald R., ed. *Menno Simons. A Reappraisal*. Harrisonburg, VA: Eastern Mennonite College, 1992.

Cornelius, Carl Adolf. *Die niederländischen Wiedertäufer während der Belagerung Münsters 1534 bis 1535*. München: K. Akademie (G. Franz), 1869.

De Bakker, William John. "Civic reformer in Anabaptist Münster: Bernhard Rothmann, 1495-1535." 2 vol. Ph.D. dissertation, University of Chicago, 1987.

Decavele, J. *De Dageraad van de Reformatie in Vlaanderen (1520-1565)*. Verhandelingen van de Koninklijke Academie voor Wetenschappen, Letteren, en Schone Kunsten van Belgie, Klasse der Letteren; vol. 37, nr. 76. Brussel: Academie voor Wetenschappen, Letteren, en Schone Kunsten van Belgie, 1975.

Decavele, J. *De Dageraad van de Reformatie in Vlanderen. Deel II. Indices en Bijlagen*. Brussel, 1975

De Hoop Scheffer, J. G. *Geschiedenis der Kerkhervorming*. Amsterdam: G.L. Funke, 1873.

Deppermann, Klaus. *Melchior Hoffman: soziale Unruhen und apokalyptische Visionen im Zeitalter der Reformation*, Göttingen: Vandenhoeck und Ruprecht, 1979.

Dickens, Arthur Geoffrey and Tonkin, John, and Powell, Kenneth. *The Reformation in historical thought*. Cambridge, Mass.: Harvard University Press, 1985.

Duke, Alastair, "The Face of Popular Religious Dissent in the Low Countries, 1520-1530." *Journal of Ecclesiastical History* 26(1975): 41-67.

Dyck, Cornelius J. "The Place of Tradition in Dutch Anabaptism." *Church History* 43(1974): 34-49.

Dyck, Cornelius J., ed. *A legacy of faith: the heritage of Menno Simons. A sixtieth anniversary tribute to Cornelius Krahn*. Mennonite historical series, 8. Newton, Kan.: Faith and Life Press, 1962.

Epp, Frank H. *Mennonites in Canada, 1786-1920: the history of a separate people*. Toronto: Macmillan of Canada, 1974.

Epp, Frank H. *Mennonites in Canada, 1920-1940: A people's struggle for survival*. Toronto: Macmillan of Canada, 1982.

Friedmann, Robert. *The theology of Anabaptism: an interpretation*. Studies in Anabaptist and Mennonite history, 15. Scottdale, Pa.: Herald Press, 1973.

George, Timothy, "John Calvin and Menno Simons: Reformation Perspectives on the Kingdom of God." In *Calviniana: ideas and influence of Jean Calvin*, edited by Robert V. Schnucker. Sixteenth Century Essays & Studies, 10. Kirksville, Mo.: Sixteenth Century Journal Publishers. 1988.

Goertz, Hans-Jürgen. *Die Täufer: Geschichte und Deutung*. Edition Beck. München: C. H. Beck, 1980.

Goertz, Hans-Jürgen, ed. *Radikale Reformatoren: 21 biograph. Skizzen von Thomas Müntzer bis Paracelsus*. Beck'sche schwarze Reihe, 183. München: C. H. Beck, 1978.

Goertz, Hans-Jürgen, ed. *Umstrittenes Täufertum: 1525-1975; neue Forschungen*. Göttingen: Vandenhoeck und Ruprecht, 1975.

Horst, Irvin Buckwalter. *Anabaptism and the English Reformation to 1558*. Nieuwkoop: B. de Graaf, 1966.

Horst, Irvin Buckwalter, ed. *De gemeente als vertolking van de nieuwe tijd*. Amsterdam: Algemene Doopsgezinde Societeit, 1980.

Horst, Irvin Buckwalter, ed. *The Dutch Dissenters. A critical companion to their history and ideas, with a bibliographical survey of recent research pertaining to the early Reformation in the Netherlands*. Kerkhistorische bijdragen, 13. Leiden: E.J. Brill, 1986.

Horst, Irvin Buckwalter. *The radical Brethren: Anabaptism and the English Reformation to 1558*. Bibliotheca humanistica et reformatorica, 2. Nieuwkoop: B. de Graaf, 1972.

Houtte, J. A. van, ed. *Algemene Geschiedenis der Nederlanden*. Vol. 4, *De Bourgondisch-Habsburgse monarchie, 1477-1567*. Utrecht: W. de Haan, 1949.

Kawerau, Peter. *Melchior Hoffman als religiöser Denker*. Haarlem: F. Bohn, 1954.

Keeney, William Echard. *The development of Dutch Anabaptist thought and practice from 1539-1564*. Nieuwkoop: B. de Graaf, 1968.

Kirchhoff, Karl-Heinz. *Das Phänomen der Täuferreiches zu Münster 1534/35*. Münster: Aschendorffsche Verlagsbuchhandlung, 1989.

Kirchhoff, Karl-Heinz. *Die Endzeiterwartung der Täufergemeinde in Münster. 1534/35*. Jahrbuch für Westfälische Kirchengeschichte, 78. Lengerich/Westfalen, Germany: Komm.-Verlag F. Klinker, 1985.

Kirchhoff, Karl-Heinz. *Die Täufer in Münster 1534/35: Untersuchungen zum Umfang und zur Sozialstruktur der Bewegung*. Veröffentlichungen der Historischen Kommission Westfalens, 22. Geschichtliche Arbeiten zur westfälischen Landesforschung, 12. Münster in Westfalen: Aschendorff, 1973.

Klaassen, Walter. *Anabaptism: neither Catholic nor Protestant*, 3rd edition. Kitchener: Pandora Press, 2001.

Klaassen, Walter. "Menno Simons research, 1937-1986." *Mennonite Quarterly Review* 60 (1986): 483-96.

Klaassen, Walter, "Menno Simons, Vormgever van een traditie." *Doopsgezinde Bijdragen* Nieuw Reeks 12-13 (1986-1987): 226-47. As "Menno Simons: Molder of a tradition." *Mennonite Quarterly Review* 62(1988): 368-86.

Knappert, Laurentius. *De Opkomst van het Protestantisme in een Noord-Neder-landsche Stad: geschiedenis van de hervorming binnen Leiden van den aanvang tot op het beleg.* Leiden: S. C. van Doesburgh, 1908.

Krahn, Cornelius. *Dutch Anabaptism: Origin, spread, life and thought (1450-1600).* The Hague: Martinus Nijhoff, 1968.

Krahn, Cornelius. *Menno Simons (1496-1561): ein Beitrag zur Geschichte und Theologie der Taufgesinnten.* Karlsruhe: H. Schneider, 1936.

Kühler, Wilhelmus Johannes. *Geschiedenis der nederlandsche Doopsgezinde in the zestiende eeuw.* Haarlem: H. D. Tjeenk Willink & Zoon, 1932.

Laubach, Ernst. "Jan Mathys und die Austreibung der Taufunwilligen aus Münster Ende Februar 1534." *Westfälische Forschungen* 36(1986): 147-158.

Leendertz, Willem Izaak. *Melchior Hoffman.* Verhandelingen uitgegeven door Teylers godgeleerd genootschap; nieuwe serie, 11. Haarlem: F. Bohn, 1883.

Littel, Franklin Hamlin. *Das Selbstverständnis der Täufer.* Kassel: J. G. Oncken (Thiele & Schwarz), 1966.

Loeschen, John R. *The divine community: trinity, church, and ethics in Reformation theologies.* Sixteenth century texts and studies. Kirksville, Mo.: Sixteenth Century Journal Publishers, 1981.

Meihuizen, H. W. "The concept of restitution in the Anabaptism of Northwestern Europe." *Mennonite Quarterly Review* 44(1970):141-158.

Meihuizen, H. W. *Menno Simons: ijveraar voor het herstel van de Nieuwtestamentlische gemeente 1496-1561.* Haarlem: H. D. Tjeenk Willink & Zoon, 1961.

Mellink, Albert Fredrik. *Amsterdam en de wederdopers in de zestiende eeuw.* Sunschrift, 120. Nijmegen: Socialistiese Uitgeverij Nijmegen, 1978.

Mellink, Albert Fredrik. "De beginperiode van het Nederlands Anabaptisme in het licht van het laatste onderzoek." *Doopsgezinde Bijdragen* Nieuw Reeks12-13 (1986-1987): 29-39.

Mellink, A.F. "De sociaal-religieuze revolutie van het Herformingstijdvak. " *Wetenschap en Samenleving.* 1968.

Mellink, Albert Fredrik. *De Wederdopers in de nordelijke Nederlanden 1531-1544*. Leeuwarden: Uitgeverij Gerben Dykstra, 1981.

Oosterbaan, Johannes Arnoldus. "De reformatie der Reformatie: Gronslagen van de doperse theologie." *Doopsgezinde Bijdragen* Nieuw Reeks 2(1976): 36-61.

Oosterbaan, Johannes Arnoldus. "Een doperse christologie." *Nederlands Theologisch Tijdschrift* 35(1981): 32-47.

Oosterbaan, Johannes Arnoldus. "The Theology of Menno Simons." *Mennonite Quarterly Review* 35(1961): 187-1996,

Ozment, Steven E., ed. *Reformation Europe: a Guide to Research*. St. Louis: Centre for Reformation Research, 1982.

Ozment, Steven E. *The Reformation in the cities: the appeal of Protestantism to sixteenth-century Germany and Switzerland*. New Haven: Yale University Press, 1975.

Packull, Werner O. *Mysticism and the early South German-Austrian Anabaptist movement, 1525-1531*. Studies in Anabaptist and Mennonite history, 19. Scottdale, Pa.: Herald Press, 1977.

Packull, Werner O. "The sign of Thau: The changing conception of the seal of God's elect in early Anabaptist thought." *Mennonite Quarterly Review* 61(1987): 363-374.

Pater, Calvin Augustine. *Karlstadt as the father of the Baptist movements: the emergence of lay Protestantism*. Toronto: University of Toronto Press, 1984.

Post, Regnerus Richardus. *Kerkelijke verhoudingen in Nederland voor de Reformatie van 1500-1580*. Utrecht: Spectrum, 1954.

Posthumus, N. W. *De geschiedenis van de Leidsche lakenindustrie I. De Middeleeuwen*. 's-Gravenhage: M. Nijhoff, 1908.

Schöps, Hans Joachim. *Vom himmlischen Fleisch Christi: eine dogmengeschichtliche Untersuchung*. Sammlung gemeinverständlicher Vortrage und Schriften aus dem Gebiet der Theologie und Religionsgeschichte, 195-196. Tübingen: J. C. B. Mohr (Paul Siebeck), 1951.

Sepp, Christiaan. *Verboden Lectuur: Een drietal Indices librorum prohibitorum toegelicht*. Leiden: E. J. Brill, 1889.

Stayer, James M. *Anabaptists and the Sword*. Lawrence, Kan.: Coronado Press, 1972.

Stayer, James M. *The German Peasants' War and Anabaptist community of goods*. McGill-Queen's studies in the history of religion, 6. Montreal & Kingston: McGill-Queen's University Press, 1991.

Stayer, James M. "Oldeklooster and Menno." *The Sixteenth Century Journal* 9(1978): 51-67.

Stayer, James. "Polygamy as Inner-worldly Asceticism," in *DAN* Bulletin Nos 12&13. 1980-1981, 59-67.

Tonkin, John. *The Church and the secular order in Reformation thought*. New York: Columbia University Press, 1971.

Trapman, Johannes. *De Summa der godliker scrifturen (1523)*. Leiden: New Rhine Publishers, 1978.

Valkema Blouw, P. "Drukkers voor Menno Simons en Dirk Philips, " in *Doopsgezinde Bijdragen* (Nieuwe Reeks 17, 1991) 31-74.

Verheyden, A. L. E. *Anabaptism in Flanders 1530-1560: a century of struggle*. Studies in Anabaptist and Mennonite history, 9. Scottdale, Pa.: Herald Press, 1961.

Voolstra, Sjouke. *Het Woord is vlees geworden: de Melchioritisch-Menniste incarnatieleer*. Dissertationes Neerlandicae. Series theologica, 8. Kampen: J. H. Kok, 1982.

Voolstra, Sjouke. *Menno Simons. His Image and Message*. North Newton, Kansas: Bethel College, 1997.

Vos, Karel. *Menno Simons, 1496-1561: zijn leven en werken en zijne reformatorische denkbeelden*. Leiden: E. J. Brill, 1914.

Vries, O. H. de. *Leer en praxis van de vroege dopers uitgelegd als een theologie van de geschiedenis*. Leeuwarden: Dykstra, 1982.

Waite, Gary K. *"Spiritualizing the Crusade: David Joris in the context of the early Reform and Anabaptist movements in the Netherlands, 1524-1543."* Ph.D. dissertation, University of Waterloo, 1986.

Williams, George Huntston. *La Reforma Radical*. Seccion de obras de historia. Mexico: Fondo de Cultura Economica, 1983.

Williams, George Huntston. *The Radical Reformation*. Philadelphia: Westminster Press, 1962.

Woltjer, Jan Juliaan. *Friesland in hervormingstijd*. Leidse historische reeks van de Rijksuniversiteit te Leiden, 7. Leiden: Universitaire Pers, 1962.

Zijlstra, S. "*Nicolaas Meyndertsz. van Blesdijk: een bijdrage tot de geschiedenis van het Davidjorisme.*" Doctoral dissertation, Rijksuniversiteit te Groningen, 1983.

Zschäbitz, Gerhard. *Zur mitteldeutschen Wiedertäuferbewegung nach dem grossen Bauernkrieg.* Leipziger Uebersetzungen und Abhandlungen zum Mittelalter, Reihe B, 1. Berlin: Rutten & Löning, 1958.

About The Author

Helmut Isaak was born August 5, 1939, in Filidelfia, the current capital of the Paraguayuan Chaco. After secondary and teachers' school training in Paraguay, he received a Licentiate in Theology from the Mennonite Seminary in Montevideo, Uruguay (SEMT).

A generous grant from the Dutch Mennonite Conference (ADS) made it possible for Helmut to study Mennonitica at the University of Amsterdam where he obtained a further degree in Theology.

Returning to Paraguay, Helmut taught for eight years at the Colegio de Loma Plata, Menno Colony, Paraguay, where he also was involved in environmental and development projects as well as working as youth leader with local Mennonite churches.

A second grant from the Dutch Mennonite Conference made it possible for Helmut to do graduate research in the Netherlands and in Northern Germany in 1977 and 1978, on the early development of the Anabaptist Reformation.

After moving to Canada in 1980, Helmut served as senior pastor in three different churches as well as one church in Regensburg, Germany. Along with pastoral work, he has given intensive seminars on Anabaptist History and Theology in Santiago de Chile, in Bogota, Columbia, at Bethel College in Newton, Kansas and at the Faculty of Theology of the Universidad Evangelica del Paraguay.

Now a Canadian citizen, Helmut's academic and pastoral work continues to be carried out in multiple countries and cultures. He is fluent in Low German, High German, Spanish, Dutch and English.